EUROPEAN
MEDIA STUDIES

EUROPEAN
MEDIA STUDIES

Kevin Williams

Hodder Arnold

A MEMBER OF THE HODDER HEADLINE GROUP

First published in Great Britain in 2005 by
Hodder Education, a member of the Hodder Headline Group,
338 Euston Road, London NW1 3BH

www.hoddereducation.com

Distributed in the United States of America by
Oxford University Press Inc.
198 Madison Avenue, New York, NY10016

Hodder Headline's policy is to use papers that are natural, renewable and
recyclable products and made from wood grown in sustainable forests.
The logging and manufacturing processes are expected to conform to the
environmental regulations of the country of origin.

The advice and information in this book are believed to be true and
accurate at the date of going to press, but neither the authors nor the publisher
can accept any legal responsibility or liability for any errors or omissions.

British Library Cataloguing in Publication Data
A catalogue record for this book is available from the British Library

Library of Congress Cataloging-in-Publication Data
A catalog record for this book is available from the Library of Congress

ISBN-10 0 340 71902 8
ISBN-13 978 0 340 71902 2

1 2 3 4 5 6 7 8 9 10

Typeset in 10/13 Adobe Garamond by Servis Filmsetting Ltd, Manchester
Printed and bound in Malta

What do you think about this book? Or any other Hodder Education title?
Please send your comments to the feedback section on www.hoddereducation.com.

Acknowledgements

This book could not have been written without the cooperation of a number of people. The impetus for the whole endeavour comes from the formidable combination of a Danish man and a Dutch woman. Over a decade ago Professor Hans Henrik Holm of the Danish National School of Journalism in Arhus and Professor Marianne Peters of the Hogeschool in Utrecht brought together students from all over Europe and the world in their *Europe in the World* programme. They forced teachers and students alike to examine issues of journalism, media and society in a European context. In particular they forced me to take off my Anglo-American blinkers – which are firmly tied to the study of the media and communication in the United Kingdom – to discover the European dimension of journalism and media studies. I am eternally grateful to them for liberating me from my conceptual cell. My knowledge and understanding of European media comes from a number of colleagues on this and related programmes in Arhus and Utrecht: Jens Henrik Hahr, Kim Minke, Nancy Graham Holm, Peter Vasterman, Peter Verwey, Gerd Smit, Peter Schurs and Paul de Lange. Inge Munk, Mari Anne Verdonk and Anna Nerjup also deserve thanks; without their help and skill these programmes would not have run so smoothly. I would also like to thank the late Geoff Mungham of Cardiff University, who overcame his narrow English upbringing to become a wholehearted and committed European teacher. His contribution to these programmes was immense and his untimely death a great loss. I am so sorry he was not able to comment on the final text of this enterprise.

Others who also played a key part in my European voyage of discovery are Tor Ekevall, Judy Gladwell, Brian Winston, John Eldridge, Bob Franklin, Colin Sparks, Diana Brand and Rob Melville. I would also like to thank my American colleagues who were part of the EU–US exchange programme, especially Ralph Izard, Byron Scott and Jim Crook. Particular thanks go to all the students who went through the European Journalism Studies Masters programme from 1993 to 2001. Their patience, good humour and contribution to my classes in European Media played a crucial role in developing this book. Thanks are also due to all my colleagues at Swansea, especially Ieuan Williams and Debbie Rideout, Louise Stoddard, Mike Bromley and, above all, Clare Hudson, who continues to support my academic endeavours between the chinks of everyday life.

Crucially there are all the people at Edward Arnold who waited so long for a manuscript. Thank you to Lesley Riddle, Abigail Woodman, Eva Martinez and Colin Goodlad. Finally I would like to thank the usual suspects, Edmund, Margaret, Frances, Alan, Griff, Rowley, Pam and Barry, and Ie, who despite his many shortcomings still has his sedentary job at the BBC. None of these people are responsible for the limitations of the book. They are entirely my fault.

Contents

Introduction

Why write a book about European media? Colin Sparks (1998: xvii) is not interested in the location of the supposed cultural boundaries of Europe, nor whether certain kinds of behaviour are properly 'European'. Like the term 'British', 'European' is simply 'another ludicrous ideological construction' that is 'not open to serious analysis [or] useful to illuminate reality'. He might be right; most probably he is. But ideological constructions have personal consequences.

My starting point is a struggle with something called 'Britishness', which has been alleviated in some part by discovering a European identity. Being 'imprisoned inside the misrepresentation and misunderstanding of others can', as Anthony Smith (1980: 27) has said, 'be a withering form of incarceration'. Being 'Welsh' inside the British State has been a real and emotionally charged struggle against someone else's view of who and what I am. The latter decades of the twentieth century have provided an opportunity for many living on the margins of the United Kingdom to escape the straitjacket of 'Britishness' to explore an allegiance to something beyond these shores. Being European has been and still is an attractive proposition in several ways. It has provided the opportunity for previously subsumed collective identities to explore what it means to be Welsh, Catalan, Basque, Scottish, and so on. By undermining the nation state, the European supranational experiment has allowed space to examine and debate new or renewed identities. It has also enabled exploration of the extent to which there are similarities – in practices, attitudes, beliefs, opinions and tastes – between Europeans, in contradistinction to the bonds which formally tie citizens to their nation states. This journey of enquiry has led to an interest in the structures, practices and performances of the media across Europe.

This basic introductory text seeks to make a small contribution to the neglect of the Europe-wide dimension of the study of the mass media, thereby challenging the Anglo-American dominance of the 'discipline' of media studies. As a media scholar, my studies of the press, broadcasting and film have focused largely on what has happened and is happening to the media in Britain and North America. What is happening elsewhere in the world is sometimes touched on, usually in order to understand the extent to which western, or more accurately Anglo-American, structures, practices and representations are replicated or reinforced. The 'self-absorption and parochialism' of much of the study of the mass media has been criticized by Curran and Park (2000: 3), who refer to the 'routine' way in which 'universalistic observations about the media [are] advanced in English-language books on the basis of evidence from a tiny handful of countries'. Downing (1996: xi) talks of the conceptual impoverishment of extrapolating theoretically from such unrepresentative nations as Britain and the USA, a concern shared by Sparks (1998). Until recently this 'bias' has been supplemented by the tendency to concentrate on national approaches to understanding media systems. Comparative studies of the operation of the mass media in different countries and nation states are few and far between. The nation state plays and will continue to play a considerable part in shaping the nature of media systems, and national differences account for the distinctions between them. Ironically it is the debate in the academic community about the process of globalization – in particular, whether there are trends towards media standardization and cultural homogenization – that has led scholars to begin to explore other parts of the world and compare and contrast what is happening in different countries. The discovery of other media systems around the world has presented the study of European media with certain problems and challenges.

Europe is often lost in the discussion of global media and culture, being subsumed as part of the 'West' or the 'western bloc'. Media scholars have written extensively about the 'westernization' of the world. What is meant by the West is often imprecise (Latouche 1996). Usually it is shorthand for Anglo-American domination and its consequences. Tunstall (1977) argues that each of the world's mass media was invented and developed in the USA (with some British contribution and support) and then imported and copied by other nations. Most of the styles and patterns of media forms around the world are shaped and influenced by imported Anglo-American media. In media terms, Europe, and particularly the larger European countries, can claim nothing more than modest global accomplishments (Tunstall and Machin 1999: 2). Rather it has been one of the most profitable markets for US media exports. To speak of the 'eurocentrism' of the global media is a misnomer. We should be talking about American- or Anglo-American-centrism. While it may be possible to talk about European countries as geographically and ideologically part of the West, historically, in media terms, they have been victims of Anglo-American media imperialism in the same way as the rest of the world. By assuming their involvement as part of the 'western media', media studies has ignored or neglected the examination of the characteristics that differentiate the media and media systems in Europe from those in Britain and America, as well as the rest of the world. In the process, comparing the similarities and differences between European media systems has been passed by.

What are the European media? Determining what is European – a question at the centre of current debates about the development of the European Union (EU) – is not easy. The vast outpouring of words and images of Europe in the media presents a more certain notion of something called Europe than actually exists. Within the geographic boundaries of the European continent – which stretch from the Atlantic coast to the Urals – there are many different political and cultural entities. This diverse collection of nations, sub-nations, regions and cities has in common a history of conflict, competition and dislike. Deep-seated differences distinguish Europeans from one another and are still expressed today in the media. For example, the British tabloid newspaper the *Sun* trumpets headlines such as 'Hop off Frogs' and 'Up Yours Delors'. Elsewhere in Europe, especially in those parts of the continent which have emerged recently from behind the Iron Curtain, old animosities have resulted in open warfare and conflict. Older minority cultural groupings, such as the Catalans, Scots, Bretons and Sorbs, are also re-emerging to challenge the European nation state, and the migration into Europe of peoples from the former colonies of the now defunct European empires adds to the cultural and political complexity of the continent. These are just some of the social, cultural, political, linguistic, historical and geographic differences that set apart from each other European nations, regions and peoples.

Is it possible, then, to argue that behind this diversity the peoples who live in the nations of Europe have things in common? Is there a common heritage of shared experience which unites all Europeans? According to the European Commission there is. 'European culture is marked by its diversity of climate, countryside, architecture, language, beliefs, taste and artistic style . . . but underlying this variety there is an affinity, a family of likeness, a common European identity' (Commission of the European Communities 1983). While it is easy to say Europeans have much in common, it is more difficult to detail exactly what this is. Pieterse (1991) sums up what for many determines and characterizes European culture. 'Europe is formed by the . . . community of nations which are largely characterised by the inherited civilisation whose important sources are: The Judaeo-Christian religion; the Greek-Hellenistic ideas in the field of Government, philosophy, art and science and finally the Roman views concerning law' (Pieterse 1991: 3). These attributes, however, are part of what Pieterse and others label 'mythic Europeanism'. They are rooted in the imperial expansion of Europe in the nineteenth century, which emphasized the superiority of European civilization and the mission to spread its 'benefits' to the rest of the world. Today they are encapsulated in the views of many Europhiles, who seek to forge the 'divisive potential of sovereign states' into a single sociocultural entity called the European Community (Husband 1993). Halloran (1993) points out that while Europe has been defined in a number of ways, to suit a range of needs and interests, whatever boundaries people draw around Europe, everyone associates their mapping with an assumption of a social and cultural similarity, or 'community of culture', across the continent. The contradictions of commonality and disunity are at the heart of any discussion of Europe and what is European.

The European mass media are no different. In the latest edition of *The Euromedia Handbook*, a reference book outlining the main features of media systems in Europe, McQuail talks of 'the paradox of unity and dissimilarity of this set of national "stories"' (Kelly et al. 2004: 1). The shape of individual media systems reflects the histories of the different European nations, regions and peoples. This means that each of Europe's media systems will react differently to the vast changes that are occurring as a result of the information and communications revolution. The influence of newspapers, as well as the extent of newspaper consumption, varies across the continent. The form public service broadcasting takes differs enormously from country to country, as do the regulatory mechanisms established to oversee the running of the media. The arrangements for the reporting of politics are as diverse as the political structures that have emerged in the different nations of the continent. Europeans' media consumption habits and cultural tastes and activities have been shaped by their own societies and reflect their own specific traditions. National and local audiences, as Wieten (2000) notes of television programming across Europe, tend to gravitate towards media texts that reinforce a sense of themselves and who they are.

Nevertheless, the media in western Europe and the newly liberated eastern Europe increasingly have more in common. McQuail (2004) identifies several features. Broadcasting in European media systems is organized around the commitment to public service. State intervention in the operation of the media is accepted, to a greater or lesser extent, in every national media system as necessary to safeguard the public and national interest. Political parties have featured prominently in the shaping of European media systems, including the development of party political media. A shared set of principles of law, human rights and democracy underpin the regulation and operation of the media across Europe. The EU, in its many institutional forms, exerts pressure on every media system to adopt and accept standard forms of media regulation. There are common habits that make Europeans different from audiences elsewhere in the world, particularly in North America: Europeans read more newspapers, and per capita consumption of books and magazines is much higher. Hujanen (2000: 72) draws attention to the 'aesthetic tradition of European television', with its preference for the 'arts and high culture over the popular'. The extent to which these and other habits distinguish Europe from the rest of the world is a matter of debate. What is not is that the media in Europe are undergoing a radical transformation. Perhaps most significant today is the complex set of economic, technological, political and ideological forces that are pushing European media systems in roughly the same direction. It is possible to argue that every media system in Europe is facing a crisis in public communication, brought about by political, economic, technological and ideological changes which threaten – or promise, depending on your perspective – to erode national differences. It is possible to argue that the media are becoming more 'Europeanized'. Similarities are appearing not only in what Europeans read, watch and listen to, but also in the nature and structure of Europe's print, broadcasting, film and music industries.

This book compares and contrasts what is happening in different European media systems and explores the broad trends and developments that are threatening to erode national differences and promising to create a distinct 'European dimension' to the mass media. The basic argument underlying the description and analysis of what is happening is that, in the process of responding to a similar set of technological, political and economic changes, European media systems are beginning to converge. Some will highlight the impossibility of generalizing about the European media. This book does not seek to minimize national differences and variations; in fact, the centripetal forces which are fragmenting media into more local and regional entities are discussed. Rather the emphasis is placed on examining the forces that are producing similarities in the structure, content, practices and performances of the mass media across Europe. Not all media are experiencing or responding to these forces in the same way or to the same extent. We are not talking about a homogenization of the European media, but exploring the process by which differences between national media systems are diminishing and greater commonality is developing. It is possible to identify two main arguments in this respect. Hallin and Mancini (2004: 252) believe it is possible to 'summarise the changes in European media systems as a shift toward the Liberal model that prevails in its purest form in North America'. They identify external forces, such as 'Americanisation' and the development of a 'global media culture', and internal changes, such as 'commercialisation', as being responsible for this. Others explore the ways in which these changes are furthering the emergence of a 'European public sphere' or a 'European sphere of communication', in which a sense of 'Europeanness' is growing among the nations and peoples of Europe (Weymouth and Lamizet 1996: 202–12). European media are seen as playing a role in disseminating information about and representations of Europe which are helping to create an 'imagined community' that has nothing to do with national boundaries and particular cultural histories.

Chapter 1 outlines the transformation that has occurred in the European media landscape since 1980. It describes the nature of the changes that have led to this transformation, highlighting the way in which the national foundations of Europe's media have been shaken by the developments. The trend to an ever decreasing number of large corporate 'empires' or 'media moguls', owning and controlling Europe's media, is singled out as one of the key changes. Chapter 2 compares and contrasts the development of the press across the continent. Compared to other parts of the world, Europe is 'still the stronghold of the daily press' (Gustafsson and Weibull 1997). However, the newspaper industry is in decline and the structure of the European press is going through a profound change, the nature and shape of which are examined. Chapter 3 describes and discusses the development of European broadcasting. The distinguishing feature of European broadcasting – the concept of public service – is analysed, along with the challenges to this philosophy posed by new technological, political and socio-economic circumstances. Chapter 4 looks at the practice and performance of journalism across Europe, including the ways in which journalists define their roles in society. The different traditions with respect to news, opinion and comment, as well as the organization of the relationship between reporters and their sources, are discussed. The chapter asks whether it is possible to identify a European model or tradition of journalism distinct from its Anglo-American counterpart. Chapter 5 explores the state of the European film industry, with special reference to its relationship with Hollywood. The Americanization of European media and culture has been a long-standing matter of concern. This has been acutely manifest in the film industry, and the relationship between Hollywood and European film-makers became a key part of the General Agreement on Tariffs and Trade (GATT) negotiations in the 1990s. The consequences of this for European cinema are discussed.

Chapter 6 asks whether the media played a significant role in the collapse of communism in Eastern Europe. The images and discourse around the events of 1989 are examined in answering this question. The chapter also examines the emergence of the media in Eastern Europe since the end of communism. What has been the involvement of western media interests? How have they shaped the nature of the media that are emerging? Are the emerging media capable of building citizenship and political democracy in Eastern Europe? Chapter 7 focuses on the role of the EU in the development of the media and media policy in Europe. The factors that have shaped the EU's attempts to promote a collective identity through the media as well as the national resistance to such efforts are analysed. The internal tension within the EU and the clash between the economic and cultural objectives of the EU's media policy are explored. Finally, the chapter discusses the EU's response to one of the features of the new media landscape in Europe – the rise of regional TV channels, radio stations and newspapers, which articulate new or revived sub-national and local identities. Chapter 8 explores whether a changing media landscape is leading to a Europeanization of the output, practices, performance and structures of national media systems throughout Europe. It also asks how far 'more' European media are contributing to the development of a greater sense of 'Europeanness' among the peoples of Europe?

One final point. Throughout the book, a range of statistics is drawn on to indicate and illustrate the changes and developments taking place in the European media. Gathering these statistics is not without its problems. Information on the media in Europe is not easy to obtain, often out of date and sometimes contradictory. When data is located, facts and figures suffer from different definitions of what Europe is. What is included in and excluded from what constitutes Europe can skew figures such as those about Europeans' leisure time or newspaper consumption, or the number of television channels operating across the continent. Non-EU countries, such as Norway and Switzerland, are sometimes omitted in data about European media. In addition, national figures sometimes mask regional or sub-national variations. The term 'Europe' is often used in different ways, a problem compounded by the political changes brought about by the enlargement of the EU and the emergence of post-communist European societies. Where possible, care has been taken to identify the reference point of the statistics used.

chapter one

The European media landscape

The media in Europe have undergone considerable transformation since the end of the Second World War. Weymouth and Lamizet (1995: 8) identify two stages in their development: from 1945 to 'approximately' 1980, and from 1980 onwards. While all divisions are slightly arbitrary, it is commonly accepted that in the late 1970s a shift began to take place in the nature of mass communication and the structure and content of the media industries. The shift can be associated with a range of unprecedented technological, social, economic, political and ideological developments, which have impacted the media in several ways, the most important of which has been to undermine the national foundations on which the European media had operated since 1945. Up to 1980 the media played a key role in reinforcing national identity and providing people with their sense of belonging. Since 1980 their ability and capacity to reflect and represent national communities has been called into question. What, when and how Europeans watch, hear and read has changed, and changing media consumption habits are central to understanding new forms of group identities and allegiances that are emerging. The processes by which the media are produced have also been fundamentally restructured, including the demise of public service broadcasting, which singled out European media systems from their counterparts elsewhere in the world. One crucial aspect of this restructuring has been the growth of a small number of Europe-wide conglomerates who have come to dominate the media landscape in Europe. The political, economic and cultural consequences of the concentration of media ownership in Western and Eastern Europe are open to debate.

The media in 1945

In order to examine the changes that are taking place in the European media landscape it is important to understand what has happened to European society in the post-war period. The Second World War profoundly weakened the media, as it did every other aspect of society. After five years of fighting the basic infrastructure of European society had been destroyed. In 1945 the primary objective was the rebuilding and reconstruction of economic, social and political life. Most Europeans craved political stability. The initial impetus for the establishment of what was to become the EU was not simply the economic reconstruction of the continent, but also the desire to ensure that national differences and political conflicts would never again result in war. The peoples of Europe wanted to see an end to the traditional enmities that had divided them. They also demanded social and economic reform, to alleviate the plight of ordinary men and women who had suffered most during the war. There was a conviction among working people that the social and economic deprivations of the Depression years would not return. The result was that national governments – with a huge influx of US aid in the form of the Marshall Plan – set about reconstructing their societies on the basis of a more egalitarian economic and social order. The clearest manifestation of this was the birth of the welfare state, which promised to take care of European citizens from cradle to grave. For the next thirty years, until the mid-1970s, the welfare state extended its reach. Accompanied by steady, consistent economic growth – most spectacular in West Germany – Europe witnessed the reassertion of democracy (with outside help in the cases of Italy and Germany), a high degree of political stability (albeit frozen in by the cold war) and a level of social harmony never before experienced.

The role of the media in this period was to help to 'revitalise democratic principles and reinforce the national identities of the newly liberated European nation-states' (Weymouth and Lamizet 1995: 13). To do this the press had to undergo a process of political re-education. Fascist newspapers in Germany and Italy were closed down, as were newspapers in occupied Europe that had collaborated with the enemy. Newspapers that continued to be published in occupied France were banned in 1944; only 28 of the 206 daily newspapers published in 1939 were allowed to remain in business (Kuhn 1995: 54). New newspapers, such as *Le Monde*, were born of the effort to rebuild a new press suited to the process of reconstruction. They did this by reporting and reflecting a broad range of political viewpoints; the following decade witnessed a high degree of political pluralism in the west European press. However, it was during this period that newspapers lost their pre-eminence as the primary medium of mass communication.

From the 1960s, broadcasting, and television in particular, became the main (as well as the most trusted) source of information for a significant majority of western Europeans about what was happening around them. A recent survey found that 99 per cent of the population of the EU watch television regularly (Eurobarometer 2002). A similar picture emerges from the candidate countries who joined the EU in 2004. Unlike the press, broadcasting in Europe had been organized as a public service, rejecting the market as an effective mechanism for the allocation of resources and the provision of choice. The public service mission to educate as well as inform and entertain ensured broadcasting played a key role in the development of citizenship and the rebuilding of national communities. The history of European broadcasting up to 1980 is a history of national broadcasters, such as the British Broadcasting Corporation (BBC) in the United Kingdom, Danmarks Radio (DR) in Denmark and Norsk Rikskrinkasting (NRK) in Norway. These organizations saw their role as providing entertainment, information and education to the whole nation, attaching great importance to the role of broadcasting in building citizenship, encouraging political participation, fostering a sense of national unity and identity and defending the public interest. To do this they were provided with a virtual monopoly on broadcasting, most Europeans having only one or two channels to watch. Regional or local broadcasting usually formed a subsidiary part of the national broadcaster's operation, with the exception of Germany (whose broadcasting system was rebuilt after the war on a regional basis), Switzerland and Belgium. National governments were closely involved in the running of broadcasting and, as a result, used the medium in varying degrees to promote their plans for post-war reconstruction (Weymouth and Lamizet 1995: 14). In the process of reconstruction, the medium was often paternalistic and committed to forms of representation which emphasized the values of the national community at the expense of minority social groups.

The political and economic reconstruction of Western Europe in the late 1940s and the 1950s took place against the background of the social and moral values that had characterized the old order. Traditionally European societies were highly stratified, divided into social groupings who knew their place in the social hierarchy. The distinctions between these groups were based on clear differences in their ideological commitments, rooted in their class or religious affiliations. Individuals defined their personal identity and material well-being in terms of social class and religion (Hallin and Mancini 2004: 263–7). Social life was structured around institutions such as the church, trade unions and political parties. These bodies organized leisure activities, sports and voluntary activities, as well as schools, hospitals and welfare. They also had their own media. As the dominant media prior to the Second World War, the composition of the press reflected class loyalties and allegiances. Newspapers served the interests of different classes and social groups, many acting as the official mouthpieces of political parties or religious communities. The first half of the twentieth century had witnessed a gradual decline in the social influence of these groups, as the state began to take over more of their functions and develop people's allegiance to the nation, but the clear cultural, social and economic divisions in European society lasted into the immediate post-war period. Individuals still derived their social and moral values, attitudes, assumptions and behaviour from their class and group identity, which was reflected in the structure and consumption of the European media. Traditional social mores and attitudes were not to endure with a corresponding change in Europe's media.

Forces of change

Since the late 1970s there has been a fundamental change in the European media landscape. Technology is often seen as the driving force of the radical and extraordinary changes. Technological change has led to a proliferation of the ways of delivering information and entertainment to European households. Satellite and cable have provided the opportunity to create more media which are instantly available across national boundaries. The videocassette recorder (VCR) and interactive services such as the television remote control enable media consumers to have more say over what they consume and when they consume it. Computers have helped to reduce the costs and increase the efficiency of newspaper and magazine production. The internet offers individuals and groups new forms of expression, which threaten the traditional role of journalism in collecting and processing information. We are now embarking on a greater technological leap forward with the advent of digital technology, which 'represents the most significant innovation since the advent of television' (Chalaby and Segell 1999: 352). Digital technology, by increasing exponentially the amount of frequency space, not only speeds up considerably the transmission of information and images, but also increases the capacity to transmit more material and provides for interactive services for listeners and viewers. It promises a new 'media revolution' in that it will result in 'the definitive end of the analogue Gutenberg era' (de Bens and Mazzoleni 1998: 165).

Technological developments hold out a range of possible changes in the media industries. However, many in these industries, as well as those who comment on them, are easily led astray by what they perceive as the power of technology. They see technological change as the primary determinant of what is happening to the European media and often ascribe a degree of certainty and predictability to the process. But there is great uncertainty as to the changes new technologies are generating. Sociologist Tony Giddens talks about 'living on a high technological frontier which absolutely no-one understands and which generates a diversity of possible futures' (quoted in Chalaby and Segell 1999: 354). Chalaby and Segell (1999) speculate about the increased sources of uncertainty and the level of risk created by digitalization for those in the broadcasting industries. The changing media landscape in Europe cannot be explained solely and simply in terms of technological developments. Political policy and socio-economic and cultural factors are as important, if not more so. Winston (1998: 11) points out that these factors can act as a brake on the 'potential of the device to radically disrupt pre-existing social formations', while Levinson (1997: 10) highlights the 'profoundly unintended consequences of any information technology'. Ultimately it is only possible to understand the changing media landscape in Europe by locating technological advances in the context of political, economic, social and cultural changes.

Politics has played a crucial role in the restructuring of Europe's media landscape. Since the late 1970s, the election of European governments, of both left and right, committed to a free market ideology has been of great significance in shaping the development of the European media. They have passed legislation which has resulted in the liberalization and deregulation of the media industries. What is happening in the media industries is part of a wider neoliberal reaction against government intervention in all aspects of social and economic life. Unlike the immediate post-war years, belief in the market as the proper determinant of what the public is offered and what it chooses to consume has taken hold across the continent. Policymakers varied in their commitment to the market and, as a result, the pace of media deregulation differed from country to country. Many smaller countries were caught up in the slipstream of the changes in the larger media markets of Britain, France and Germany, while rampant deregulation took hold in Italy as a result of politicians' inability to produce any broadcasting policy. The pro-market stance of many European governments and policymakers since 1980 is based on the view that the market will increase consumer choice, promote the growth of the media industries and bring greater economic benefits (Humphreys 1998, cited in Steemers 2004: 36). This ideological shift reflects, in part, developments in the broader socio-economic environment which have stressed individual choice and consumerism.

Since the mid-1960s Europe has experienced unprecedented social and economic change, which has led to declining loyalty to the institutions that used to structure European social life. This has had a significant impact on the organization, structure, performance, practice and content of the media. Perhaps the most significant development is the expansion of the economies of Europe. Increased affluence and the emergence of the consumer society produced a fundamental transformation in people's lives. Leisure time has expanded enormously and today it is estimated that the average European spends more hours per week on leisure activities than work. Central to these activities is the use and consumption of the media, which increasingly constitutes an important part of our daily lives. More crucially, affluence and economic growth have brought about a secularization of European society which has weakened the social bonds that characterized pre-war European society (Hallin and Mancini 2004: 178–9, 263–77). Economic growth in post-war Europe emphasized individual economic success. Together with increased educational attainment, this has reinforced the individual's sense of self, shaking his or her allegiance to social and political groupings.

Traditional allegiances have been weakened further by the fragmentation of European society. Urbanization hastened the decline of rural life and the proportion of people working on the land declined massively in the immediate post-war period, resulting in the demise of the peasant and farming communities who had played a considerable political and economic role in both Southern and Northern Europe. Rural decline was followed by the collapse of the heavy industries of coal, steel and iron from the 1970s onwards, which helped to break down the solidarity of the industrial working classes (see Weymouth and Lamizet 1995: 14–15). Regular churchgoing and other forms of religious piety have diminished drastically (Kascuba 1993: 200). Membership of political parties declined as social and economic change weakened the foundations on which the mass political parties of the early twentieth century were built. Without strong attachment to religious or class faith, political parties built up around distinct social groups, and particular ideological lines were replaced by 'catch-all parties' whose primary aim was to capture votes rather than represent groups or ideologies (Hallin and Mancini 2004: 265). New social groups and divisions are emerging as the conventions and norms that traditionally shaped everyday life have waned. This can be seen across various aspects of daily life in Europe.

There has been a revolution in the lives of young people. Youth cultures emerged in the post-war period. In the 1950s and 1960s increased leisure time and rising purchasing power were responsible for young people's growing independence. This independence was celebrated by the creation of lifestyles and activities which brought young people into conflict with the older generation. Women's roles are changing. Women are escaping the domestic sphere of home and family to participate more broadly in society. This represents a challenge to the male-dominated and male-oriented nature of European society. While European society may still be organized on patriarchal lines, women today have more opportunity to shape how they conduct their lives. The migration of peoples into Europe has resulted in the rise of new demographic groups. The increased presence of so-called ethnic minority, or 'othered', groups poses a number of challenges to Europe and European institutions. Husband (1993) draws attention to the contradictions in the EU's response to migration. The EU stresses the rights of ethnic minorities, challenges racism, promotes equality and celebrates a multicultural Europe, while at the same time constructing 'Fortress Europe' through sealing the continent's borders to the entry of migrants and affirming a 'Euro-kultur' which marginalizes othered identities. Similarly, Sorbs, Catalans, Scots, Occitans and other peoples or nations without states have asserted themselves, demanding that their voices be heard and their values, ways of life and myths acknowledged (Iorwerth 1995). The outcome is not simply the fragmentation of the social structure that underpinned European society, but what some have characterized as a 'crisis of identity' (Morley and Robins 1995). The emergence of these 'new' identities in the post-war period represents a challenge not only to the values and myths of European nation states, their identities and consciousness, but also to the development of pan-European identity and consciousness.

Mass media and European identities

The media are seen as playing a central role in how Europeans are re-imagining themselves. There is a close and intimate connection between the media and identity. The media in the post-war period have played their part in giving expression to national identities across Europe (Scriven and Roberts 2003: 1). Broadcasting, film and, to a lesser extent, the press were national in their organization, outlook and output. The 'great newspapers' of Europe claimed more and more to speak on behalf of the nation, address a national agenda or speak out on the national issues of the day. Media policymaking was framed in a national context, formulated by government in keeping with the social customs, attitudes and traditions of the national community. Variations in political structures, economic conditions, language and culture, as well as social mores and attitudes, ensured that national media systems across the continent were distinct. Media consumption patterns reflect the ways of life in different parts of Europe. The division of labour, the organization of leisure, the pattern of the workday, the nature of the education system, the traditions of politics, the ability and capacity to access the media and even the weather are among the factors that have determined the ways in which Europeans consume their media and the kinds of media products that are popular. How Europeans buy their newspapers, the peak times for watching television, the types of magazines that are popular, the practice of journalism, the relationship between the media and politics and the regulatory mechanism for ensuring plurality, fairness and privacy differ from country to country. The most noticeable differences are between Northern and Southern Europe. However, the transformations in European politics, economy and society since the late 1970s have brought about a gradual erosion of these differences.

Some commentators argue that the weakening of older institutions and structures, such as the church, the family and political parties, has strengthened the power of the media to shape our sense of identity (Hallin and Mancini 2004: 263). More crucially, the changes have affected the capacity and ability of the media to reflect and represent national identity on a number of levels. Perhaps it is developments at the supranational level that are most noticeable. The economic and political change brought about by the growth of the EU and the European common market has undermined the nation state and national institutions, including the media. Since its inception in the late 1940s, what has become the EU has promoted European economic integration, which has led to a standardization and harmonization of markets in Europe. Media economic activity and media policy increasingly occur in a European context and are less subject to the whims and peculiarities of national systems. Policies, practices and actions in media markets are becoming 'Europeanized'.

Furthermore the decision to embark on the process of economic liberalization and deregulation has opened up national media markets, thereby helping to erode national differences. Since the 1980s and, in particular, the Maastricht Treaty, efforts to develop economic cooperation and integration have been accompanied by moves towards closer political and cultural cooperation and integration. The pace at which national authorities have ceded decision-making power to pan-European institutions accelerated in the wake of Jacques Delors' call for 'ever closer union'. The scale of these efforts has expanded since 1989, with the end of Soviet occupation and control of Eastern Europe. The former European countries of the communist bloc have been freed to rediscover their European identities. The alacrity with which they embraced these identities is shown in the recent enlargement of the EU, which brought several of these nations into the European project. Recent political transformation in countries such as the Ukraine promises further enlargement. The move to greater political integration is controversial in parts of Europe such as Denmark and Britain, where it is strongly resisted. While political integration may be an unimaginable endeavour for some, it is clear that since the 1980s Europe has become 'much closer to its desired unity' (quoted in Halloran, 1993).

The media have been identified by the EU Commission in their efforts to build a unified Europe as a 'crucial tool in the realisation of a European identity' (Bakir 1996: 177). Pan-European media are necessary to foster European integration and unification. As one MEP stated in 1982: 'Information is . . . perhaps the most decisive question for European unification . . . a European consciousness will only arise if Europeans are suitably informed' (quoted in Kleinsteuber et al. 1993: 129). Not all media were seen as playing an equal role in this process. The 'Television Without Frontiers' directive, passed in 1989, stressed the importance of the medium to the process of European cultural and political integration (see Humphreys 1996: chapter 8). Television was regarded as a more influential and less nationally encumbered medium than print; and technological developments, most crucially the advent of satellite broadcasting, made Europe-wide television feasible. By building a European audio-visual space, supporters of the directive saw cross-border, pan-European television programming taking a lead in building a European identity. To realize this aim, the EU set about creating the economic conditions for the development of Europe-wide television, which meant breaking down national media markets that had dominated European broadcasting until the 1980s. Deregulation and liberalization were seen as essential components in breaking down the regulatory mechanisms that protected national broadcasters, and the EU began developing a European media policy which supported the deregulatory steps of national governments. The connection between media deregulation and European integration was made clear in the Bangemann Report in 1994, which stated: 'Competition policy is a key element in the [EU] strategy. It is especially important for consolidating the single market and for attracting the private capital necessary for the growth of trans-European information infrastructure'. The aim was to encourage the enlargement of firms to operate at a European or international level, thereby facilitating pan-European programming. Bangemann also stated that regulation was necessary at the supranational level to ensure there were no regulatory disparities between member states (Wheeler 2004). As a result of the EU's activities, the media were placed at the heart of the struggle to build a unified Europe. We can see at the supranational level that the economic, political and media policies of the EU are loosening national sovereignty and changing the media's relationship with the nation and individual viewers, listeners and readers (see chapters 7 and 8).

If the efforts of the EU represent a top-down approach to using the media to construct a collective identity, pressures from 'below' are as important as those from 'above' in understanding what is happening to the European media. National media systems not only have to react to the supranational challenge of the EU, but also to those forces that are pushing for the devolution and decentralization of European politics and society. These sub-national forces are also having an impact on media structures and output. New social groups, including ethnic groups, women, young people, social movements, regional and sub-national communities, became increasingly critical in the post-war period of the ways in which they were denied access to or marginalized by the media (see Scriven and Roberts 2003). Campaigns for greater access to the airwaves or fairer representation were common in most European countries in the 1970s and 1980s. The result was that national media, in particular TV networks, began to incorporate programming which reflected these groups, communities and identities. Some groups established their own media. Zee TV-Europe is one example of how satellite television is being used to respond to the needs of minority social groups for wider audio-visual representation. Set up in 1996, Zee TV-Europe broadcasts to the South Asian diaspora across Western Europe (Dudrah 2002). Of particular significance to the debate about European identity was the development of regional media across Europe. In the late 1970s and early 1980s there was a huge growth of regional television, which took many forms, from new stations, working for established national broadcasters, to autonomous, independent channels, representing linguistic and cultural minorities (Garitaonandia 1993). The decentralization of the broadcast media represents a different version of Europe: a 'Europe of the Regions', which conceives of European identity in terms of a mosaic of difference and diversity. The tension between this view of Europe and the melting-pot approach of those supporting the development of a common culture and shared European identity is an important factor in shaping the EU's audio-visual policy. The media industries in Europe 'are supposed to articulate the "deep solidarity" of our collective consciousness and our common culture; and, at the same time, they are asked to reflect the rich variety and diversity of European nations and regions' (Robins 1993: 80). For some these views are not reconcilable. Nevertheless, the national construction of Europe's media was identified by both supranational and sub-national forces as an impediment to the development of their objectives and aspirations. Since the late 1970s the European media have contributed to the process of building sub-national and regional consciousness in Europe.

How Europeans imagine themselves is also subject to the spectre of Americanization. Throughout the twentieth century, in common with people in many other parts of the world, Europeans have felt that their cultural identity is being undermined by the relentless flow of American popular culture into their continent. Hollywood, Tin Pan Alley, jazz, rock 'n' roll, comic books, *Dallas* and *Dynasty* and computer games such as 'Tomb Raider' are all examples of American media products that have captured the imaginations and wallets of European audiences. While concern about the impact of American media and cultural products is long-standing, since the advent of television in the 1960s the flow of US material has increased rapidly, accelerating with the arrival of satellite and cable television. This increased flow is not only accompanied by the fear that the growing consumption of American culture is eroding national cultures in Europe and acting as a major barrier to the development of a common European cultural identity, but is also seen as threatening the industrial base of European media and cultural production. The importation of American products is seen as destroying European jobs and companies, making Europe less competitive in the global media markets (see Morley and Robins 1995: chapter 3). The flow of American media products and practices has led to a growing similarity in what people watch, see and hear and the way in which the media in Europe operate. European broadcasters and media executives are increasingly turning to America for knowledge and assistance on how to work in a more competitive and commercialized environment (Hujanen 2000). The EU has justified Europeanization as a necessary antidote to the process of Americanization. The growth of large European media firms and conglomerates is in part seen as increasing Europe's ability to counter US influence and play a role on the world stage. However, the audio-visual policy of opening up national media markets presents the real and clear danger of enhancing Americanization through an increased flow of US programmes into Europe. The market context which is driving the EU's audio-visual policy is not seen by some critics as compatible with expectations of the media's capacity to promote integration (Robins 1993; Schlesinger 1993). This dilemma highlights the importance of the connection between identity and economics in shaping the European media landscape.

Europe's media market

Europe has developed into the largest media market in the world. If you consider the member states of the enlarged EU, together with the population of Russia and the ex-communist countries of Eastern Europe, plus Norway and Switzerland, a potential market of nearly 700 million people exists, almost three times the size of the US domestic market. Several features can be identified in the development of this market since 1980. The first feature is that Europe's media market has undergone a huge expansion.

Europeans and their media consumption habits

Virtually every household in the EU owns a television set, with nearly half of them possessing two or more. Nine out of ten households possess a transistor radio, while almost two-thirds of households are equipped with a videocassette recorder and one-third a personal computer. Every person within the EU watches on average 3 hours and 26 minutes of television per day, broadcast by more than 2600 television channels/stations (Sequentia 1995). They listen to a comparable amount of radio, 3 hours and 11 minutes daily, supplied by over 8000 radio stations (European Music Office 1996). Newspaper circulation per capita is higher than anywhere else in the world. More than 2115 daily newspapers are published in Europe, with a total circulation of 190 million (UNESCO 2003). It is estimated that around 11,000 consumer magazines and 25,000 specialist titles are published in Western Europe (Braithwaite 1996: 97). Europeans are keen film-goers. In 2002 there were over 933 million admissions to the cinema in EU countries (European Audiovisual Observatory 2003). More than one billion units of sound recordings, that is vinyl, singles, CD and music cassettes were sold in 1999. Nearly 60 per cent of Europeans listen to music every day, the vast majority of people listening on the radio (Eurobarometer 2002). A survey of media consumption in the countries which joined the EU in 2004 indicates similar patterns emerging. In stark quantitative terms, the amount of media hardware in European households is impressive, as is the amount of time most Europeans spend on media activities.

Based on data for the member states of the EU prior to enlargement in 2004, media consumption has grown enormously. This growth is fuelled in particular by the development of broadcasting and new media. While newspapers have declined, their electronic counterparts have gone from strength to strength. Driven by technological change and the policy of deregulation, more television channels are popping up all over Europe. According to Papathanassopoulos (2002: 14), the number of channels in Europe grew from fewer than 90 in 1989 to 580 in 2000. The multiplicity of television channels, with many more to come in the wake of the 'digital revolution', is not only accounted for by the arrival of cable and satellite broadcasting. There has also been a corresponding growth in terrestrial channels, the result of governments preferring to develop commercial channels domestically rather than have them imposed from outside. Many of the new channels are thematic, in the sense that they specialize in a particular kind of programming, such as news, music, sport, children, lifestyle, shopping, history, religion, documentary, erotica and wildlife. Thematic channels survive on smaller audiences; as a result, niche broadcasting presents a challenge to the established national channels.

The arrival of these channels has resulted in greater competition in the television market, which for ordinary viewers has expanded the amount of programming they can watch. Television today broadcasts 24 hours, from breakfast television to the late-night film and educational fare of the early morning hours. To fill the increased programming hours, more news, sport, entertainment and drama/serials are being produced than ever before. A similar development has taken place in radio. As television expanded, radio slowly shrunk, to the extent that it came to be seen chiefly as a subsidiary medium of mass communication, to be used when television was not available or accessible (Kleinsteuber et al. 1993: 146). However, the 1980s witnessed a proliferation of commercial and non-commercial radio stations across the continent. New local, city, regional and national radio stations were born, broadcasting a range of material. Most of the commercial stations are primarily music driven – although news, talk and sports stations are growing in popularity – and financed by advertising and sponsorship. At the local level, their links with the local community tend to be limited, with stations forming part of national networks, broadcasting a minimal amount of locally produced material. Non-commercial radio stations, often referred to as 'free' or 'community' radio, tended to be established by individuals or groups, committed to their neighbourhoods, political causes of one form or another or particular social or ethnic groups.

Most of these new radio and TV channels are private, which represents a fundamental shift in the media landscape. The ascendancy of public service channels has been undermined by the growth of these channels. In 1980 there were only three private television channels operating in Europe. For most countries public service monopolies were the norm. By the end of the decade there were more private channels than public, a gap which has widened ever since. Three-quarters of the 580 channels operating in 2000 were private (Papathanassopoulos 2002: 14). Cable and satellite are the primary means by which these channels are delivered to European households. Cable and satellite in many parts of the continent offer better quality reception and provide additional services, such as telephony and internet access. In some countries cable has prevailed – in the Benelux countries, nine out of ten households prefer to watch television through their cable system. Cable accounts for the majority of TV households in Denmark and Germany. Elsewhere the technology has struggled. For example, in Italy only 12 per cent of households have cable (Steemers 2004: 35). Satellite broadcasting brought a flow of programmes into countries from outside their border, from neighbouring countries in Europe and beyond. Channels were set up to bypass national regulation and controls. One example is TV3, which is transmitted from London to the Scandinavian countries. It was established in London in 1990 as a pan-Scandinavian channel in order to avoid the rules and regulations governing advertising in Denmark, Sweden and Norway, which were stricter concerning the amount of advertising, the length of commercial breaks and the advertising of certain products, such as alcohol (Mortensen 2004: 46). If technology has made these channels available, and the relaxation of regulation has assisted their development, to prosper they have had to make money. The new private channels have a different role from their public service predecessors. Driven by the need to maximize their audiences, they see broadcasting as a commodity to be sold to obtain the highest return rather than as a social good which plays a key part in building the social and political order.

Private media are associated with the growth of commercialization or marketization. The early history of mass communication associates the free market with the establishment of press freedom and the emergence of democracy (McQuail: 1998). This positive connotation has given way to the more negative identification of the process with 'the pursuit of profit above all else' (McQuail 1998: 108). This approach to the media has become more prevalent in Europe since the 1980s, subordinating the operation of the media to the interests of private individuals and companies. Opening up the media to the market, and removing rules and regulations that have governed the operation and output of the media, has led to the repudiation of the tradition of public service (see chapter 3). Running the media on commercial grounds has specific consequences. In order to maximize profits, media production is becoming, in McQuail's words, 'large-scale, low cost and low-taste' (McQuail 1998: 108). Private media entrepreneurs have to sell their products and the main method of financing their commercial operation is through advertising. It is possible to sell TV programmes directly through subscription channels and pay TV. However, as the press has found, it is only through raising advertising revenue that newspapers can make a profit;

making money based solely on newspaper sales is almost impossible (see chapter 2). Thus in the new commercial environment private broadcasters can only maximize their profits by increasing audience size while minimizing their production costs. Therefore, emphasis is placed on programmes which will bring in the largest possible audiences, to attract the maximum amount of advertising. Minority tastes are increasingly neglected. The highest rated programmes tend to be entertainment and sport. Commercial media place more emphasis on entertainment than information and education, are more concerned with keeping down costs, which impacts on the quality and range of material offered, cater to the interests of the mass rather than minorities, and seek to reduce financial risk by developing successful formats and recycling popular genres, themes and approaches (McQuail: 1998). While commercial criteria are more prevalent in private channels, they have not been without their impact on public service channels. In order to compete, public television has had to adopt a more commercial approach. Dwindling audiences have forced public broadcasters to develop programming policies similar to those of their private competitors. Failure to do so would make it more difficult to justify public finance. The increasing scope for commercial enterprise in broadcasting is also apparent in other media industries. Commercialization has undermined the rationale for state intervention in the newspaper and film industries. Press subsidies to encourage diversity are dwindling, while film production in many parts of Europe, especially Eastern Europe following the collapse of communism, has virtually disappeared with the decline of government support.

The growing commercial nature of the European media has had an impact on their content. With more airtime to fill, greater competition and the need to satisfy commercial requirements, there has been a growth in the amount of cheap programmes imported from the USA. Sepstrup (1989) has identified a strong correlation between a higher proportion of American programmes on European TV screens and the greater degree of commercialization in the European broadcasting market. From their study of the output of 36 television stations across Europe, de Bens and de Smaele (2001: 68) found that nearly two-thirds of the fictional material broadcast was of North American origin. Private channels tended to broadcast more American programming than public channels. But American influence goes beyond the amount of US programmes on the screen. Many home-produced quiz and game shows are derived from or based on US formats, such as *Wheel of Fortune*, which first aired in America in 1975, to be adapted for broadcast in Britain in 1983, France in 1987 and Germany in 1988, and subsequently in 50 other national media markets (Tunstall and Machin 1999: 30). Other popular US genres to cross the water include the daytime talk show and the reality crime series. The growing US-derived content of European television follows a pattern that has developed in the European film and music markets. Commercialization has facilitated increased US imports. How American imports are adapted for European audiences and how Europeans consume this material does raise questions about the influence of US media products and the extent to which European audiences are being Americanized.

Commercialization is also seen as responsible for the 'dumbing down', 'tabloidization' or 'boulevardisierung' of European television and media in general. While there is some debate about the exact nature of what is meant by tabloidization (see Esser 1999; Bek 2004; McLachlan and Golding 2000), broadly it refers to two trends: the growth of entertainment at the expense of information in the media, and the incorporation of entertainment values in information and news. Serious content, including politics, news and current affairs, is being either cut back or diluted to reflect the market demand for more entertainment. Specifically it means more human interest stories, less political coverage, fewer international and more local stories, hard news being replaced by sex, scandal and celebrities. This change in content applies to both the press and television, although the process is something which has only begun to occur in broadcasting over the last two decades. The extent and impact of entertainment taking priority and the rise of 'infotainment' is open to debate. Defenders of the changes argue that by making politics and news more entertaining the media are reaching people who would otherwise not be interested and 'giving the audience what they want' (see Klein 1998; Brants 1998; Brants and Neijens 1998). Critics believe they are contributing to growing political cynicism, increasing public knowledge of current affairs and encouraging mistrust of government and politicians (see Schulz 1997, 1998).

Changes in the content of the media must be seen in the context of the changing nature of media regulation. Regulation has been seen as an indispensable part of the media environment in western liberal democracies, even by those who are strong supporters of the free market. Autonomous bodies, such as Conseil Supérieur de l'Audiovisuel (CSA) in France or even the Federal Communications Commission (FCC) in the USA, have ensured that broadcasters are accountable to the public for what they report and represent. Similarly, Press Councils operate in various European countries to oversee the standards and performance of the press. Other mechanisms operating to the same end include journalistic codes of practice and right of reply and privacy legislation. Such regulatory devices in Europe have always been stronger in the broadcasting sector. The precise nature of regulation reflects the different economic conditions, attitudes to individual rights, political traditions and cultural sensitivities in each European country. Since the 1980s the trend in every European nation has been to lighter-touch regulation. In the name of encouraging economic efficiency and making Europe's media more competitive, the rules and regulations overseeing the content, obligations and duties of the media industries have been weakened. Less media regulation at the national level has been accompanied by the development of regulation at the supranational level (Wheeler 2004). This has led some to argue that what is happening is not deregulation but re-regulation, which is reinforced by the fact that no nation has abandoned media regulation completely.

New forms of media regulation are a response to the technological, socio-economic and political changes that are taking place. Above all, they reflect the rapid and radical transformations in technology. Digitalization is bringing about the rapid convergence between media and communications systems. In the analogue world each medium developed separately, with its own technologies, methods of production and distribution systems, which were for the most part incompatible with each other. Digital technology is merging technologies used in broadcasting, telecommunications and computers, and offering a variety of possible new uses and applications (de Bens and Mazzoleni 1998; Chalaby and Segell 1999; Murdock 2000). The old regulatory arrangements were based on separate consideration for each media form and each sector of the communication industry. Breaking down the barriers between media and communication services has posed huge legislative and regulatory dilemmas (Østergaard 1998). Convergence also promises to reconfigure the content of the media by bringing together all the major forms of expression in one place, as well as enabling users to interact with the new media and personalize their consumption of the mass media (Murdock 2000). The internet is a new form of mass communication, bringing together interpersonal and mass-mediated communication (Truetzschler 1998). For most Europeans it promises to revolutionize their interaction with the media. However, the claims made for the new medium, such as its democratic and emancipatory potential, are still a long way from being realized, as most Europeans still prefer to watch television and read their newspapers than surf the net.

Europeans on the internet

From the mid-1990s the growth of computer-related technologies in Europe has outstripped the growth of other communications technologies. The number of Europeans with access to a computer rose rapidly in the 1990s, resulting in the internet moving 'from the margin to mainstream in Europe' (Norris 2000b: 3). Yet today the majority of Europeans do not use a computer. A survey of European media consumption patterns found that nearly 54 per cent of those surveyed never use a computer and only one in three regularly access the internet (Eurobarometer 2002). This means the internet has some way to go to challenge the traditional means of information and entertainment retrieval in Europe. Europeans prefer TV, national and local newspapers and radio to the internet. There is also a north–south divide as in terms of access to and usage of the internet. The proportion of people using the net is highest among Northern Europeans, especially Swedes (66.5 per cent), Danes (59.4 per cent), Dutch (53.8 per cent) and Finns (51.4 per cent), and lowest among Southern Europeans, where only 14.8 per cent of Portuguese and 15.1 per cent of Greeks are users. These differences are explained partly by socio-economic factors, but with relatively affluent countries such as France and Germany low on both counts, they do not fully account for the differential take-up of the new media. Norris (2000b) identifies other factors, such as the size of the service sector, the spread of higher education, literacy, language and government policy. A large service sector facilitates access in the workplace. English is the language of the internet, and countries with a greater familiarity with the language would be expected to show higher usage. The new media have so far simply reinforced the traditional north–south divide in Europe's traditional pattern of media usage. It is also the case that the internet appeals disproportionately to the affluent, the educated and the young.

Finally, digitalization is fuelling the formation of new media corporations seeking to take advantage of the convergence of media sectors. Industrial convergence is creating giant media conglomerations, whose growth represents not only the changing nature of media ownership, but also the decrease in the number of firms that own and control Europe's media market.

Changing nature of ownership

If national government and public media organizations were the main actors on the European media landscape prior to 1980, today's primary movers are large corporate 'empires' or 'media moguls'. Their economic activities are no longer contained by national boundaries. Their operations are less constrained by rules and regulations. Their commercial needs lead them to standardize their products. Their power and influence are a major determinant of the contemporary media landscape. Since the early 1980s these firms have come to dominate the media in Europe. The large number of television and radio channels brought into existence by deregulation and liberalization is controlled by an increasingly small number of media conglomerates. Berlusconi, Murdoch, Hersant, Springer, Messier are the names of but a few of the media moguls whose firms have exploited the changing media environment to amass more and more of the press, broadcasting, film and music industries across Europe. Unlike the press barons of Britain and North America, their European counterparts developed more slowly, but today Europe's media moguls have been propelled into positions of influence and power almost unparalleled in the history of mass communication. Of the world's top 50 media companies, half were European; eight in Germany, seven in Great Britain, four in France, three in Italy, two in the Netherlands and one in Luxembourg (Meier and Trappel 2000: 48). Some of these groups have a long tradition: Havas and Hachette in France and Bertelsmann in Germany can trace their origins back to the 1830s, while others, such as Silvio Berlusconi's Mediaset, have emerged in the last two decades of the twentieth century (Mazzoleni and Palmer 1992: 26). All have extended their power and influence as a result of the transformation of the European media.

The emergence of mega media corporations is based on an 'unprecedented wave of mergers, acquisitions and partnership agreements' (Mazzoleni and Palmer 1992). To exploit the potential monetary rewards offered by the newly liberalized broadcasting markets and compete in a climate of rapid technological change, media firms have had to expand and adjust to maintain themselves. Today's media empires are involved in a relentless search for markets. Competition and financial considerations, such as the escalating cost of media production, mean that firms must continue to grow and expand. Large-scale production is everything as it assists firms to cover their costs, minimizes their risks and makes them competitive. For European firms lacking the language advantage and market share of their US rivals, growth has become essential. Hachette's chief executive states that 'if you're involved in advanced technologies, you have no choice but to diversify and internationalise' (quoted in Mazzoleni and Palmer 1992: 34).

The mergers, takeovers and partnerships that have been the primary means by which Europe's media empires have expanded have not been without their problems. Empires can fall as well as rise, as Europe has seen in the case of Kirsch. The 47-year-old Munich-based group filed for insolvency in 2002, with immediate debts of around 6.4 billion euros (*Financial Times* 2002). Kirsch's intervention into the pay-TV market was costly, losing the company 2 million euros per day during 2002; together with a downturn in the German media market, this resulted in the group's collapse. Vivendi is another European conglomerate which got into difficulties. Under the leadership of Jean Marie Messier, Vivendi (which started life as a 149-year-old French water company), added a crateful of media assets, including Universal Studios and other US media operations, and was thereby transformed into one of the largest media conglomerates in the world by the late 1990s. Rapid expansion hit the buffers in 2002, following problems in the pay-TV part of Vivendi's diversified entertainment empire, compounded by disagreements within senior management and injudicious comments by Messier to the effect that defending French culture was of no interest to him and his company. The experience of Kirsch and Vivendi highlights the fact that the media empires of the late twentieth century were often built on shaky foundations; in Picard's words, they are not necessarily 'permanent and omnipotent' (Picard 1996).

These media empires are characterized by several features that single them out from the previous companies that had owned and controlled Europe's media. These firms are international in scale. Companies such as Bertelsmann own media assets around the world, including in the USA. Even medium-size companies in Europe operate in several countries. The German WAZ Group owns media in Austria, Switzerland and several Eastern European countries, while the Finnish publisher, Sanoma WSOY, is the largest media group in the Nordic region, with interests in the Netherlands (following its purchase of the country's oldest and largest magazine publishers, VNU, in 2001), as well as the Baltic States, the Czech Republic and Hungary (Kelly et al. 2004; International Federation of Journalists 2003). Sweden's Bonnier Group, which controls over 25 per cent of the newspaper market in Sweden, has a presence in more than 20 European countries (International Federation of Journalists 2003). Ownership of the European media is no longer national in reach. It is also increasingly cross-media in nature, as firms diversify into a variety of sectors of the media industries. Previously confined to particular media, primarily as a result of regulation, which prevented newspaper groups owning more than a certain share of the broadcasting market and vice versa, firms have extended their ownership across the media industries. Mediaset owns television in Italy, Spain, France and Germany, as well as newspapers, magazines, journals, advertising firms, film production and distribution interests, a video rental company, telecommunications operators, internet and teletext services and mobile phone companies (International Federation of Journalists 2003). Sanoma WSOY has interests in newspapers, magazines, book publishing, broadcasting, multimedia, a photo agency, business information services, cinema and film distribution, internet and video sales and rentals.

Most of Europe's media firms have also diversified into other areas of business, industry and finance. Media production often forms part of broader industrial concerns with other interests. They are no longer simply media empires. Many companies have bought into the media industry as perceptions of their profitability have risen. One example is Berlusconi's empire, which started as a property development and construction company. Deregulation led him into the media, and success led him to diversify his operations into businesses as diverse as life insurance, pension funds, sporting ventures – such as AC Milan football club – department stores, restaurants and supermarkets. The range of influence is such that the term 'Berlusconism' has been coined to describe 'a way of life in which people live in houses built by Berlusconi . . . watch television controlled by Berlusconi, shop in supermarkets owned by Berlusconi, eat in restaurants built by Berlusconi and relax on Berlusconi tennis courts or watch his soccer team' (International Federation of Journalists 2003: 24).

The Italian experience is replicated in other European countries, as media ownership ceases to be located in family concerns specializing in a particular form of media production and distribution and is integrated into the heart of financial capital. This development raises questions about the independence of the media from the business sector, fear of which is accentuated by the concentration of ownership of these media giants. Growth, deregulation, internationalization and diversification have whittled away the variety of firms who have owned and controlled the European media. Concentration was first noticeable at the national level. In the mid-1980s, as the leisure sector grew, there was a general trend to the centralization of control of every sector of the media. The top three, four or five companies came to own an increasingly larger share of their respective markets, and through cross-ownership the domestic media in Europe were subject to the growing political and economic interests of a few media moguls. This trend is now apparent at the European level as these firms grow out of their national markets and seek to exploit the liberalized media markets across Europe and beyond. Some perceive the enlarged influence of these firms and their owners as a potential threat to democracy.

Euro media conglomerates

Two European media conglomerates that have become major players on the worldwide stage are Bertelsmann and Vivendi.

Bertelsmann is the largest media enterprise in Europe and one of the world's top ten companies. Bertelsmann began life as a publishing and printing company in the nineteenth century. It has a controlling interest in Europe's largest TV and radio group, RTL, with 24 television stations and 14 radio stations in 10 countries. RTL produces around 10,000 hours of programming annually. It owns content production companies in several European countries, including Regent and Thames Talkback in the UK. It owns more than 100 magazines and newspapers in 14 countries, including France, Spain, Italy, Austria, Russia, the Netherlands, Germany and the USA. Its publishing arm extends across the world and includes Random House, one of the top five publishers in the world, a book club with 28 million members and a scientific and technical subsidiary which owns over 700 trade magazines. Bertelsmann Music Group operates in 54 countries and owns over 200 labels, including RCA.

At the height of its success, in 2002, Vivendi Universal was valued at $55 billion. It started life as a French water company, Compagnie Générale des Eaux, changing its name in 1998. In the same year it merged with Havas, France's largest books publisher and business information provider, and in 2000 it joined with Canal Plus and the Canadian media and distilling company, Seagram. Its music group includes, among other record labels,

MCA, Decca, Polygram, Motown and Deutsche Grammophon. Its has a large stake in telecommunications companies in France, as well as a mobile phone network and phone services in Europe and Africa. It was Europe's largest trade publisher until 2002 and owns newspapers and magazines such as L'Express, L'Expansion and La France Agricole in France, and Spain's leading paperback publisher, Alianza Bolsillo. Through Universal it owns television, cinema, video and video games companies. Universal TV Group owns US cable networks, such as Newsworld International. Ownership of numerous pay-TV companies comes through Canal Plus. In 2002 financial problems led to the departure of its charismatic chief executive, Jean Messier, and some of its media interests were sold off.

Are changes in ownership harmful?

There is considerable debate within most European countries concerning the effects of the extension and concentration of media ownership. Should European societies fear the influence of the media moguls and their media empires? Some commentators emphasize the economic advantages of such enterprises. They argue that the economies of scale of large-scale production bring benefits to consumers in the form of a wider range of products of better quality at lower costs. Using the less pejorative term 'consolidation', they talk of the synergies of large companies which support creativity and allow for the cross-promotion of their products (see *Economist* 2002: xx). Critics point to the negative effects, including the loss of political, intellectual and cultural diversity. The variety of ideas and opinions, they argue, will be reduced as a result of the concentration of ownership. Control over the process of production is also seen as having the potential to lead to standardization in both the cultural content and format of the product (Humphreys 1996: 73). Too few owners also raises the question of political bias. Humphreys (1996: 74–5) identifies several ways in which powerful media groups have exerted pressure on politicians and the political process. First, political bias is seen as having an influence over the outcome of elections. He cites as examples Murdoch's support for Mrs Thatcher and Tony Blair and Springer's support for Helmut Kohl and the right-wing coalition at the 1994 Bundestag elections. Second, media moguls are seen as using their influence to change public policy on issues of national concern. Third, owners and editors have exerted indirect influence by 'playing on the natural sensitivities of politicians about how they are represented in the media'. Fourth, they determine who gains access to the media, and finally, they can attain a position of influence at the heart of decision-making inside political parties and governments. For example, Robert Hersant became a Gaullist member of the National Assembly in France, along with 11 of his employees (Mazzoleni and Palmer 1992: 145). More significantly, Silvio Berlusconi used his media power to become prime minister of Italy – twice.

Berlusconi's rise to political office is seen as the ultimate example of the power of media moguls. He is Italy's 'Mr Broadcasting', coming to prominence with the deregulation of Italian broadcasting in the mid-1970s (see chapter 3). A highly successful building entrepreneur, he acquired a monopoly of private television. His ability to attain this position was assisted by his close relationship with the socialist prime minister, Bettino Craxi. In 1984 Craxi overturned a court order which stopped Berlusconi from broadcasting, and in 1990 pushed through legislation which confirmed his private monopoly of commercial television. Today Berlusconi's company, Mediaset, owns three channels, which have a 45 per cent audience share and 60 per cent of total advertising. Up until 1992 Berlusconi played the 'normal' role of a media tycoon who 'lurks behind politics, but is not in politics' (Ginsborg 2004: 57). The events of 1992 propelled him into politics. Corruption charges levelled at senior politicians of all the established parties brought down the Italian political system and the power of the elites who had controlled it. Former prime ministers were called to account and Berlusconi's protector, Bettino Craxi, fled abroad, where he was to die eventually. National collapse was accompanied by a personal reversal of fortune. Diversification into the retail business and the purchase of the pay-TV channel, Telpiu, had proven disastrous (Ginsborg 2004: 64). With profits tumbling and political stability crumbling, Berlusconi took the plunge into Italian politics.

Setting up a new political party, Forza Italia, Berlusconi fought the 1994 elections as part of a right-wing alliance, achieving a remarkable victory. Forza Italia obtained 21 per cent of the vote and Berlusconi became prime minister. The techniques used in Berlusconi's campaign, especially his use of the media – television, in particular – are regarded by some scholars and commentators as crucial to his success. The media mogul's entry into politics is seen as turning the Italian political system into a 'videocracy' (Mazzoleni 1995). His party was only four weeks old when it attained power; the formidable 'media armoury' he brought onto the electoral battlefield is seen as decisive in promoting the new political party. Forza Italia was a new development in Italian party politics. Described as a 'media-rooted party' it had no policy baggage nor bureaucracy, and loose ties with the voters. It only served to 'amplify its leader's message' and was dependent on the media to reach the electorate (Mazzoleni 1995: 302). Using his marketing and advertising firm, Pubitalia, Berlusconi polled Italians to find out their likes and dislikes, packaged his party accordingly and promoted Forza Italia through his media. According to some commentators, the result was 'a populist message, delivered in an appealing and persuasive style' (Mazzoleni 1995: 303). Opponents were denied access to his channels as he and his party tied up the airwaves. The message for some was that Berlusconi's media power had delivered him into political office. The balance between the media and politicians had changed for ever.

Berlusconi's first term in office did not last very long. Dissent within his coalition led to his resignation in December 1994. However, this did not mark his departure from politics, even though many at the time believed his political career was over. His defeat at the 1996 elections seemed to confirm this and repudiate the videocracy thesis. Between 1996 and 2001 he rebuilt his party and put his business interests back on a sound commercial footing. His coalition won the 2001 election easily. Research shows that he and his campaign were an overwhelming presence on his own channel and the public service channels (Ginsborg 2004: 95). As prime minister, he now controls 90 per cent of Italian television, the main source of information for 80 per cent of Italians. Mediaset receives its licences to operate from the state that he heads up (European Federation of Journalists 2003). Since becoming prime minister,

Berlusconi has acquired additional media interests and done nothing to resolve the conflict of interest between his media power and political power. Instead he has exploited the situation to extend his control of the media. Presenters known for their opposition to the government were dropped by the public service broadcaster, RAI, only months after they were criticized by Berlusconi (Cozens 2002; Fisk 2002). RAI also banned a special edition of the satirical programme *Blob* on Berlusconi's attempt to bring the state broadcaster to heel (Reporters Sans Frontiers 2002). The programme referred to the efforts of the prime minister to pack the RAI board with his own followers. In 2003 he finally got his way. Following the resignation of the board, some of whom objected to the prime minister's 'non-stop occupation' of their work and the lack of respect shown to news diversity, Berlusconi appointed the members of the new board, in an act of unprecedented interference (Reporters Sans Frontiers 2003). In 2004 he attempted to bypass the nominations system again to have the head of McDonald's in Italy appointed president of the board (Arie 2004). Dissident voices in Italian society have virtually disappeared from television screens since 2001. According to Paul Ginsborg (2004: 113) the 'multiple associations of Italian civil society simply do not exist, except when they become of such proportions that they cannot be ignored, as with the European Social Forum's peace march in Florence in November 2002'. RAI's ratings have fallen since 2001. In January 2004, Mediaset's channels surpassed RAI's rating in prime time for the first time (Arie 2004). The public service broadcaster's deficit has risen and the claim is being made that Berlusconi's government is trying to put RAI at a disadvantage *vis-à-vis* Mediaset (Reporters Sans Frontiers 2003). The unparalleled concentration of the political and media power in a single person's hands has led the president of Italy to call for legislation to 'better guarantee the fundamental rights of the opposition and minorities by means of press pluralism and impartiality', without which 'there is no democracy' (Reporters Sans Frontiers 2003). Attempts to introduce media ownership laws have failed.

Berlusconi's rise to power in Italy is seen as an example, albeit an extreme one, of the dangers of the concentration of media power in the hands of one person or organization. However, the extent to which media determine people's political loyalties and opinions is open to debate (Mazzoleni 1995; Roncarolo 2002; Ginsborg 2004). The success of Forza Italia in the last decade has as much to do with social and political changes inside Italy – such as the introduction of a new voting system in the early 1990s, the collapse of public trust in the political elite, the discrediting of the established parties and the rise of regional discontent – as one man's hold over television. Some commentators argue that Berlusconi's rise must be placed in the context of the failure of the Italian political system (Roncarolo 2002: 82). He was able to exploit the 'vacuum left behind after the fall of the First Republic' (Mazzoleni 1995: 311). Unlike Berlusconi, media moguls in Europe are happy to exercise their influence behind the scenes. Many have a personal approach to politics, favouring relationships with individual politicians, rather than involvement with political parties or causes (Tunstall and Palmer 1989: chapter 5). The motivations of media moguls vary enormously. Prestige, profit, propagandizing and political influence are some of the reasons to build a media empire. Some see the driving force behind the expansion of Europe's media empires as commercial, stating that control by an individual tycoon or entrepreneur is becoming less common as 'men in suits' take centre stage. Individual chief executives, such as Messier at Vivendi and Thomas

Middelhoff at Bertelsmann, are seen as more typical of those who run media conglomerates. Interested in making money, they adhere to a strictly commercial agenda, leaving their employees alone editorially, as long as they are maximizing profits; while they, in turn are left alone by the owners who reap the monetary rewards. If they set themselves up as bigger than the organization they can incur the displeasure of their employers and shareholders, as both Messier and Middelhoff found out when they lost their jobs. While media moguls such as Berlusconi, Hersant and Murdoch are increasingly happy to let managers oversee the daily operations of their media empires, they exercise the final say. They appoint managers, define the structures within which journalists, producers and editors work, determine the strategy and control the investment and finances. Public standing and private influence count as much as financial acumen and profit maximization in their ability and capacity to acquire and control media interests.

Conclusion

The changing nature of the media in Europe is creating what some have labelled a 'new order', characterized by a huge increase in the amount of media, less government regulation and intervention in the media, the decline of public monopolies and the notion of public service, increasing scope for commercial enterprise and private ownership, the tabloidization and Americanization of media content, the convergence of media and communications and the growing influence of a small number of media conglomerates and entrepreneurs (McQuail 2004: 2). European media are big business, with the communications and media industries among the most vibrant and productive areas of most European economies. Satisfying and shaping what Europeans see, read and hear is the responsibility of a continually decreasing number of firms that grow ever larger, with potential consequences for democracy and economic development in Europe. The future of the European media is increasingly in the hands of these corporations. One crucial question is the extent to which the new order is bringing about the Europeanization of the media and encouraging the development of a greater commonality in the practices, output and performance of the European media. This is a matter for discussion as we explore a variety of media sectors in the following chapters.

chapter two

The press in Europe

Since 1945 predictions about the imminent demise of the newspaper industry in Western Europe have always proved unfounded. Seen as an 'endangered species' since at least the late 1960s, newspapers have survived (Schoenbach et al. 1999). Certain sections of the industry have turned out to be more resilient, with local newspapers in parts of Europe showing particular staying power. Nevertheless, newspapers have changed considerably. Newspaper readership and circulation numbers have fallen. There has been a radical restructuring of the industry. Traditionally, the European press was affiliated with political parties and was highly partisan in its coverage. Since the 1970s the close links between political parties and newspapers have been severed and there has been a 'depoliticization' of reporting. Newspapers in Europe are becoming more like their Anglo-Saxon counterparts – commercial entities. The rapid decline of the party press corresponds to the introduction of new kinds of newspapers, such as 'free sheets', which were pioneered in Scandinavia. The ability of newspapers to survive has been enhanced by subsidies and economic incentives, which have encouraged the plurality and diversity of the press in many countries. These press subsidies have caused some debate, as have changes in the content of newspapers. Finally, newspapers have had to adjust to technological change. The internet is altering the nature of information delivery and the press everywhere has had to respond. European newspapers are no different, establishing online versions and reconfiguring the way in which they are produced.

Europe's newspapers

Newspapers are Europe's oldest means of mass communication; given their longevity, it is not surprising that more newspapers are read in Europe than in any other part of the world. Nearly half of all Europeans read a newspaper 5 to 7 times a week (Eurobarometer 2002). On average, Europeans spend about 40 minutes per day reading their newspapers (Coste-Cerdan and Minon 1993: 47). According to UNESCO (2003), for every 1000 inhabitants, 261 Europeans buy a newspaper every day, compared to 141 Americans and a world average of 96. Nevertheless, there are significant variations in the levels of newspaper consumption within Europe. Northern Europeans buy and read more newspapers than their counterparts in the south. Norwegians, Finns and Swedes read the most; Italians, Spaniards, Portuguese and Greeks the least. The significance of these differences is a matter of judgement, however, because of the variety of ways in which European nations measure newspaper readership and the range of definitions of what constitutes a newspaper (Gustafsson and Weibull 1997). Newspaper consumption is highest in Norway, where in 1997 598 per 1000 inhabitants read a daily newspaper, and lowest in Greece, with only 69 per 1000 (Papathanassopoulos 2001a: 109). While around 85 per cent of Norwegians are exposed to a newspaper every year, the same is true for only 38 per cent of Spaniards, 44 per cent of Italians and 47 per cent of Greeks (Gustafsson and Weibull 1997). A number of factors – from economic underdevelopment, climate and religion – have been put forward to account for the disparity. De Bens and Østbye (1998: 17) highlight the higher levels of urbanization in the north and illiteracy in the south. They also draw attention to the stronger sense of class politics in Northern European societies, which facilitated the development of the habit of newspaper reading among working people. There are also media factors to explain the difference. Press distribution systems in Northern Europe are more efficient, and subscribing to newspapers – the most common means of receiving a newspaper in Northern Europe – tends to foster a stronger sense of loyalty.

Newspaper reading habits

Europeans obtain their newspapers in several ways. Most Northern Europeans subscribe. In the Netherlands over 90 per cent of newspapers drop through the letterbox onto the mat every morning. Newspaper subscription coincides with higher rates of product loyalty. In Southern Europe and France newspapers are usually purchased from a kiosk or news-stand. Kiosks are a common feature of most cities and towns in this part of the continent, as well in the newly constituted democracies of Eastern Europe. Europeans do not read their newspapers at the same time. In some countries evening newspapers are more popular than morning dailies. Greeks enjoy reading their newspapers in the evening. 'Nearly three-quarters of the circulation of Greek newspapers is made up of evening and Sunday editions (Terzis and Kontochristou 2004). Sunday newspapers do not exist in France and Germany.

The newspaper market in the EU is dominated by three countries – Germany, France and Britain – which, between them, supply 60 per cent of newspaper sales (Papathanassopoulos 2001a: 109). The market is skewed in other ways. National newspapers only exist in a small number of European countries. Britain has a highly developed national press, but other countries, such as France and Germany, are dominated by regional, local or city newspapers. Regional newspapers are the main actors in the French market, accounting for nearly 80 per cent of circulation, with the Rennes-based *Ouest France* the best-selling newspaper in the country (de Bens and Østbye 1998: 9). Newspapers such as *Le Monde* or *Le Figaro*, which enjoy an international reputation, sell primarily in the Paris area, traditionally the weakest region in France for the consumption of daily newspapers (Kuhn 1995: 31). Germany's best-selling newspaper, *Bild-Zeitung*, has national reach, but the majority of the country's daily newspapers are regional. Unlike in France, regional newspapers in Germany are high quality, prestige newspapers. The elite opinion-forming newspapers that emerge from urban centres such as Frankfurt and Hamburg have no equivalents in France.

There is also a distinction made in the European newspaper market between mass-selling popular newspapers and serious quality publications. In Britain the division is between tabloids, or 'red-tops', and broadsheets, with the size of the paper distinguishing the content until recently. Tabloids are less serious. In Europe there is no such correlation. Newspapers such as *Le Monde* in France, *Ta Nea* in Greece, *La Repubblica* in Italy and *El País* and *El Mundo* in Spain are serious quality publications, despite their tabloid size. Nevertheless, newspapers with an emphasis on entertainment exist, with the term 'boulevard press' being coined to describe them. They are firmly entrenched in Germany, where *Bild-Zeitung* and its Sunday equivalent, *Bild am Sonntag*, have established huge circulations, based on a format of sensational reporting, attractive visual presentation and gossip. *Bild-Zeitung* is Europe's most popular paper, selling around 4 million copies every day. Nevertheless, *Bild* is not typical of the German press. In some countries sports dailies are very popular. *Marca* is one of Spain's leading sports daily newspapers, with a national circulation of only about 35,000 fewer copies than the country's best-selling daily newspaper, *El País* (de Mateo 2004: 235). Sports dailies also thrive in Italy and Portugal. *La Gazetta dello Sport* is one of the best-selling dailies in Italy, while Portugal sustains three daily sports newspapers, two of them – *A Bola* and *Record* – selling over 100,000 copies. Despite the presence of a strong boulevard press and sports newspapers in some parts of Europe, newspaper markets across the continent are dominated by the more serious newspapers. As a medium, newspapers are associated more typically with serious content and political journalism, which accounts for their underdevelopment as a means of mass communication in certain European countries.

The decline of the European press

There has been a slow and gradual contraction of the number of newspaper titles, sales and readers in Western Europe since the end of the Second World War. This decline was noticeable and rapid prior to 1980, when the industry entered a period of general stability. Stability lasted a relatively short time, as decline returned in the 1990s to become the most prominent feature of the European press. This picture is more noticeable in certain parts of Europe and certain parts of the industry. National and regional/local newspapers have experienced some downturn, but it is daily newspapers in the EU that have suffered most, experiencing a 'sustained' decline in the 1990s (Papathanassopoulos 2001a: 109). The number of daily newspaper titles in France fell from 142 in 1950 to 69 in 1994, while neighbouring Belgium experienced a 50 per cent drop between 1950 and 1996, from 51 to 26 (de Bens and Østbye 1998: 9). In Denmark 78 newspapers closed between 1945 and 1990, and by 1999 only 35 daily titles remained (www.ejc.nl). In the Netherlands 29 newspapers existed in 1996, compared to 115 in 1950; while Norway has seen a comparatively small decline over the same period, from 91 to 85 newspaper titles (de Bens and Østbye 1998: 9). Some countries have been better able to resist the trend. An expansion of titles has taken place in countries such as Spain, Portugal and Germany, which have emerged relatively recently from long periods of dictatorship. The collapse of the Berlin Wall resulted in new titles being founded in the former

East Germany (see chapter 6). In the 1990s the readjustment to democracy in Spain and Portugal witnessed the development of new regional daily papers or the emergence of independent regional editions of older newspapers (Gustafsson and Weibull 1997). Gustafsson and Weibull (1997) note that the decline in the number of daily newspapers titles has been somewhat more pronounced in countries where there has been a higher exposure to the press, where more newspapers are sold per million inhabitants.

Since the 1960s newspaper circulation and readership have fallen steadily. Fewer Europeans are buying and reading newspapers than 30 years ago. This is particularly noticeable among the younger generation, but it is also the case for the less well educated. In Northern European countries such as Sweden there has been a small fall in the number of less educated people reading newspapers, while in Southern Europe farmers and blue-collar workers are the main non-reading groups (Gustafsson and Weibull 1997: 262). Nevertheless, there are differences across the continent, which reflect the different reading habits of Europeans. In their study of newspaper readership, Gustafsson and Weibull (1997) found that in some parts of Europe newspapers have maintained their attractiveness. Spain is one country that has seen an increase in reading. Political change is one of the main reasons for the increased demand for newspapers. However, it is socio-economic developments since 1976 that have proven more decisive. For example, the liberation of women from domestic confinement and their entry into the labour market resulted in more women reading newspapers and magazines. Traditionally low levels of newspaper consumption allow the press greater opportunities for expansion, as is the case in Spain, Italy, Greece and Portugal. In Northern Europe the peculiarities of the Dutch commitment to the three 'k's – 'koffie', 'krant' and 'kachel', that is, coffee, newspaper and stove – have helped to maintain a higher level of newspaper reading than is true of its Northern European neighbours, ensuring that decline has not been as rapid (Hemels 1997: 330). The picture of declining readership has to be qualified, but a slow and gradual contraction of the print media is a feature of post-war Europe.

Explaining decline

The gradual decline in the press is explained in a number of different ways. The most common explanation is the competition from other media, including broadcast and, more recently, new media. The growth of television since the 1950s is often seen as having had an adverse impact on newspaper reading habits. The evidence to support this viewpoint is flimsy. Gustafsson and Weibull (1997: 259) conclude from their study of the Western European press that it is 'very hard to find a strong influence from radio and television on the general position of newspapers'. This is not to say that television has not influenced the development of the press. In response to the rise of television, newspapers have introduced facelifts, more pictures, more colour and new layouts, including shorter articles, more eye-catching typography and articles that are easier to digest. Unable to compete with the immediacy of the broadcast media, the press have placed more emphasis on editorial content, commentaries, columns and opinion. The 'scarcity of information' on television – the information in a half-hour news bulletin almost fits onto one page of a broadsheet newspaper – has enabled newspapers to compete by providing background information in more detail and depth (Svegfors 1998; de Bens and Østbye 1998). Papathanassopoulos (2001a: 117–18) argues that the tight government control over television in Greece up until the 1990s provided the press with a 'comparative advantage'. Limited and staid television and radio coverage ensured people would turn to their newspapers for a broad range of information about domestic affairs. The deregulation of broadcasting has created more private, commercial television and radio stations, which have provided increased competition for the press in every European nation state.

Rejecting the impact of television, other variables are identified to account for the decline in the press. Some see changing socio-economic circumstances as significant. The increase in disposable income since the 1950s has allowed people to spend more money on leisure activities outside the home. Young people in particular have exerted their spending power on a range of other media and leisure activities, such as popular music, drinking, clubbing and eating out, which are seen as more preferable pastimes than newspaper reading. The secularization of European society has loosened the ideological, religious and political reasons for buying and reading newspapers. Newspapers in early twentieth-century Europe acted as collective organs for sectional interests, sponsored, funded and supported by political parties, churches, rural communities and trade union and business interests. The decline of collective allegiances and the rise of individualism have eroded the social basis for newspaper consumption. While changing social and economic conditions can and do undermine newspaper consumption, Gustafsson and Weibull (1997) point out that they also provide opportunities. They note that the changing position of women in Southern Europe has brought new readers into the industry. Perhaps of more significance is the changing economic structure of the press.

Changing economics of the press

The press in many parts of Europe in the immediate post-war years received artificial protection as a result of the rationing of newsprint and paper in a period of economic austerity. In Britain, such rationing limited newspapers to four to eight pages, and therefore news-hungry readers of the post-war years would buy more than one newspaper. The end of rationing in 1956 saw a swift rise in the size of newspapers and a rapid end to the habit of reading more than one. As a consequence, circulation declined and titles disappeared, including the *News Chronicle* and the *Daily Herald*, which could not compete. In the Netherlands, a similar downturn in the number of newspaper titles came in the wake of the relaxation of newsprint controls (Wieten 1988). In what was then West Germany, the press was protected by the Allied efforts to rebuild democracy in the former Nazi State. Newspapers were licensed to ensure a range of opinion was represented, and a platform was provided for the press to play its part in the development of democratic citizenship in the country. The establishment of a democratic system saw the relaxation of Allied press policy and the return of fierce competition in the West German newspaper market, with a corresponding shrinkage in the number of titles (Hardt 1988).

Increasingly, competition has determined the fate of European newspapers since the end of rationing in the late 1950s. Competition in the newspaper market has been 'cut-throat', with smaller publications succumbing to the competitive pressures (Humphreys 1996: 69). The cost of keeping a newspaper going has risen alarmingly, with price wars, heavy borrowing and downsizing the order of the day. Cutting prices might increase sales in the short run, but once they returned to their previous level, readers departed. Increased costs remained, however. The competitive pressures have mounted over the decades. These have come from within the industry – such as the advent of 'free newspapers' in the 1980s – and from other media, most significantly the privatization of broadcasting in the 1980s (see chapter 3). Newspapers operate in two markets: advertising and readership. Most newspapers do not make a profit on the basis of their readers. Cover price is usually inadequate to offset the costs of production. Hence the importance of advertising revenue, which has become more significant in the running of newspapers throughout twentieth-century press history. Today advertising is the main source of revenue for the majority of European newspapers, contributing between 50 and 75 per cent of the revenue of a 'healthy' newspaper (de Bens and Østbye 1998: 19). It is difficult to see how any newspaper can survive in the contemporary market unless it can attract substantial advertising. The growing importance of advertising is represented in the increased number of pages in newspapers, as well as the addition of supplements, which advertisers can direct at specific target audiences. The search for advertising revenue is having as much impact on the content and the shape of the European press as television and television journalism.

The rise of commercial television – cable and satellite – free newspapers and direct mail and telephone advertising threatens the economic foundations of the business of newspapers. The 1990s witnessed a noticeable drop in the newspaper industry's share of media advertising expenditure in nearly every Western European country (Papathanassopoulos 2001a: 113; Gustafsson and Weibull 1997: 268). Until 1980 the amount of advertising on television in most European countries was, with a few exceptions, non-existent or highly restricted. Since 1980 deregulation has liberalized broadcasting, freeing up the airwaves for advertising. Some channels continue to forbid advertising and restrictions do still apply in some countries; for example, in France, supermarkets, lawyers, cinemas, publishing companies and the press are prevented from advertising on the television and radio (European Federation of Journalists 2002). Commercial television has loosened the hold newspapers traditionally had over advertising. This is most noticeable in Southern Europe, where newspaper advertising share was always weak; television attracts over 60 per cent of media advertising expenditure in Italy, Greece, Portugal, Spain and France (Papathanassopoulos 2001a: 113). In spite of declining advertising revenue in most media systems, in Europe paid-for newspapers still attract the bulk of media advertising. However, within the industry there has been a shift in advertising from paid-for newspapers to free sheets. Launched in 1995 in Sweden, *Metro* is an example of a successful daily free newspaper. Distributed free on the underground and commuter train system of Stockholm, the newspaper is made up of adverts and short articles taken from the wire services. A small staff has kept production costs down and led to the newspaper being successfully adapted in other countries. By 2002 there were 22 editions of the paper published in 14 countries (Hulten 2004: 239). The emergence of the internet provides another source of competition for advertising revenue. Television competes with the press for display or brand advertisements. There has been no competition for classified advertisements, which constitute about 30 per cent of all press advertising revenue in most European countries (de Bens and Østbye 1998: 19). The internet represents a potential threat to this source of revenue, as the cost of classified advertising on the internet is estimated to be about 3 per cent of the cost of advertising in the press (Knee 1998). Competition for advertising revenue has clearly intensified, with the press share falling. Yet to attribute the economic problems of the industry to the expansion of television and other forms of media advertising has been described as a 'simplification' (Gustafsson and Weibull 1997: 269). There are other equally significant problems.

Mismanagement and poor industrial relations have characterized the press throughout Europe. Strict employment laws, inefficient management and strong unions, often referred to as the 'aristocracy of the labour movement', have contributed to a state of industrial relations which can be described as difficult, at best (Humphreys 1996: 38). Overmanning and resistance to technological change have dominated the newspaper industry in Europe. Print workers have been one of the most highly paid, organized and politically inclined groups of workers. Their political and industrial muscle enabled them to impose the 'closed shop', which helped to protect their employment rights. However, over time it also led to abuses within the industry, including practices which encouraged overstaffing and engineered inefficiency. In the 1960s, when advertising revenue was high and newspapers profitable, employers colluded in making agreements that perpetuated this situation. When hard times came along, strikes, closures and the shutting down of the presses became features of the industry. The 1970s witnessed major long-drawn-out disputes, which contributed to the disappearance of several newspapers. The most celebrated strike lasted 29 months, when the leading French print union, Fédération du Libre, led a walkout at the *Le Parisien Libere* after its owners announced they were to move their printing operation to a new plant outside Paris and lay off several hundred workers (Kuhn 1995: 42–4). Management eventually won, but the cost was high – the circulation of the paper almost halved during the strike, never to regain its market position. Similar disputes took place in West Germany in 1976 and 1978, when for a couple of months workers at 325 newspapers were locked out, and in Denmark in 1980, when 35 out of the country's 45 dailies were shut down (Hollstein 1983: 253). The year-long Wapping dispute in Great Britain in 1986 was the culmination of the wave of strikes associated with the introduction of new print technology. The transition to new print technology had been more peaceful in Scandinavia and the Netherlands, where workers' councils aided the transition, although tensions in management–union relations were exacerbated. Eventually agreements were reached in most countries, but the consequences of these agreements and the new technology were the decline of union power, the diminution of print workers and an increase in the freedom of press owners to run newspapers as they liked. Periodic economic recessions since the oil crisis of 1974 have added further to the problems of the press. The struggle to remain economically viable has become more difficult. Faced with rising costs of production and distribution, the weaker European newspapers have had limited choices: closure, merger or takeover.

Restructuring the newspaper industry

The decline in titles and circulation and changing economic circumstances have brought about the restructuring of the newspaper industry across Europe. The most obvious change is in the nature of ownership. In most Western – and Eastern – European countries the newspaper market is dominated by an increasingly small number of large business concerns. Concentration of press ownership is not a new phenomenon in Europe. During the interwar years industrialists such as Hugenberg in Weimar Germany, Prouvost in France and the press barons in Britain exerted control over vast swathes of the newspaper business. By 1930 Hugenberg had some form of control or influence over 50 per cent of the German press (Tunstall 1977: 152). Since the end of the war, concentration of newspaper ownership has proceeded at an unprecedented pace, accelerating as the economic circumstances of the industry have worsened. Takeovers, mergers and acquisitions have been the main response to the ailing plight of Europe's newspapers. Multiple ownership of titles is common in every sector of the newspaper industry – as well as the print and publishing industry more generally – as Europe has witnessed a dwindling number of chains dominating the market. These large business enterprises are better able to deal with the economic circumstances. They are able to pool editorial resources, rationalize the workforce, share administrative, production and distribution facilities and negotiate better terms with advertisers (Humphreys 1996: 68).

The growth of these chains was facilitated by the lack of regulation limiting concentration of ownership of the press in several European countries, including Denmark, Greece, the Netherlands, Spain, Belgium, Portugal and Luxembourg. Elsewhere owners were able to circumvent or bend the regulations to suit themselves. In 1990 Robert Hersant in France owned 35 per cent of the circulation of the national daily press and 18 per cent of the regional press, as well as holding interests in other regional publishing companies which appeared to contravene the antitrust provision of France's 1984 press law (Mazzoleni and Palmer 1992: 32). Strong connections with government, in this case with France's current president, Jacques Chirac, have ensured that exemptions are possible and legal measures not applied (de Bens and Østbye 1998: 12). Countries with strict ownership regulations, such as Germany, fostered an early internationalization of press ownership. German print groups, such as Springer, Burda, WAZ, Gunner and Jahr, and Bertelsmann, limited by the opportunities in their domestic market, expanded more rapidly into foreign media acquisitions.

Compared to the television and other print media forms, such as magazines and books, foreign ownership of European national newspaper markets has been rare until recently. However, European press groups are extending their influence into neighbouring markets. Foreign ownership of newspapers in Eastern Europe is common (see chapter 6), and it is increasingly a feature of markets in the West. For example, the Norwegian industrial conglomerate, Orkla, bought Denmark's largest newspaper group, Berlingske, in 2001; and another Norwegian company, Schibsted, owns Sweden's two largest newspapers, *Aftonbladet* and *Svenska Dagbladet* (Østbye 2004: 159). In the process, newspapers are becoming part of larger media groups whose interests are far removed from traditional newspaper owners, who tended to see themselves as publishers rather than capitalists, concerned more with serving their communities than making profits. The domination of newspaper markets around Europe has made it more difficult for new newspapers to appear; *Today* and *News on Sunday* in Britain, *Infomatin* in France, *Super!Zeitung* in Germany and *24uur* in Belgium are examples of new entries that have disappeared almost as quickly as they hit the news-stands (de Bens and Østbye 1998: 11). The major shift in the European newspaper industry has been the virtual disappearance of political party-owned newspapers. Growing public indifference and disillusionment with politics, the demise of ideology and the changing economics of the industry have combined to undermine what had been the most prominent feature of the European press, the ownership and control of newspapers by political parties and organizations such as trade unions.

The depoliticization of the press

Historically, newspapers in Europe have had strong links to political parties and organizations. In the nineteenth century newspapers were tied intimately to the struggle for political rights and political freedom. In Britain, the *Northern Star*, the best-selling newspaper in the world in the 1840s, was the mouthpiece of the Chartists, the first organized political movement of working people struggling for the vote and rights in the workplace. Politically partisan papers, with a few noticeable exceptions, disappeared relatively rapidly in Britain with the extension of the franchise, the rise of parliamentary democracy and the industrialization of the press in the late nineteenth century. In North America and Britain 'political conflicts were efficiently codified by parliamentary bipartism and confined to party politics' (Chalaby 1997: 636). This created the conditions for the development of a commercial press, not openly committed to any particular political party or ideology. Such newspapers flourished in the Anglo-American world, supported by a set of favourable economic circumstances. The advertising market spread more quickly in Britain and America than it did in mainland Europe. This provided Anglo-American newspapers with a source of revenue that could sustain their independence. This is not to say that advertisers and advertising was without political bias; newspapers which were unable to deliver readers with sufficient purchasing power or advocated policies inimical to business or against the national interest could not attract sufficient advertising and therefore struggled to survive (Curran et al. 1980). By 1910 it is estimated that advertising constituted 60 per cent of the total revenue of American newspapers and periodicals (Chalaby 1996: 320).

In Europe political and economic circumstances were to maintain a 'party press' well into the twentieth century. Advertising grew more slowly and, as a result, newspapers were financially dependent on political and other interests for longer. Commercial newspapers did emerge, however. For example, in France newspapers modelled on the American press were highly successful. *Le Matin* was launched in the last decade of the nineteenth century, stating that it would be a 'unique newspaper . . . that will not have any political opinion', while *Le Petit Parisien* became the best-selling newspaper in the world on the eve of the First World War, with a circulation of more than 1.5 million (Hallin and Mancini 2004: 255; Kuhn 1995: 19). However, these papers did not displace the party press as they had done in Britain and America. Class conflict, political division and ideological differences remained more entrenched in European society. The years between the two wars, a time of profound political upheaval compounded by economic crisis and depression, accentuated the intensity of political struggle. With political and ideological differences running deep, it was unsurprising that newspapers were extremely partisan and highly political (Humphreys 1996: 23). The party press enjoyed its heyday in the interwar years. Newspapers of opinion and party organs multiplied and their circulations grew rapidly. In France 8 of the 11 Parisian newspapers with the highest circulation were party papers, from *L'Humanité*, the official publication of the French Communist Party on the left, to *Le Croix,* the mouthpiece of the political wing of the Catholic Church – Catholic Action – on the right (Chalaby 1996: 321). In Germany each political camp had its own newspapers. Humphreys (1996: 23) states that 'one-third of the press sector was accounted for by "party papers": the Catholics had over 400, the Social Democrats around 200 and the Communists around 50'. The rise of the Nazis corresponded with the growth in the number of newspapers supporting their cause.

It was not only in countries with overt political conflict that the party press thrived. Dutch society in the nineteenth century had produced highly organized groups that were labelled *zuilen,* or pillars. Modern, mass-based and well-organized social movements of Protestants, Catholics, Liberals (secular) and Labour emerged, which for ordinary people became 'objects of personal, social and political identification' (Van der Eijk 2000). In 1917 a negotiated political settlement recognized and established the existence of these pillars. Newspapers were usually closely associated with different pillars or subgroups within them. In Denmark the press was traditionally 'less a means of information and still less considered as a business venture, but was a weapon in a political conflict both in fighting political adversaries and – no less important – in organising supporters' (Sollinge 1999: 39). The four major political parties had their own newspaper in every middle-size town across the country. The 'four-paper system' was the basis of the Danish press. Press reform in 1905 saw a loosening of party political affiliations in some parts of the press and a slow decline in the political content of newspapers, but up until the 1970s Danish newspapers maintained their political partisanship.

Elsewhere in Scandinavia the political loyalties of the press were as firmly entrenched. The interwar years were the 'grand era' of the party press in Finland. Salokangas (1999: 95) illustrates the extent of the party press in Finland by highlighting that in 1939 only 19 of the 127 general newspapers in the country did not have a party political affiliation. Hadenius and Weibull (1999: 134) note the close links between newspapers and political parties in Sweden at all levels. Political and trade union organizations dominated the ownership of the Social Democratic newspapers; party sympathizers made up almost their entire readership, with party affairs taking prominence and the content promoting party objectives. The same was true of other political parties. In Norway all the major political parties had their own newspapers in most of the country's major cities and towns between the wars. Nearly 60 per cent were closed down during the war, most never to be restarted (Østbye 1997: 169).

In Southern Europe, authoritarian political systems tied newspapers to party or government agencies. Dictatorships in Spain, Portugal and Greece turned newspapers into propaganda instruments for the regimes. Party newspapers have been a feature of the Italian press. A close relationship between newspapers and politics began with the struggle for the unification of Italy in the 1870s. *L'Unita,* the newspaper of the Italian Communist Party (PCI), was established in 1924 by (among others) the Italian political theoretician, Antonio Gramsci, attaining a circulation high of 300,000 in the 1960s (Hallin and Mancini 2004: 94). Other party papers, most notably *Il Popolo* for the Christian Democrats and *L'Avanti* for the Socialists, were set up at the same time. In the late 1940s 50 per cent of the Italian press consisted of party papers (Hallin and Mancini 2004: 95). In Eastern Europe, following the collapse of communism in 1989, party political newspapers flourished as part of the rebirth of democratic politics (see chapter 6), but even in countries more associated with commercial, free enterprise systems there are examples of political newspapers existing in the post-war period. In Britain the *Daily Herald* was set up as a strike newspaper just before the First World War. During the interwar years it was partly owned and managed by the trade union movement and closely identified with the political agenda of the Labour Party. It was one of the best-selling newspapers of the period and, when it was closed in 1963, it still sold well over a million copies. The failure to attract advertising was a key reason for its downfall.

The post-war period has witnessed the depoliticization of European newspapers, a process which began in earnest in the late 1950s and early 1960s. The party press had been discredited by the war and the events leading up to it. Newspapers closely associated with the political excesses of the 1920s and 1930s were banned at the end of the war. In Germany, the Allies suppressed the newspapers that had paved the way for the Nazis' rise to power. Newspapers had to be licensed by the Allied authorities and, when the Federal Republic of West Germany was created in 1949, attempts to re-establish party newspapers failed as they could not compete with the licensed newspapers which had already established themselves in the market (Hickethier 1996: 105). In other countries newspapers tainted by their association with Nazi occupation or fascism were closed down. In France there was a clean sweep of the press, with newspapers that had published during the occupation forbidden to reappear; out of 206 dailies published in France in 1939, only 28 were able to resume operations after the war (Kuhn 1995: 54). The realization that the pre-war political conditions had been partly responsible for the calamities of the war resulted in political changes that undermined the party press. Readers were hostile to polemical politics and the press reluctant to re-engage in the old-style politics (Humphreys 1996: 28). Party newspapers and partisan reporting did not disappear immediately; it was more like a slow fading away. Socialist papers affiliated to political parties and unions could be found in France (*Le Populaire*) until 1970, the Netherlands until 1969 (*Het Vrije Volk*) and in Belgium (*De Morgen* in Flanders and *Le Peuple* in Wallonia) until the mid-1980s (de Bens and Østbye 1998: 15). *L'Humanité* had the largest circulation of any French newspaper in the years after the Second World War. Since 1947 the newspaper has slowly lost readers and influence, dropping to 60,000 readers in 1996 (Hallin and Mancini 2004: 95). Its survival, albeit in a highly weakened form, indicates the traditional value attached to political newspapers in Europe.

Party newspapers lasted for longer in Scandinavia than elsewhere in Europe. Weakened by the war, they never regained the heights of the 1930s. However, in Norway and Sweden as late as the early 1970s more than 80 per cent of the press was made up of newspapers with party political allegiances (de Bens and Østbye 1998: 14). The loosening of political affiliations has developed since 1980. Newspaper closures in Denmark put an end to the 'four-paper system'. Local newspapers that remain often have a monopoly in their locality, which has led them to tone down their politics in order to attract readers from the former newspapers of their political opponents (Hallin and Mancini 2004: 179). Politically owned newspapers in Sweden had problems as early as the 1960s, when trade union ownership could not prevent the *Stockholm Tidningen* from closing (Hood 1972: 73). The most significant event in the decline of party papers came in 1996, when the National Organization of Labour Unions (LO) sold one of the country's best-selling newspapers, *Aftonbladet*, to Norway's largest newspaper publisher, Schibsted. This represented the symbolic end to the close connections between party and press. In Norway the publishing group A-pressen had been a group of Labour Party newspapers, each organized locally, with shares held by trade unions, local party organizations and Norsk Arbeiderpresse, a central holding company (Høst 1999: 121). Reorganized and renamed in 1989, the group started to 'behave as a typical commercial media corporation', and by 1996 foreign shareholders, including Chase Manhattan Bank, owned more than a quarter of the company's shares. Today all the newspapers in Norway and Sweden claim to be non-partisan and politically independent. Elsewhere party affiliations have been dropped quietly as partisan publications have been replaced by larger commercial newspapers.

De Bens and Østbye (1998: 15) account for the depoliticization of the press in a number of ways. They highlight the poor management of the press by political parties, especially those on the left. Another explanation is the problem left-wing or radical newspapers had in attracting advertising revenue from the business community. It is also the case that since 1945 the reading public has become less interested in politics. People are increasingly less likely to read newspapers for their party political partisanship, preferring to have more neutral or 'objective' news accounts. Newspapers associated with parties have experienced harder times in a more apolitical period. In Denmark and Sweden the contraction of titles is explained by the declining fortunes of the Social Democratic party press, while the decline of *L'Humanité* can be explained by the failing fortunes of the official newspaper of the French Communist Party. Papathanassopoulos (2001a) accounts for the demise of partisan papers in Greece in terms of political parties losing touch with voters and the growing public disillusionment with both politicians and journalists. The consequence is that sporting and financial newspapers in Greece are booming. Without parties' financial support, along with the effective system of distribution they provided, the political press has dwindled in numbers (Kuhn 1995: 73). The key characteristic of this decline is that it has been slow, which is explained partly by the efforts of the state to intervene in the newspaper market to ensure that some form of political diversity is maintained.

State subsidies of the press

In certain parts of Europe the intervention of the state has been crucial to the economic survival of the press. State aid to newspapers has taken a number of different forms across the continent. Most countries provide indirect support to the press in one form or another. One of the main forms of indirect support is preferential treatment over value added tax (VAT). Newspapers in nearly every Western European country are either exempt from paying VAT or pay reduced rates. In Britain the total exemption of the press from VAT has been carefully guarded and when suggestions were made to introduce the tax in 1993, dire predictions about the impact of such a move on the health of the newspaper industry forced the government to back down (Humphreys 1996: 102). Preferential post rates and telephone and telex charges are given to newspapers and magazines in some countries, while a subsidy is provided for the purchase of newsprint in France and Italy, for example. In countries such as Italy, Belgium and Portugal reporters have access to cheap transport to undertake their reporting responsibilities. All these forms of assistance enable newspapers to reduce their costs production and are by and large 'uncontroversial' (Humphreys 1996: 103). However, other forms of subsidy are contentious.

Governments became more directly involved in subsidizing the press in the 1960s. Direct state aid to the press has been flirted with by nearly every European country, with the exception of Britain, Germany, Ireland and Switzerland (Humphreys 1996: 103). State subsidies have come and gone in some countries. Spain briefly operated press subsidies in the 1980s (Hallin and Mancini 2004: 121; de Mateo 1989). Other countries are more committed to such intervention, with France, Italy and the Nordic countries being the most enthusiastic proponents. State financial assistance to newspapers was adopted by the French in the late 1940s as a reaction to the excessive control exercised over the press during the interwar years by financial capitalism (Kuhn 1995: 40). The intention was to ensure that readers had access to a variety of sources of information. The value of subsidies is not insignificant; according to Kuhn (1995: 41), they amount to between 12 and 15 per cent of the total turnover of the press. In Italy subsidies were introduced in the mid-1970s, in the wake of a serious financial crisis in the daily press. In 1975 only 17 out of the 74 daily newspapers broke even (Sartori 1996: 139). Fear of widespread bankruptcies led the government to introduce a law granting aid to the press, which helped to alleviate the situation. The closure of established newspapers, including the 133-year-old *La Gazetta de Popolo* in the early 1980s, strengthened the subsidy system (Hollstein 1983: 250). An economic revival in the late 1980s breathed some life back into the Italian press, only for the winds of recession to blow hard once again in the 1990s. State aid has been invaluable in helping the Italian press to weather the changing economic climate. Other countries, such as the Netherlands, Austria and Denmark, set up funds in the 1970s and 1980s to support newspapers in financial difficulties. However, the most developed systems of state subsidies are found in Norway, Finland and Sweden.

The Swedish press subsidy system is regarded as 'the model system' (Humphreys 1996: 106). Financial aid to the press begin in 1964, when the Swedish Parliament decided to provide ten political parties with money to help with the cost of distributing their party newspapers. This failed to stop the decline in daily newspapers which, by the early 1960s, had seen the number of cities in Sweden with more than one newspaper fall to seventeen, almost a 50 per cent drop since the early 1950s (Hollstein 1983: 249). Particularly badly hit were the papers of the Social Democratic Party, which had been the major governing party in Sweden for more than 40 years. In 1971 it was decided to support the press financially by providing grants to assist with the production costs of newspapers whose circulation was smaller than that of their competitors in relevant markets. The scheme of supporting 'second newspapers' was funded partially by a tax on the advertising of daily and weekly newspapers, which meant that the stronger newspapers were subsidizing their weaker rivals, albeit indirectly. The system is administered by the Swedish Press Subsidies Council, an independent agency, which has been generous in the amount of aid that it has provided over the years. Two large daily newspapers, the Social Democratic *Arbetet* and the conservative *Svenska Dagbladet,* have survived only because of state support (Humphreys 1996: 106). Overall, 57 newspapers received some degree of support in 1997. Among the second newspapers in metropolitan areas it is estimated that state press subsidies account for between 5 and 35 per cent of their revenue (Hadenius and Weibull 1999: 142).

The decline in newspaper titles has not been as acute in Norway as elsewhere in the Nordic countries. However, the death of local competition in the Danish press and the disappearance of Labour newspapers in Sweden were seen as a portent of what would happen in Norway (Skogerbø 1997: 102). In the late 1960s there was considerable support across the Norwegian political spectrum for the introduction of press subsidies to support newspapers particularly vulnerable to competition and to maintain political diversity at the local level. The bulk of the financial aid has been allocated to second newspapers in local markets and smaller local newspapers, in the form of production subsidies. In addition, newspapers serving the minority Sami community have been subsidized, as well as newspapers in the northernmost province of the country, Finnmark, a relatively inaccessible and sparsely populated region (Skogerbø 1997: 105).

Finland also has a highly developed system of subsidies. Subsidies are paid to newspapers in economic difficulties as well as to political parties, in line with their strength in parliament. The latter may use their subsidies to support newspapers other than formal party organs (Salokangas 1999: 99). The subsidies paid to the Finnish press reached a peak in 1991. Subsequent decline is accounted for by the diminishing power of the political parties to direct subsidies and the deterioration of state finances, as well as concerns about the role of subsidies in preventing reform in the newspaper sector.

Denmark is the only Scandinavian country not to embrace press subsidies fully. In spite of the rapid decline in newspaper numbers, especially in the party press in recent years, there has been a reluctance to use government aid to save newspapers. The Finance Institute of the Press was established in 1970 to channel 'modest funds' to 'needy newspapers', which has seen small amounts of money provided as loans for the modernization of newspaper production and the establishment of new newspapers (Petersen and Siune 1997: 38). More direct intervention in the finances of the press has been resisted.

The impact of these subsidies on the industry is open to debate. It cannot be denied that the countries with the most developed system of press subsidies have the highest per capita number of newspapers and highest levels of newspaper consumption. It is also true to say that subsidies have not prevented the developments they were meant to counteract. Newspapers and newspaper reading are still in decline, concentration continues to increase and political diversity is shrinking. In Norway the number of 'second newspapers' has continued to fall, from 30 in 1972 to 10 in 1997, which for one commentator represents a 'partial success', since without subsidies all these newspapers could have died (Horst 1999: 115). In Sweden the Press Council believes that in the difficult economic conditions of the 1970s over half the subsidized papers would have closed without state aid (Hollstein 1983: 249). Similarly, in Finland the party press was maintained by state subsidies in the 1970s and the early 1980s, but the decline in state subsidies has corresponded with falling circulation and declining titles (Salokangas 1999: 95, 102). Critics, however, highlight the detrimental consequences of press subsidies.

State subsidies of the press: good or bad?

Subsidies are a response to the economic plight of the newspaper industry. By providing economic support the state can assist the press sector to stand up to market forces that are reducing the number of newspapers and the number of people who own them. However, the justification for subsidies in most countries is political. They encourage and support a broad range of opinion and comment in the press. As a result they are a vital instrument in the state effort 'to safeguard the principle of freedom of opinion' (Humphreys 1996: 107). Subsidies have been crucial in supporting the party press. Newspapers with strong party political affiliations have been the main recipients of state aid. In France *L'Humanité* and *Le Croix* were the daily newspapers that benefited most, being the only dailies by the early 1990s to receive direct state support (Kuhn 1995: 40). Not that subsidies were enough. *L'Humanité*'s survival in 2001 depended on its sale of shares to stay afloat (Hallin and Mancini 2004: 95). The party press has gained most in Sweden, where newspapers associated with or affiliated to the Social Democratic Party and the Centre Party – the two political parties most favourable to the press support system, have received the bulk of the aid (Hadenius and Weibull 1999). In Norway the Marxist-Leninist daily newspaper, *Klassekampen*, founded in 1973, survives only because of press subsidies (de Bens and Østbye 1998: 14). Across Europe politically partisan papers are in retreat, but in some countries they survive as a result of the intervention of the state.

Critics argue that their survival has come at a high price. Opposition to press subsidies takes a variety of forms, from the argument that they make the press dependent on the state and less likely to perform their basic function of critically scrutinizing politicians, to the view that they act as an obstacle to press reform. Anglo-American critics see press subsidies as an unwarranted intervention in the free market. They are seen as embodying 'the danger of excess of power from the state over the press' (Grisold 1996: 503). They make newspapers economically dependent on the very institutions and authorities they should monitor and criticize (Skogerbe 1997: 103). The application of subsidies is cited to support this argument. Murschetz (1998: 302) examines how vested political interests appeared to shape the application of subsidies in several European countries, including Sweden, where subsidies in the 1970s 'were tailored to the needs of the newspapers of the then governing parties'. Subsidies have been seen by some as part of the process by which the French State undermined the efforts of the press to perform its watchdog function (Humphreys 1996: 47, 63; Chalaby 2002b). While press subsidies may not be politically neutral in France, there are a range of other factors that restrain the French press, including strict privacy laws and the *étatiste* tradition of the French State (see Lamizet 1996; Kuhn 1995; Texier 1998). Deciding on whether subsidies politically restrict newspapers is often a matter of the way in which they are applied. Some countries make provision for some negative effect on political journalism, as in Norway and the Netherlands, where grants are conditional on guarantees of editorial freedom (Humphreys 1996: 107). Sweden and Norway have developed a strict set of economic criteria, supported by a transparent system of regulation, to ensure the 'politically neutral allocation of subsidies' (Murschetz 1998: 303). Subsidies in other countries are allocated less clearly and hence more open to political abuse. There is a distinction to be made between general subsidies provided to all newspapers, irrespective of their needs, and selective subsidies targeted at specific papers. It is the latter that poses problems. In France and Austria aid aimed at weaker party or politically committed newspapers has made political factors appear 'more formidable and pervasive' (Murschetz 1998: 303; Grisold 1996: 503). However, the evidence to indicate that subsidized newspapers are less critical of the state is weak. Persistent critics of government, such as *Klassekampen* in Norway and *L'Humanité* in France have been major recipients of state aid. Newspapers, particularly in the Nordic countries, were more deferential to political elites in the 1950s before press subsidies were introduced (Hallin and Mancini 2004: 163).

A more significant criticism of press subsidies centres on their economic costs outweighing their benefits. Some argue that 'state aid to the press is too indiscriminate, not differentiating between the needy and the already well off' (Kuhn 1995: 42). In many countries indirect and general subsidies help the better-off newspapers. Austria's leading newspaper is *Neue Kronen Zeitung*, selling over 1 million copies daily in 2001, which represented nearly 43 per cent of the total circulation of the press in the country (Trappel 2004: 5). The provision of indirect and general subsidies to this newspaper has assisted it in maintaining its dominance of the market, which is out of all economic proportion in a country of Austria's size. In France, with postal aid helping only larger newspapers and newspapers receiving 80 per cent of their revenue from advertising still eligible for state aid, subsidies have 'an inherent bias favouring the already economically better off newspapers, so harming competition and diversity' (Murschetz 1998: 304; Kuhn 1995: 42). One of the reasons for scrapping subsidies in Spain was that, in practice, they favoured newspapers with large circulations. In 1987 *El País*, *La Vanguardia* and *ABC* – three of the country's largest newspapers – together with *El Periódico*, received 33 per cent of the total subsidy available (de Mateo 1989: 222). While they may ensure that financially weak newspapers survive, subsidies do not address the structural problems in the newspaper market, preventing the press from addressing management inadequacies and inefficiencies, imbalances in the workforce, and distribution and promotion failings. They also enable policymakers and regulators to shy away from tackling more crucial questions regarding press diversity, namely legislation on media ownership. Press subsidies, as Kuhn (1995: 42) notes of the situation in France, tend to favour the status quo and discourage economic initiatives.

Newspapers and the net

Technological changes had a major impact on the newspaper industry in the post-war period, but not always in ways that were foreseen. New print technology helped to reduce the costs of production, improve the layout and design of newspapers and, in certain countries, provide the basis for a fundamental shift in relations between management and unions, with a decline in the power of the print unions and the number of print workers. The net has increased the speed and efficiency as well as reduced the costs of news gathering. In this way technology has helped to improve the competitive position of the European press. This is contradicted by the increased competition that the net provides for advertising revenue and the vast investment that is required to develop online newspapers and electronic publishing. Most European newspapers have their own websites. These help them to target younger, potential readers who no longer read newspapers in large numbers. However, it has also opened them up to new competition from internet service providers who often offer their product for free. Some scholars envisage that the net will require newspaper publishers to alter their businesses completely. Others have argued that hard copies of the newspapers will disappear to be replaced by online versions. Such digital dreams still appear a long way off; as de Bens and Østbye (1998: 20) stress, 'readers want to turn the pages of their "familiar" newspaper, feel and smell the paper and "zap" through at their own pace'. And while the net has had an impact on newspapers, it is also the case that there has been a 'mediatization' of the net. Fortunati (2005) argues that rather than changing the formats and manifestation of newspapers, traditional media organizations are dominating and shaping the presentation of news on the net. A survey of print and online newspapers and their competitor online-only news services in several European countries found relatively little difference between the outlets in relation to their content (Van der Wurff 2005). The survey also provided evidence to show that traditional media were increasingly dominant on the net and that full use was not being made of the new technology. Online newspapers, the survey concluded, were still searching for their role.

Conclusion

The European press has survived longer than many have predicted. However, in face of challenges from other media, including new media technologies such as the internet, newspapers have changed their form and content considerably. Increased commercial pressures and growing competition have changed fundamentally the economics of the industry and the management of newspapers. The result is that the ownership and operation of the European press, which for most of the twentieth century was a political activity, is now more of a business enterprise than it has ever been. Depoliticization has not prevented newspapers from expressing political opinions, but it has meant that politics are less central to what newspapers are producing and how they are produced. Changes driven by economic and market developments have posed political dilemmas for governments and policymakers. To ensure that a broad range of political opinion is expressed, many governments have intervened to provide subsidies to ailing or financially weak newspapers. In trying to ensure political diversity, however, state intervention may well hamper the introduction of reforms necessary for the economic survival of the press.

chapter three

Public service and the deregulation of European broadcasting

Broadcasting in Western Europe has been described as a 'mixed model' (McQuail 1990). European nations at the advent of radio broadcasting in the 1920s rejected both the unregulated, free market model developing in the USA and the directly regulated, state-controlled system emerging in the Soviet Union. They adopted a distinctive model which combined components of commercial and state-regulated broadcasting and is usually called public service broadcasting. A variety of public service broadcasting systems developed across the continent, some of which placed broadcasting in a closer relationship with the state than others. Some countries rejected the market playing any part in the financing of broadcasting, while others developed a dual role for the state and the market in raising revenue. This model had the support of most of the significant forces in Western European society until the late 1970s. However, support was gradually eroded by a range of technological, financial, political and social changes. Since 1980 the consensus behind public service broadcasting has broken down and, as a result, broadcasting has undergone considerable change (Petley and Romano 1993). This chapter examines the technological developments and new regulatory mechanisms that have ushered in a world of multi-channel, market-driven television and explores the readjustment of broadcasting structures, output and audiences that has resulted. While there is a general crisis of public service broadcasting in Western Europe, with public funding for television being cut and the audience for public service television falling, these readjustments have differed nationally.

European public service broadcasting

The public service system that took hold of Western European broadcasting in the period following the Second World War was characterized by a number of key features. McQuail (1995) identifies the 'old order' as being distinguished by a programming policy catering for all tastes, public accountability, monopoly, national scope, independence from vested political interests and non-commercialism. The overall end product could be seen as 'quality' programming for all. Programme-makers were freed from the commercial need to make profit and governed by guidelines that ensured, among other things, access for minority groups and fair and impartial political coverage, and, as a result, they produced programmes that had broad appeal. Public service broadcasting made available a far wider range of representation than other media. Accountability was put in place through regulatory bodies and Western European legislatures usually had ultimate control over the funding of public service broadcasting. The most common means of financing broadcasting in Western Europe was by a licence fee, set by governments and collected by a government agency. Broadcasting tended to be a monopoly in most countries, with one broadcaster licensed and funded by the government. Monopoly was justified by the technical argument that there was a scarcity of airwaves and hence only a few channels were available. However, most Western European governments were reluctant to allow such a potentially powerful means of communication to operate outside their control.

Politics was central to the development of public service television in Western Europe. Blumler (1992: 12) points out that public service broadcasting bodies are 'highly politicised organisations'. The state played a crucial role in the formation of these organizations, but public service broadcasters have taken their responsibilities to the performance of the political process and maintenance of a healthy civic culture 'far more seriously' than their colleagues elsewhere in the media and in commercial systems in other parts of the world, such as the USA (Blumler 1992: 12). This does not mean that public service broadcasting was closely controlled by government. Day-to-day editorial control often rested in the hands of the broadcasters, who achieved considerable independence of government in many, if not all, Western European nations. The independence of broadcasting was guaranteed by a number of different political arrangements. Kelly (1983) identified three different forms which bring television and politics together. There are formally autonomous systems, in which arrangements have been established to separate decision-making from the government of the day. Such arrangements exist in Britain, Ireland and Sweden. Politics in broadcasting systems ensures that the governing bodies of broadcasting organizations have representatives from all major political parties, as well as other social groups and movements associated with them, as in Germany, Denmark, the Netherlands and Belgium. Finally, there are what Kelly terms 'politics over broadcasting systems', in which the government and other organs of the state can intervene directly in the day-to-day decisions of broadcasters, as in Greece, Italy and France. Sensitivity to state involvement in broadcasting has always been a matter of concern in every European country. The rationale for the state's role in the broadcast media is that broadcasting is too important to be defined as a market commodity. It is a social good, a commonly valued resource that must be organized for the collective good to ensure that all citizens have an equal right to be educated, informed and entertained. The public broadcasting system in Western Europe was supported by a wide range of groups and interests in western society.

Prior to the 1980s a broad consensus surrounded the public service concept. Political elites supported public broadcasting as it enabled them to exercise some form of control over a potentially disruptive social force. For intellectuals and cultural elites, public broadcasting allowed them access to the airwaves to educate audiences about the finer aspects of literature and the arts, and to raise standards of knowledge and understanding. Many saw it as a crucial tool in promoting social harmony. Bureaucrats in Europe, more accustomed to state intervention than their North American counterparts, saw it as natural that a government department should oversee broadcasting. The press were grateful as the rejection of commercial broadcasting prevented broadcasters competing for what was a limited amount of advertising revenue. For audiences the range of programming appeared to satisfy their viewing requirements. However, from the early days of radio and television, after the novelty of the new medium had worn off, audiences were increasingly dissatisfied with what was served up. In Britain in the 1930s listeners drifted away from the BBC to tune into European channels such as Radio Luxembourg and Radio Fecamp, private services banned in the UK, to receive a range of entertainment in preference to what they saw as the dull and worthy output of Reith's public service station. These concerns did shape the development of programming policy, but remained hidden by the consensus surrounding public service.

The European public service model was destabilized by a number of changes in the late 1970s and early 1980s. Technological change was critical as it undermined the 'scarcity of the airwaves' argument, which had justified the monopoly of broadcasting. The original rationale for public service broadcasting in Western Europe was the scarcity of frequencies, making regulation necessary to avoid the confusion and chaos of airwaves wrought by competing radio signals. Monopoly was seen as 'natural' in such circumstances (Negrine 1998: 228). The arrival of the new media technologies of cable and satellite in the late 1970s brought to an end the problems of scarcity. New systems of delivery undermined terrestrial services by liberating the airwaves to more and more channels. As significant was the arrival in positions of political power of right-wing libertarian governments, opposed to public regulation and state intervention, which they saw as inhibiting the operation of the free market (Humphreys 1996: 161). Free marketeers, such as Mrs Thatcher in Britain, Jacques Chirac's Gaullist neoliberals in France and the neoliberal faction of the Christian Democrats in Italy, committed themselves to liberating broadcasting from the 'nanny state' and ensuring that consumer choice, as determined by audience tastes and preferences, would prevail. They embarked on the process of deregulation and liberalization which represented a direct challenge to public service values. These governments were lobbied hard by a range of commercial interests. The business lobby behind deregulation was a formidable amalgam of cable and satellite operators, advertisers, independent television producers, the press and publishing industries, broadcasting facilities and financial interests, all of which believed that opening up European broadcasting would be favourable to their enterprises (Humphreys 1996: 174). The advertising industry in Europe was particularly effective at lobbying for change, at a national and a European level (Humphreys 1996: 172; Mattelart and Palmer 1991: chapter 4). By breaking the public service monopolies, the advertising industry hoped to reduce the rates they had to pay to advertise on television. Other powerful interests supported the coalition against public service broadcasting on political grounds. The European Commission believed that breaking down national public service broadcasting monopolies would assist the process of European cultural and political integration (see chapter 7). It also sought to prioritize economic aims in the television industry in order to build European production to counter the increasing flow of US programming into the continent (Humphreys 1996: 259–61). Commercial pressure came from the new media moguls, who sought the relaxation of national rules and regulations to facilitate their entry into the increasingly lucrative broadcasting market. The press saw broadcasting as an investment opportunity rather than a competitor, and with newspaper groups becoming incorporated into larger media enterprises, the larger potential profits to be made in television pushed concerns about the newspaper business into the background. Finally, fuelled by the social and cultural changes of the 1960s onwards, audiences increasingly demanded and asserted their right of access to information and a range of programming. Increased prosperity meant that more people were able and willing to pay for what they wanted to see on their television screens. The result was that the forces for change became overwhelming and in 1976 Italy became the first European country to 'deregulate' television.

The Italian affair

The Italian state broadcaster Radio Audizioni Italiana (RAI) had held a monopoly of broadcasting from the end of the Second World War. Deregulation in Italy was as much a response to political factors as technological innovations such as satellite and cable, which promised a multi-channel system. The stifling hand of the Christian Democrats, who had been the majority party in Italy since 1945, brought forth calls in the 1970s for greater diversity on Italian television. Their defeat in the 1974 election provided the opportunity to do something about the situation. The resulting changes brought about a radical shift in the 'ecology' of Italian broadcasting. In its first phase, deregulation led to the setting up of hundreds of private television stations throughout the country – about 600 local television stations and more than 2500 radio stations were born (Mazzoleni 1997:129). Lacking the public subsidy of the state broadcaster, RAI, and relying heavily on advertising revenue to fund their operations, the output of these stations was variable. Sartori (1996 :156) identifies three kinds of organizational types: independent stations, the 'pioneers of private television', which produced their own programming and sold their own advertising; the so-called 'circuits' established by advertising sales agencies, which began to incorporate television programmes; and 'networks', which centralized programming, advertising sales and management through the merger and affiliation of channels. The audience share of these early networks rose from 4 per cent in 1977 to 24 per cent in 1979. However, their programming was described as combining 'artless idealism with naked profiteering'. Before long the television explosion encountered meltdown as local stations closed. The end of the first phase of Italy's television experiment came when the 'big operators' began to buy up strings of local stations. The main beneficiary of this process was the TV entrepreneur, Silvio Berlusconi, who came to own three major national channels – Canale 5, Retequattro and Italia 1. The means by which most of private television was delivered into the hands of one man and one corporation, Berlusconi and Fininvest, is attributed to 'a mixture of contradictory factors – managerial skill and lack of it, far-sightedness and obtuseness, active and passive political cronyism' (Sartori 1996: 158; see also Mazzoleni 1991).

The kind of programming Berlusconi's channels offered was organized around 'high advertising appeal', relying heavily on a schedule of quiz shows, 'sanitized nudity', bought-in old US situation comedies and sport. Games and variety shows seemed to be on all the time. The most notorious was *Colpo Grosso* — put out by another private TV station – which had stripping housewives and, as a main prize, the chance to undress the show's dancers. Italian television pioneered the 'TV sex show' (see Blain and Cere 1995). Soap operas purchased from the USA and Latin America and dubbed into Italian also became part of the service. The invasion of foreign imports into Italy has been described as 'the most extraordinary collection of international programming stock ever seen in the history of television' (Sartori 1996: 160). The increase in foreign-made material was a response to the need to produce programmes at the lowest possible cost; bought-in soaps at the time were five times cheaper than the home-made product. The new ecology of Italian broadcasting soon settled into the following pattern. RAI's share of the audience had fallen to around 45 per cent, while the share of Berlusconi's channels had risen to roughly the same amount. The remaining 10 per cent or so was fought over by myriad local and regional stations, including those run by the Catholic Church, Italian political parties, trade unions and hard-core porn interests. However, in order to survive, RAI had to drop part of its public service mission and become involved in a ratings battle. Sartori (1996: 156) details how a number of traditional programmes disappeared altogether from its schedule during these years, which he labels the period of 'tactical degeneration'. First the Friday night drama series disappeared, then the slots for children's programmes were reduced and finally cultural offerings were relegated to later and later in the evening. In an effort to compete, RAI had been driven downmarket, increasingly embracing the formats adopted by Berlusconi's channels. Criticized and pressured to concentrate on 'serious' programming, RAI argued that this would further diminish its audience. The changes were necessary if RAI was to secure its future and the future of public service broadcasting.

The 1980s was an era of unremitting competition in Italian television. Mazzoleni (1997: 129) compares the period with the Wild West, with 'unregulated competition, births and deaths of hundreds of broadcasting enterprises, rocketing programme costs and, above all, the consolidation of a private broadcasting industry, monopolized by a single trust'. In the end there was 'trench warfare involving two combatants – the RAI and Fininvest' (Sartori 1996: 160). During this period the amount of broadcasting hours increased considerably: annual hours of television rose from around 6000 in 1976 to about 34,000 in 1986 (Wolf 1989: 53). However, advertising time on Italian television grew even more quickly. In 1983 RAI carried 40,000 advertising slots on its three channels, a figure which rose to 60,000 by 1987; meanwhile, Fininvest channels had no fewer than 284,800 slots in the same year (Wolf 1989: 53). RAI was operating on an income two-thirds of which came from licence fees and one-third from advertising (Henry 1989). This saturation of advertising meant that 'programmes, schedules, tones and even the appearance of on screen personnel were all determined by the need to satisfy the needs of advertisers' (Grundle 1997: 69). Demands were made for limits on advertising, but it was in the area of programme quality that concerns became most pronounced. Informational programmes were virtually absent from Fininvest's channels, although prior to 1991 Berlusconi's channels were prevented from broadcasting live, which hampered their attempts to develop a news service (Grundle 1997: 63). However, the amount of time devoted to what was the centre of the public service schedule – news and current affairs – declined on RAI. Qualitatively, there were changes in the presentation of information programmes on RAI, as more sensational, cinéma-vérité-type formats – of programmes such as *Yellow Telephone*, *I Confess* and *Public Prosecutor* – replaced the more traditional and less spectacular news and current affairs output (Wolf 1989: 59). Public concerns at the more market-oriented nature of RAI's news selection and presentation led to calls for a television journalism 'freer, more autonomous and more respectful of professional integrity' (Wolf 1989: 62). Only with such changes could the threats to journalistic standards and, hence, the national and civic culture be countered.

In these circumstances, the government did nothing to put order back into the broadcasting sector. It was not until 1990 that a bill was passed to address the chaos. The Mammi law, however, only served in the eyes of critics as a 'legalization of the status quo' (Mazzoleni 1997: 129). While the law introduced new programming responsibilities and a number of measures to ensure transparency in the industry, it made no attempt to reform the system and left intact existing patterns of ownership (Sartori 1996: 159). Backed by what was then the 'biggest commercial TV network under single ownership outside the US', Berlusconi became prime minister in 1994 and wasted no time trying to appoint new executives to RAI to ensure that the political bias of the organization went his way (Hutton 1994). By the 1990s RAI had split its service into three channels, each supporting a particular political persuasion – RAI 1 remained in the hands of the Christian Democrats, RAI 2 was run by the Socialist Party, while the Communist Party controlled RAI 3. The result was an open civil war inside RAI, with journalists passing votes of no confidence in their news directors, and broadcaster pitted against broadcaster (Glover 1995). Internal competition was dropped in the 1990s as RAI sought to fight off the threat from the centre right government and Berlusconi's media empire. The close connection between the broadcasters and political parties was also abandoned, having been discredited by the corruption scandals of the early 1990s. In the process, public service was redefined and RAI's distinctiveness abandoned (Pandovani and Tracey 2003).

The 1990s witnessed a convergence in the output of Italian television. The new 'technocratic' management team that took over the running of RAI in the mid-1990s, following Berlusconi's electoral defeat, decided that the organization should become more competitive and broadcast even more popular programmes. The amount of fiction formats on RAI channels grew enormously: in 1992, 9242 hours of fictional programming were aired, compared with 2259 in 1982 (Pandovani and Tracey 2003: 145). RAI had taken 'a conscious decision to fight its commercial competitor on its own terrain', which resulted in a radical departure from its traditional programme formats (Hibberd 2001: 237). Hardly any effort was made to prevent the ever-increasing amount of low quality programming. In 1994 the Constitutional Court belatedly declared Fininvest's near monopoly of the commercial system illegal, but its decision was nullified in 1995 when the Italian public voted in a referendum in favour of Fininvest keeping its channels and the partial privatization of RAI. Locked into the ratings battle, which inflated the costs of programming, the amount of imported material on RAI increased. Anglo-American programmes and formats are now the most watched programmes on the channel. There is increasingly less difference between RAI and Berlusconi's channels. RAI's strategy enabled it to maintain its audience share, but at the expense of its public service commitments, which are ever more marginalized in its output.

Crisis of Western European broadcasting

The Italian experience is seen as a good illustration of what is happening to broadcasting in Western Europe. Deregulation brings about the growth of privately controlled television networks, and the increased competition they present undermines public service broadcasting. The number of people who watch the public service channels is drastically reduced. In response, public service channels are forced to 'imitate commercial television in an effort to try and beat the competition' (Siune and Hulten 1999: 28). As a result, there is a decline in the traditional mixture of programmes catering for diverse audience tastes and interests that characterizes public service television. Public service channels come to resemble their commercial competitors more and more. Serious programming devoted to information, education and culture disappears from the peak viewing hours – prime time – to be replaced by more entertainment-oriented shows. The market-driven imperatives of the new television lead to a lessening of the range of programme output and actually work to restrict choice for the viewer. While the amount of television broadcast expands, the variety of programmes on offer is reduced. The profit motive results in a relentless search to produce television at the lowest cost. In the case of Western European broadcasting, this means importing more cheap television programmes from the USA. The reliance on American and other foreign imports and the growth of low-cost, entertainment-driven programmes is seen as presenting a threat to national cultural identity and cultural standards (see Tunstall and Machin 1999). The impact of commercialization on the content of television is summed up in an official report in 1994 on the consequences for German television (quoted in McQuail 1998: 119):

> . . . we can observe a surplus of programmes, both in entertainment and information. The TV programme itself has become more sensational, more negative, focusing more on scandals and rituals in politics. Entertainment has increasingly focused on sex and violence, on simplistic stereotypes, more rapid editing as part of a slowly developing 'video clip aesthetic', a new confusion of realities and television realities . . .

At the heart of Western European broadcasting has been its 'delicate and often symbiotic relation to politics' (Brants and Siune 1998: 128). The new commercial order is changing the nature of politics and political communication. The maintenance of 'serious' programmes is seen as a particularly acute problem in the reporting of politics. The raison d'être of public service broadcasting is to provide a range and diversity of political coverage that enables the citizen to play his or her full part in the political process. News and current affairs was at the centre of the traditional public service schedule. Most commercial channels regard political coverage as marginal. As a result, the amount and quality of political information is falling. Competition is forcing public channels to scale back on politically informative news or push it to the margins of the schedule. The nature of political reporting on television is also changing. It concentrates more on the rituals and personalities of politics than on the substance and issues (Brants and Siune 1998: 137–9). Investigative journalism is changing. There is also a significant alteration in the style and mode of the presentation of politics across the commercial and public channels, emphasizing immediacy and emotion at the expense of explanation and elucidation. Shorter, snappy and sensational items are more newsworthy. One writer has dubbed the new product as 'newszak' (Franklin 1997). The explosion of newszak and the changing nature of political reporting both raise questions about the role of television in democracy. These developments are seen as favouring political parties and personalities that trade on the emotive, and contributing to the degradation of public debate, which accounts for the growing cynicism about politics, the rise of voter apathy and the decline of public participation in the political process. Blumler and Gurevitch (1995) have referred to this as the 'crisis of public communication'.

National variations

The generalized crisis suggested above points to the imminent death of public service television in Europe. For some it is already dead: in Tracey's words, public service broadcasting is a 'corpse on leave' and any attempt to save it is more akin to 'the preservation of primeval bugs in amber than the continuation of any vibrant cultural species' (Tracey 1998: 33). However, as Curran (1996) notes, the decline of public service broadcasting across Western Europe has not been uniform. In some parts of the continent public service channels have been better able to resist the pressures of commercialization; in others, public broadcasters have improved their performance to fight off the competition; and elsewhere the public have rallied around public service to defend it. The picture of what is happening to public service television is varied and the reasons for this are found in a range of social, political and cultural factors.

It is important to point out that the concept of public service has been interpreted differently across Western Europe. While scholars (for example, Blumler 1992; Broadcasting Research Unit 1986) have striven to identify the common features of European public service broadcasting, national economies, cultures and politics have determined considerable variations in practice. As Brants and Siune (1992: 101) state, 'public service broadcasting in Europe is relatively lacking in norms; in fact there is no uniformity even in the terminology used'. Three factors in particular have underpinned this difference: the ways in which public television is financed; the nature of the relationship between broadcasters and the state; and popular attitudes to and understanding of the public service mission to explain. Today pure public service systems, funded only by public subsidy, usually through a licence fee, do not exist (Humphreys 1996: 125). It was in the late 1980s that the handful of Western European countries – Belgium, Denmark, Norway and Sweden – that supported systems of public subsidy only began to run ads. There are still some channels, such as the BBC in the United Kingdom, Norway's NRK and Sweden's SVT, which are still financed only by a licence fee. However, most public service channels have been financed by a mixture of public and state subsidy and advertising revenue for a long time.

Spanish state television, Televisión Española (TVE), had always raised the vast proportion of its revenue through advertising – in 1977, 94.1 per cent of its financing came through advertising (Maxwell 1995: 27). Spanish television was exceptional in the extent to which advertising played a role in the financing of public broadcasting, but it has been present in most European broadcasting systems. The revenue for German public service channels is raised through a mixture of advertising – which is limited to certain hours and may not be shown within a programme – and a licence fee. France introduced commercials to state television in 1968, and by 1977 advertising accounted for 25 per cent of the revenue of the monopoly state broadcaster, ORTF (Kuhn 1995: 131). Figures for 1979 show that in Greece advertising accounted for 29.2 per cent of the revenue of the public broadcaster, while the figures were 38 per cent in Portugal, 48.9 per cent in Ireland and 25 per cent in Holland (Maxwell 1995: 27). In Britain commercial broadcasting was introduced as early as 1955, with the launch of ITV (see Williams 1997). While BBC and ITV were kept separate in their sources of finance, British television audiences were introduced to advertising on their screens earlier than most other Western Europeans. Some form of mixed revenue has been the reality for most Western European broadcasters prior to the commercial deluge. Where the commitment to public subsidy has been strongest, public service broadcasting has remained more firmly entrenched.

Countries in which public service broadcasters have been able to maintain some independence from the state, or which have been able to ensure some degree of equality of representation in their coverage of politics, have been better able to defend the ideals of public service, by and large. The political arrangements of broadcasting in Northern Europe, in particular in Scandinavia, have ensured that the traditional public service model has been defended most rigorously. What some have labelled 'savage deregulation' (Traquina 1995) has been more apparent where public perceptions of the state and its intervention in broadcasting have been most negative. In Southern Europe – primarily Spain, Greece, Portugal and Italy – the new commercial order has advanced more quickly as a consequence of public service broadcasting's close association with years of authoritarian government or clientelism. It also explains why the advance of commercial broadcasters in these countries is closely tied to the importance of news and political information at the centre of the media agenda.

Crucially there is the matter of public and political support for the ideals and objectives of public service broadcasting. Western European countries which are more culturally homogeneous, and have experienced a long period of political consensus in the post-war years, have been better able to provide more sturdy foundations for public service broadcasting. The social democratic welfare states of Northern Europe contrast noticeably with the more politically and ideologically divided polities of Southern Europe. Serving the nation, building a national culture and maintaining balance and objectivity in news and political reporting are more straightforward in a climate of cultural homogeneity and political consensus. Popular support for the process of public enlightenment is another important factor. Social democracy in Scandinavia emphasized the importance of education as well as the role of radio and television in serving as the 'social cement' during periods of change (Sondergaard 1996: 12). Dahlgren (2000) relates how the Social Democratic Party's implementation in Sweden of the 'folkheim' – the people's home – with its emphasis on economic and social security and opportunity for all citizens, shaped the structure and output of the media. In such circumstances mass commercial culture was seen as 'vulgar, if not downright threatening to an enlightened democracy' (Sondergaard 1996: 11). Thus it is not surprising that in response to the efforts of the Norwegian Broadcasting Corporation (NRK) to adapt to the new competitive environment in the mid-1980s, there was a 'public outcry at what was seen as a trivialisation of television output' (Syvertsen 1991: 105).

Based on these factors, it is possible to suggest that what is happening to public service broadcasting in Western Europe is far more varied and complex than the picture of an impending process of eclipse painted by some commentators. To examine these variations in more detail, comparison is made between what has happened in Scandinavian countries and in the countries of Southern Europe, and between two of the big players in Western European media systems, France and Germany.

Northern exposures

Scandinavia has been exposed to the forces of the new commercial broadcasting order as much as elsewhere in Western Europe, but until the late 1980s the Nordic countries had maintained their public service broadcasting monopoly with only minor adjustments (see Bondebjerg and Bono 1996). The case of Denmark is typical (see Holm 1998; Sondergaard 1996; Bondebjerg 1996; Petersen and Siune 1997). One institution – Danmarks Radio (DR) – had a monopoly on radio and television broadcasting until 1983, with a single television channel, which broadcast six hours every day, during which 50 per cent of the programmes were news and culture. The monopoly was broken when local broadcasting began on an experimental basis in 1983, leading, in 1988, to the creation of a second channel, TV 2, which carried both national and regional television. TV 2 has been described as a 'reaction to the challenge from foreign channels broadcast to Denmark via satellite and . . . cable' (Petersen and Siune 1997: 36). This channel was funded by advertising and the licence fee from the outset. By the beginning of the new millennium both the amount of television and television viewing had increased in Denmark. The two terrestrial channels, DR and TV 2, have been joined by TV 3, a wholly commercial channel, broadcast by satellite from London to all of Scandinavia, and exempt from national laws, and by DR 2, a satellite channel set up by the public service broadcaster to reach the younger and better-educated segments of the population. Since 1997 local television in Denmark has been allowed to network and is now called TV Denmark, behaving, in effect, like a third terrestrial channel. It is a commercial channel. Cable penetration is high in Denmark (around 60 per cent), which allows Danes access to many foreign TV channels. Thus from a single channel 12 years ago, the Danish viewer today is presented with a variety of channels.

The result is that the Danish public spends more time watching television – viewing has doubled in the last decade. Danish channels are watched much more than foreign channels. DR is watched by around 25 per cent of the audience, TV 2 by about 35 per cent, with the remaining 40 per cent split between the other channels (Tufte 1999: 86). The growth of commercial practices has had an impact on programme content. Fictional programmes grew rapidly in the early 1990s; for a fully commercial operation, such as TV 3, this category accounts for more than 80 per cent of output. But such programming also increased on the other channels – nearly 50 per cent of TV 2 and 30 per cent of DR was devoted to entertainment and fictional programming in the mid-1990s. News programmes, however, have also increased. Petersen and Siune (1996: 45) describe Danes as 'news freaks'. In 1996 one-third of the population watched the main news on TV 2, while nearly 50 per cent tuned in for the main bulletin later on DR. By 2000 the amount of news in prime time had increased on both channels, rising on TV 2 from 17.7 per cent of output in 1995 to 22.3 per cent in 2000, and on DR from 19.4 per cent to 26.9 per cent for the same years (*Jyllands Posten*, 15 February 2000). (Figures are based on prime-time viewing – 6 p.m. to 11 p.m. – from 18 to 23 January in the years stated.) News has become more central to the programming policy of both channels as the entertainment content has declined, for example, series (mainly soaps) fell between 1991 and 2000 from 21.5 per cent to 3.9 per cent on DR, and from 15.2 per cent to 3.6 per cent on TV 2.

The growing amount of news on Danish television has been accompanied by a debate about the nature of news programming. A recent study of Danish TV news found that TV newscasts today are more likely to contain shorter items and more feature material (Hjarvard 1999). The increased sensationalism of news reporting, with more focus on conflict and scandal, crime, 'soft news' and news presentation, in terms of style and angles, has been identified by other researchers as a change in Danish news (cited in Brants and Siune 1997: 138). The Media Committee – set up by the government in 1994 to monitor the state of the Danish media – identified politically relevant information on TV news as having become 'sporadic and incoherent' (Holm 1998). Some journalists argue that these changes mean that 'television as a medium is just now coming of age in Denmark' (quoted in Graham-Holm 1999). They contend that Danish television in the public service era was simply 'radio with pictures'. Bondebjerg (1996: 51) refers to the 'ideology of objectivity which made it difficult to produce investigative and in-depth journalistic programmes'. He welcomes the growth of 'more personal and controversial forms of documentary' since the 1980s. In 1988 DR – followed a year later by TV 2 – established a documentary group whose only function was to develop documentaries. Despite recent cuts in DR's documentary group, the result has been high ratings, international recognition and documentaries becoming a 'powerful element in modern Danish television culture' (Bondebjerg 1996: 54). The two main tracks developed in these documentaries have been the first person participant observation and investigative reporting. The decline of government intervention and the loosening of party affiliations in broadcasting appears to have provided an impetus to the development of a more independent, personal and critical journalism.

The situation in Denmark is reflected to a greater or lesser extent in other Northern European broadcasting systems. The shift in the schedules as a result of commercialization and deregulation has been gradual. The emphasis is still on news and current affairs, which have adapted to the new realities of the market on their own terms and in accordance with what Danish audiences want, within the parameters of Danish society and its traditions. Similar developments are observable in Norway (see Syvertsen 1992) and Sweden (see Djerf-Pierre 2000). There is evidence to show that trends in Northern Europe do not support the argument there is a convergence in the content of television. Research indicates that across the Nordic region news, current affairs, documentary and domestic fiction have increased on public service television (Siune and Hulten 1999; McQuail 1998). It is also the case that public service criteria have been incorporated into the new commercial channels in Scandinavia, in particular in relation to the diversity and quality of programming policy commitments. While television in Northern Europe has had to change in response to the pressures of commercialization and deregulation, this change is characterized as a 'modernization' of the concept of public service rather than its demise.

Due south

The ethos of public service has never been as deeply ensconced in Southern Europe as it has been in the Nordic nations. The sharp decline of the public broadcaster is a noticeable feature of this part of Europe. Within the very first year of their operation, 1989, two private entertainment channels, Mega Channel and Antenna TV, dominated Greek television (Papathanassopoulos 1997). The public channels saw a steady erosion of their audience, falling from 61.6 per cent of viewers in 1989 to 7.9 per cent by 1995; by 1997 their cumulative debt was reported as 45 million drachmas. Similar experiences are found in Spain and Portugal. In Spain RTVE built up huge debts, which were covered by the government as its audience plummeted from 76.6 per cent of the television viewing market in 1990 to 34 per cent by 1997 (Lopez et al. 1999: 353). In Portugal the two channels of public broadcaster Radiotelevisao Portuguesa (RTP) could claim just over 39 per cent of viewers by 1996, having collapsed from a near monopoly of the national audience in 1993 (Rui Cadima and Braumann 1999).

The demise of the public broadcaster in Southern Europe has been accompanied by a shift in the nature of programming. The rise in the number of television hours has seen the growth of cheap-and-cheerful programming. Traquina (1995) has shown how soaps and quiz shows came to dominate the main public service channel, RTP 1, in Portugal following the introduction of commercial television. He found that in 1993 entertainment programmes (films, soaps and game shows) were more prevalent in prime time on the main public service channel than on the two main commercial channels. The three genres took up 68 per cent of prime-time programming on RTP 1. The output of Greek television has also seen an increase of game shows, soap operas and films. This has led critics to describe private channels as 'glorified versions of tabloid newspapers' (Papathanassopoulos 1997: 362). The sluggish response of the public television channels to such fare was one of the main reasons behind their decline. In Spain the arrival of private television channels produced a 'serious shortage of programmes', which threw the industry into a 'state of great uncertainty' (Vilches 1996). By 1995 fiction, films and TV drama accounted for 43 per cent of the total output of Spanish television. The influx of North American and foreign programming has been a noticeable feature of the situation in all these countries. For example, of all the films shown on Spanish television in 1994, 58 per cent were American (de Mateo 1997: 205). However, the unrestricted competition in the television market in these countries has led to a spiralling upwards of the cost of programmes and programme-making, which has hampered the development of the service. There are too many stations and channels for the relatively small domestic advertising market. In Portugal, to ease this situation, in 1997 the government decided to remove advertising from the second public channel and reduce its amount on RTP 1. The insufficiency of advertising revenue to cover the financial needs of operators has resulted in the rising cost of bought-in programmes as channels compete for their purchase. The result is that for much of the period since deregulation the general state of the television business in Southern Europe – with some exceptions – has been very precarious. Both private and public channels have made considerable losses and the production of 'quality' programmes, that is, high-cost productions, has suffered.

The fate of public television in Southern Europe is intimately tied to a history of excessive direct state control over the media. In all three countries discussed above broadcasting was regarded as an arm of the state until the mid-1970s. Public service was compromised by politicians using television as an instrument of propaganda and political interest. The underdevelopment of civil society ensured that policy-makers focused on what was politically expedient. Papathanassopoulos (1997: 365) argues that in Greece the deregulation was a 'knee jerk reaction to the politics of the time and to electoral speculation rather than a response to the needs of the industry'. Syngellakis (1997) explains how the chaotic system of deregulated television was introduced in response to the internal electoral needs of the socialist government of the day and the pressures being exerted on Greece to adjust rapidly to the norms of democracy in order to ensure its membership of the European Community. A similar situation was found in Portugal and Spain, as media interests and owners made their deals with politicians, steeped in the tradition of the state intervening directly in the business of television (see Traquina 1995; Bustamente 1989). The use of television as an 'instrument' outlived the authoritarian military regimes. In Greece, for example, director generals of the public service broadcaster, ERT, changed on average every 12 months, well into the 1990s (Papathanassopoulos 1997: 364). Deregulation and privatization were fuelled by the desire to remove the shackles of dictatorship and the need to democratize. However, the tradition of a strong centralized state and political clientelism ensured that changes in the structure of television were slow to develop (see Papatheodorou and Machin 2003). When they did, the discredited public service broadcasters found it difficult to maintain the loyalty of their viewers.

The deregulation of television in Southern Europe has thus coincided with freeing it from the dead hand of direct state intervention. Starved of non-governmental news for so long has meant that there exists a considerable popular demand for news and information programmes. News is central to the output of both private and public stations. In Greece one of the advantages of deregulation is that 'contemporary TV news is faster, less boring and, at least, the newscasters are what they are supposed to be – not readers of the government's announcements as they were in the past' (Papathanassopoulos 1997: 361). Private channels, in particular, have responded to the public demand for news. In Portugal, from the very early days, the private channels carried a considerable amount of information programming in prime time – more than their public service competitor (Traquina 1995: 231–2). News has also featured in Spain, with both the public and the newly autonomous regional television channels devoting a significant part of their output to the genre (see Lopez et al. 1999), while Syngellakis (1997) states that 'Greek television programming is dominated by news and information'. The growth of entertainment on television in most of Southern Europe has been accompanied by parallel growth of news and information. However, the lack of an investigative tradition of journalism has retarded the development of a critical television journalism that challenges the entrenched power of the established political parties.

Franco-German differences

At the heart of Europe the clash between 'northern' and 'southern' responses to deregulation and commercialization has been encapsulated by the changes in the broadcasting systems in

Germany and France. Two of the 'big three' players in Western European broadcasting have taken different paths in adapting to the new broadcasting order. In both countries broadcasting was a public monopoly until the mid-1980s; the break-up of the public service monopoly took a different form in each. Following the introduction of competition in the early 1980s, France embarked on a radical change when, in 1986, the Chirac government initiated the transfer of TF 1, the leading public service channel, into private hands. The channel was sold to a consortium headed by the Bouygues construction company. One of the consequences of this development was the eventual demise in 1992 of La Cinq, one of the commercial channels introduced by the socialist government in 1985. Thus it was not only the channels that remained in the public sector, Antenne 2 and FR 3, that were affected, but some of the early commercial operators suffered too. Humphreys (1996: 233) highlights the lessons of the French experience for 'headstrong free marketeers and privatizers': more channels compete for limited advertising revenue which increases competition for programmes and media stars, driving up costs and eventually squeezing profit margins and resulting in bankruptcy. The search for cheaper programmes is part of this scenario; through the process of deregulation it adopted, France put considerable pressure on its indigenous production base. The decline of French-sourced production came at a time when the French government was leading European efforts to resist the flow of US material into the continent. The success of Canal Plus, a pay-for programmes channel, which up to 1997 was received in 6 million French households, attests to viewers' perceptions of the content of terrestrial television in France.

The situation in Germany saw the integrity of public service television maintained for longer. The decision of the Federal Constitutional Court in 1981 to end the public monopoly paved the way for the growth of commercial channels from 1984 onwards. After some initial problems the new commercial channels started to gain ground slowly and from 1992 the public service channels had lost their position as market leaders (Hickethier 1996: 113–14). With viewing figures declining, its limited share of advertising revenue falling and the government refusing to raise the licence fee, German public service broadcasting went into crisis in the mid-1990s. This gave rise to a national debate, in which calls were made for the discontinuation of the main channel, ARD (Hickethier 1996: 115). By the late 1990s Germany had six main TV channels, three public and three commercial, sharing almost equally 80 per cent of the total audience (Tunstall and Machin 1999: 198). However, there is no evidence that the content of the public service channels has come to mirror that of the commercial stations. There is much more news and information on the former: ARD and ZDF, the two leading public channels, broadcast 40 per cent and 44 per cent, respectively, information programmes on a 24-hour basis, compared to 14 per cent for the two leading commercial channels (McQuail 1998: 122). Public service has consolidated its position without copying the formats of commercial television. Hickethier (1996: 117) argues that public television was able to strengthen its position by adopting a twofold strategy: the expansion of serial-making and the augmentation of news. More up-to-the-minute reporting, the introduction of news specials and more in-depth coverage of world events were emphasized. The amount of news remained stable on public service television between 1985 and 1995, at about 18 per cent, while on the commercial channels its presence in prime time has dropped considerably, to between 4 and 5 per cent (McQuail 1998: 122). While the style and mode of presentation of news on both services has become similar, there is evidence to show that in recent years news output on the commercial channels has come to resemble that of the public broadcasters. There has been a decline of 'human interest' stories on RTL and SAT 1, the leading private channels, and both commercial and public broadcasters have increased the number of political stories on the news (McQuail 1998: 122). In her study of German television in the early 1990s, Pfetsch (1996) found that the amount of political information on both services had increased. She concluded that 'private channels caught up with public channels regarding the contents of political information while the public channels caught up with the commercial channels in their presentation formats' (Pfetsch 1996: 446). For Hickethier (1996: 118) what has happened with news and political reporting on German television is one aspect of how commercial broadcasting is being influenced by the public service model.

The differences between the situation in France and Germany can be attributed to a range of factors. However, the relationship between politicians and policy-makers and the media was important. Partisan political control dominated the development of French television. De Gaulle used to govern by television; an astute media performer, he ensured that his opponents were denied access to airtime, as well as packing all the key positions in broadcasting with his closest allies. Nothing much has changed since his departure from the scene. Successive presidents of both the left and right have used television to pursue their own advantage. The decisions of the 1980s, to introduce commercial television and privatize TF 1, were the products of short-term political opportunism. Mitterrand's decision to allow two private channels was determined by his concerns about losing the 1986 legislative elections. Placing these channels in the hands of his supporters, he hoped to fend off defeat. As Kuhn (1995: 175) notes, the legacy of governments pursuing their own political interest has been 'to the detriment of the implementation of the public service ethos'. In Germany the establishment of broadcasting was underwritten by the efforts to use the media as instruments of democracy. The lessons of the Third Reich taught post-war German governments that broadcasting should be secured 'against capture by either the state or sectional interests' (quoted in Negrine 1998: 226). The political re-education programme in Germany enhanced popular support for broadcasting encouraging social diversity and established regulatory structures to ensure that this goal was enforced. This firmly cemented public service broadcasting into foundations of political, administrative and public support, which has enabled the model to exert its influence over the development of commercial television in Germany.

Public service and the digital revolution

Digitalization promises further radical changes in the nature of European broadcasting. It enhances the capacity to deliver more TV pictures via satellite, cable or terrestrial transmission, further increasing the number of channels available for viewers. It holds out the possibility of changing not only the way in which television and radio are delivered, but also how viewers interact with what they see and hear. A variety of services, from shopping to telephony, television to banking, can now be delivered via one set-top box, making today's television receivers obsolete. Through interactive devices it allows viewers more control over what they see and when (see Murdock 2000). Digitalization poses a further challenge to public service broadcasting; however, the challenge varies across Western Europe. Kleinsteuber (1998) draws attention to the different rates at which new media technology is taken up in Europe. Some countries have high cable and satellite penetration – Scandinavia, Germany and the Benelux countries (Belgium is nearly totally cabled). Other countries, such as Italy, Portugal and Greece, have no significant cable take-up. Nations such as Britain, France and Spain have only recently come to cable and satellite. The varying degrees of penetration have implications for the development of digital television. Whether more than a small elite of viewers will take advantage remains a matter of speculation. It is clear that the pace of the introduction of the new technology will vary across Europe. The ability and willingness of viewers to pay for their television services will also be a determinant. Digital television can be free and some public service broadcasters are experimenting with such a digital service – for example, in Germany and Italy. But in addition to payments for the relevant apparatus to receive the service, it is likely that many of the new channels offered will be by subscription. In certain parts of Western Europe viewers have shown themselves to be reluctant to pay for their television. Pay-TV struggles where the range of 'free television' is wide. In Germany and Italy, for example, such services have met with limited success, while in Britain and France, with a limited number of channels, pay-TV channels such as Canal Plus and BSkyB have been very successful. Thus the market for the take-up of new digital services is highly fragmented.

There is still much uncertainty about the potential of the new digital technology. In addition to uncertainty about the level of market demand for the new digital services, Chalaby and Segell (1999) highlight the increased competition thrown up, the pace of technological progress and the exact nature of convergence. With technology producing an increasingly unpredictable broadcasting environment, the risks for investors and producers are multiplied. Such is the extent of these risks that several authors identify a small number of the largest media corporations in Europe as crucial to the growth of digital television (Kleinsteuber 1998; Murdock 2000; Papathanassopoulos 2002). Only these companies will be able and willing to take on the risks, as the costs of developing such technology are high (Papathanassopoulos 2002: 36–7); their successes in the past have been attributed in some part to their willingness to gamble on the future. But even 'inveterate gamblers' such as Rupert Murdoch are aware of the huge risks associated with the digital revolution. Europe's leading media players, including BSkyB, Canal Plus, Bertelsmann and CLT, have cooperated in planning for the future of television (Papathanassopoulos 2002: 38). Public service broadcasters face considerable obstacles in entering the digital world (Kleinsteuber 1998: 72). Huge costs are incurred in converting to the new technology and purchasing new equipment to be ready for the switch-off of the present analogue service. What is also certain is that in a new digital world more programmes will be needed to fill up the increased space on our television sets. Competition for these programmes will drive up costs, particularly of popular programme formats such as films and sport. With finances limited by the public funding, and declining audience share making it difficult to justify the continued use of public money, public broadcasters will struggle. In the future the large media conglomerates are likely to strengthen their hold over the European communications industries and exert more influence over the television market, with the likely consequence of further weakening of the public service model.

Conclusion

Following the deregulation of Western European broadcasting in the late 1970s and early 1980s, new commercial television channels and new commercial forces have established themselves in the television market. The consequence of this has been to undermine the system of public service broadcasting that had dominated European television in the post-war period. National responses to these changes have varied. In some parts of Europe the public service ethos has proven more resilient. How broadcasting systems adapt to the new conditions depends on a series of domestic factors, including the strength of national cultures, the financial regimes for funding broadcasting, popular attitudes to information, education and entertainment, the relationship between broadcasting and the state and the attitudes of policy-makers. In countries where policy-makers, programme-makers and viewers have had an understanding of and commitment to public service, deregulation has been accompanied by specific obligations on programme content and quality. Hence in countries such as Germany and Denmark we are more appropriately talking about re-regulation, with public service commitments surviving, albeit in a different form. In other countries, where no obligations have been placed on public or private broadcasters to broadcast particular kinds of programmes or meet quota requirements for domestic production, public service has withered. But everywhere public service broadcasting has changed. Now digital technology threatens to change it further. At the heart of this change is whether broadcasters delivering a diversity of programming, including programmes essential to the operation of the political process, have a future in the modern broadcasting era.

(This chapter is an amended and rewritten version of 'Demise or Renewal: The dilemma of public service television in western Europe', which first appeared in Bromley, M. (ed.), 2001, No News is Bad News: Radio, Television and the Public, London: Longman.)

> **chapter four**

The nature of European journalism

Journalism can be traced back to the emergence of print culture in early sixteenth-century Europe. However, the profession of journalism is often described as an Anglo-American invention, a discovery of the nineteenth century (Chalaby 1996). The Anglo-American model of journalism – sometimes called the 'Liberal' or the 'professional' model – is credited with the development of the modern conception of news, as well as the practices of reporting and interviewing that characterize contemporary journalism. European journalism is seen as gradually importing Anglo-American practices and adopting the ways in which British and American journalists work. The nature of the European model of journalism, including the ways in which journalists define their role in society, is the focus of this chapter.

There are of course differences in the ways in which journalism is practiced in the countries of Europe, but it is possible to identify a European model which is more literary, political and intellectual in its approach. As a result, the nature of news values and the organization of the newsroom separate European from Anglo-American journalism. The extent to which journalism in Europe is replicating the Anglo-American model is open to debate, with the European tradition seen as remaining more firmly entrenched in some countries, such as France, Italy and Spain. However, journalism is changing everywhere as a result of technology, commercialization, the development of public relations and political spin-doctoring, and a generational shift in the profession. The efforts of the profession to adapt have corresponded with a decline of public trust in the performance of journalism in nearly every European country.

Models of journalism

The roots of journalism are located in the invention of printing in Mainz in the late fifteenth century. News books or newsletters began to appear in the early decades of the seventeenth century. Licensed by the state, these prototypes of newspapers could only be distributed after going through a heavy process of censorship. Even in the most liberal of regimes, such as the city state of Venice, the publication of news and information was subject to controls. These early publications were produced by printers; their content was culled from correspondents, including diplomats, secretaries, postmasters, readers and merchants. The division of labour within the newspaper industry in the eighteenth century resulted in the emergence of a specialized person responsible for gathering material to fill out the pages of the newspaper. The term journalist first came into regular use in a public sense in Europe in the 1700s (Palmer 2001). It was not until the nineteenth century that journalism attained the status of a profession. Some press historians believe this was a product of the changes in the Anglo-American press from the middle of the nineteenth century (Chalaby 1996, 1998). The strategies and practices, norms and values that came to characterize modern journalism were developed in the USA and UK, and then disseminated to other countries. According to Chalaby (1996: 304) 'other nations . . . progressively imported and adapted the methods of Anglo-American journalism'. The comparative advantage was the result of the press industrializing more rapidly in these countries than elsewhere.

The Anglo-American model of journalism is news driven. Chalaby (1996) identifies the emphasis on speed and accuracy in the delivery of news in the Anglo-American press. The 'extent and accuracy of its information' was singled out by a nineteenth-century commentator as the reason for the supremacy of the Anglo-American newspapers over their European counterparts. The gathering of facts and eyewitness accounts of events, and their rapid transmission, became the cornerstone of the Anglo-American model. The reporter and his notebook, aided by the development of shorthand, became responsible for much of the content of nineteenth-century newspapers in Britain and North America (Smith 1978). Reporters were sent to cover events throughout the country. The advent of the telegraph and telegram meant reports from further afield were possible and international news became a feature of the Anglo-American press. Above all, the reliability of the information provided in the news reports was underpinned by a commitment to 'objectivity'. Putting aside the difficult problem of how objectivity is achieved in practice, Anglo-American journalism emphasized the importance of being objective, detached and neutral in the recording of the news (see Schudson 1978). The emphasis on facts and objectivity accorded with the commercial needs of the Anglo-American press. By presenting the facts and allowing readers to draw their own opinion of them, newspapers were able to sell to more people, across a broad range of political views and attitudes.

If Anglo-American journalism emphasizes the gathering of news and the amassing of facts as accurately and quickly as possible, the 'European model' of journalism places greater emphasis on the interpretation and analysis of events and issues. Based on a discussion of journalism in France, Erik Neveu describes this model as locating journalism somewhere between literature and politics. Neveu (2001: 12) notes that, for most of the nineteenth century, working for a newspaper was a stepping stone for a 'real career' in literature or politics. Chalaby (1997: 638) describes French journalism as a 'provisional occupation', with young men and women seeing it as 'the first step towards a brilliant literary career'. Many of the key figures of nineteenth-century journalism in France were great novelists, such as Emile Zola, Victor Hugo and Honoré de Balzac. The tradition of journalism in France is associated with the writer rather than the reporter (Neveu 2001: 14). Hence the compiling of facts was seen as secondary to serious articles or essays discussing politics and literature. Opinion and comment prevailed over news and information throughout the nineteenth century and well into the twentieth (Chalaby 1996). The French journalistic tradition does not draw a sharp line between facts and interpretation, and articles 'freely mixed news with opinions' (Chalaby

1996: 311). The most celebrated form of journalistic writing is the 'commentary', which combines analysis and comment on a topic from a specific, usually political, point of view (Chalaby 1996: 315). 'French journalism has always been more a journalism of expression than a journalism of observation: it gives precedence to the chronicle and the commentary over summary and reportage' (Albert 1983, quoted in Hallin and Mancini 2004: 98). Polemical writing dominated Italian newspapers for much of the post-war period. Political commentaries, known as *pastone romano*, appeared daily on the front page in the 1950s and 1960s (Porter 1983: 10–11). A review of major political developments of the day written by a leading journalist was the dominant form of political reporting in the Italian press. Their equivalents appear in the French and Spanish newspapers under the titles of *chronique* and *crónica* respectively (Hallin and Mancini 2004: 101). The German tradition of journalism was 'unfamiliar with the distinction between factual reporting and commentary' and also emphasized literary quality (see Kleinsteuber and Weischenberg 2001). According to Donsbach and Klett (1993: 57) '. . . the opinionated editor and commentator was seen as the epitome of the journalistic profession' in Germany, with German journalists 'more likely to make news decisions on the basis of their subjective beliefs'. While reporting and interviewing are the crucial practices of fact-centred Anglo-American journalism, opinion and intellectual analysis are central to the more literary inclinations of European journalism.

Politics also distinguish European from Anglo-American journalism. The press and media in general in Europe are, as we have seen, closely linked to political parties and factions. European society is more politically fragmented and more politicized than Anglo-American society. Bechelloni (1980: 228–43) describes how Italian journalists have traditionally been 'political clients', whose close ties to political parties enable them to benefit from political protection and patronage, in terms of finance and job security. Mancini (2000: 266) states that 'Italian journalists are advocates, linked to political parties, and very close to being active politicians themselves'. The system of 'lottizzazione' assured the representation of the major political parties within the Italian media, particularly broadcasting, in the post-war period. The so-called 'sharing out' of state broadcasting meant that each of the major political parties was given control of one of the three public television channels. RAI was divided between the Christian Democrats (RAI 1), the Socialist Party (RAI 2) and the Communist Party (RAI 3). With the disappearance of the traditional political system in the 1990s the situation has begun to change, although the direct involvement of political parties in the designation of senior managers within public television still occurs.

The political fragmentation of European societies, as in Italy, produces a more complex political situation for the journalist to negotiate. Chalaby (1996: 319) notes that it was – and still is – far easier in America and Britain for journalists to exercise political neutrality and objectivity, because of the limitation of political choice arising from the two-party political system. European journalists are confronted by an array of political forces. In France, the wide range of political positions, parties and ideologies, from communism to royalism, ensured the practice of journalism would be based on political opinions rather than news and information (Chalaby 1996: 319). Journalism in the Nordic countries, to a greater or lesser extent, is tied closely to politics through the consensus that developed in these countries around welfare state democracy (see Dahlgren 2000). In most European countries journalism and the media are the 'voices of organised groups' (Mancini 2000: 271). Whether it is through 'pillarization' in the Netherlands, 'socially relevant groups' in Germany or 'lottizzazione' in Italy, journalism has been closely attached to politics and the promotion of ideology. As Mancini (2000: 273) puts it, objectivity 'is almost impossible within an intricate and fragmented panorama in which a greater number of political forces act and in which even the slightest shades of meaning in a story risk stepping on the positions of one of the forces in the political field'.

The result is that European journalism is more ideological and more politically committed than its Anglo-American counterpart. The tradition of advocacy is more firmly established. Kocher (1986) found that German journalism places greater emphasis on opinion and less on news. According to Kocher's study, German journalists define their primary role as that of being 'missionaries' and see their profession as 'a species of a political and intellectual career'. They are more comfortable in the role of advocating a political position than their British colleagues, who tend to define their role as 'transmitters of facts' and 'neutral reporters of current affairs'. The political and ideological nature of European journalism is partly explained by the nature of European political systems, their greater diversity, partisanship and acceptance of state intervention. However, the slow development of the economic conditions that enabled Anglo-American journalism to detach itself from politics and the state is also significant. Market forces played an important and earlier role in the US and British press than they did in Europe (Chalaby 1996: 320). The rapid growth of industrial capitalism in nineteenth-century Britain and America enabled the press to build up a separate source of revenue, mainly through advertising, which allowed it to become independent of the state and political parties. The autonomy of the press from the political sphere encouraged the depoliticization of journalism; and the need to increase advertising income saw the norms of objectivity and neutrality enhanced as newspapers tried to reach out to more readers. By contrast, the growth of advertising revenue and market forces in the European press was much slower. Chalaby (1996: 321) describes the reluctance of French industrialists to spend money on advertising, while Lumley (1996: 202–4) notes how small readerships and slow urbanization held back the emergence of an Italian press. The result is that in Europe the press remained dependent on the state and political parties for longer.

Journalists were also more open to publicizing political opinions in many parts of Europe, as a result of the relatively low status of the profession. In 1918 Max Weber described journalists as belonging to 'a sort of pariah caste' (quoted in Tunstall 2001: 25). For most of the nineteenth century journalism was treated with disdain and fear, a lowly occupation which no one with any ability would willingly enter (Lee 1976). To earn a living, journalists had to supplement their income in other ways. As a consequence, they were open to bribery and political patronage. It is estimated that between 1871 and 1913 the French government spent between one and two million francs per annum on seeking to influence journalists who were in the habit of taking regular bribes from bankers, financiers and foreign embassies to conceal information or promote share sales and business ventures (Chalaby 2002b: 80). Selected French journalists were in receipt of money from the government until well into the 1960s. Porter (1983: 29–34) outlines the extent to which bribery and graft played their part in the development of modern Italian journalism, even though Italian journalists were relatively well paid compared to most of their European counterparts. In Portugal, the low status of journalism was perpetuated by dictatorship. The Salazar and Caetano regimes reduced the occupation to little more than a 'clerical sub profession' whose main task was 'to transcribe or summarise statements issued by government departments of ministerial offices' (Seaton and Pimlott 1980: 179). As a result, Portuguese journalism was a low-paid occupation with little professional pride, offering no opportunity for talented individuals. It was only in the wake of the revolution in 1974 that it began to develop greater professionalism and more autonomy. However, this only came after journalists had played their part in the anti-imperialist, anti-colonial and anti-fascist struggle initiated by the Portuguese revolution (Hallin and Mancini 2004: 103). Similar situations pertained to Spain and Greece in the wake of the collapse of military dictatorships (see Papatheodorou and Machin 2003).

In Britain and North America, journalism was rescued from low esteem and corruption in the late nineteenth century by the demands of commerce and business. In countries such as Italy, France, Spain, Portugal and Greece the failure of the press to attain a sufficient level of financial independence made it more difficult for journalism to develop as a profession and establish its autonomy from the state and political groupings (Hallin and Papathanassopoulos 2002: 183; Papatheodorou and Machin 2003: 34). The struggle to attain a distinct professional identity proceeded most slowly in Southern Europe, where the political and literary roots of journalism were deeper. Professional organizations and journalists' unions are generally weaker in the Mediterranean countries. Traditionally they were linked to political parties and membership was low. Where autonomous organizations were established, as in Italy, the main concern was the control of access into the profession rather than 'advancing common standards of professional conduct' (Hallin and Mancini 2004: 112). In Northern European countries – Scandinavia, the Netherlands, Germany and Austria – the strong political affiliations of the press did not correspond with the underdevelopment of the profession of journalism. Journalists' unions emerged in the late nineteenth and early twentieth centuries to play an important role in establishing rules and regulations and thus facilitated the emergence of a journalistic culture which transcended political affiliation (Hallin and Mancini 2004: 177). In many European countries there are editorial statutes that protect the independence of journalists. Under the *clause de conscience*, French journalists have the right to leave their newspaper with compensation if the ideological position is changed (Hallin and Mancini 2004: 116). The nature and speed of the development of the profession in Europe, as well as the lower social standing of journalism, has meant that European journalists have been more closely tied to politics than their Anglo-American counterparts.

Newsrooms and news values

The difference between European and Anglo-American journalism is not only a matter of how journalists understand their role in society and how they approach their work; it is also manifest in the organizational structures in which they work. Newsrooms in many parts of Europe operate very differently from Anglo-American offices. In Britain and America centralized newsrooms are favoured, with a high division of labour apparent in the organization of the newsroom (Esser 1998: 378). More people are employed to undertake a wider range of tasks. At least four different professional groups have been identified as performing the functions of the newsroom – reporters, sub-editors, leader writers, page planners/designers (cited in Esser 1998: 379). Reporters are divided into general reporters and specialist correspondents, and usually organized in 'beats' or 'desks', such as business/finance, home, foreign and sports. Background pieces, analysis and interpretation are for the most part written by feature writers, who are allowed to present a point of view. In recent years opinion has become the remit of columnists, whose numbers have increased significantly. There is a 'distinct separation between the tasks of the reporter, who collects the news externally . . . the sub-editor in the editorial office, who corrects texts and formulates titles and headlines and the commentator or "leader writer" who contributes texts expressing opinions' (Kepplinger and Kocher 1990: 292). News gatherers and news processors are often segregated, working in different departments (Esser 1998: 389). Anglo-American newsrooms are hierarchical structures. Their organization reflects the emphasis placed on the separation of fact and comment, as well as the importance of journalism as a business demanding the smooth operation of the production process.

Newsrooms in Europe are less centralized and journalists perform a wider range of tasks. The division of labour in European newsrooms is less apparent. In many parts of Europe one term – *redakteur* in Germany, *redactor* in Spain and *redacteur* in France – is used to describe all those working in the newsroom. The European journalist is more likely to perform the whole range of functions – news gathering and reporting, writing editorials and technical production – that are carried out by several individuals in Britain and the USA (Esser 1998: 379; Kepplinger and Kocher 1990: 292). German, French, Spanish and Italian journalists are less aware of the fundamental division inside Anglo-American newsrooms between reporters and sub-editors. In Europe the journalist will be involved in every aspect of the operation of the newsroom, investigation, editing, reporting, commentary and layout, as well as building contacts with external sources of information. The organization of European newsrooms reflects the importance attached to editorial commentaries as a yardstick of quality in journalism and the role of the journalist in conveying opinion. Compared to Anglo-American newsrooms, there are fewer structures to prevent journalists from acting out their 'advocacy' or 'missionary' roles.

The different approaches to journalism between Europe and the Anglo-Saxon world can also be seen in the way in which the news story is constructed. Professional journalism has a number of universally recognized forms of presenting information: reportage, commentary, interview, 'hard news' and the 'inverted pyramid' (Pottker 2003: 501). The inverted pyramid has come to be regarded as the professional way to write a news story. Developed in America in the nineteenth century, the inverted pyramid places the most important information in the lead sentence of a news story, which is organized to answer the so-called five 'w's questions: who? when? where? what? and, sometimes, why? (Pottker 2003: 402). The information in the rest of the story is presented in 'decreasing order of importance', with the least relevant coming at the end of the story. At the time when this form of news writing became customary in the US press, European newspapers wrote their stories in chronological order. The European style came to be seen as exemplifying 'how news should not be written' (quoted in Pottker 2003: 502). A number of explanations are provided as to how this inverted pyramid style came to be adopted in the US press (Pottker 2003). Economic and commercial factors are identified as critical: the form enhances the 'receptivity' of the product, by making it quicker and easier to read, and facilitates the process of production by enabling texts to be shortened quickly and cheaply. The spread of this form of news writing around the world is associated with the commercialization of the press and media.

The demise of the European model?

The development of European journalism in the twentieth century is portrayed as the gradual demise of the literary and political form. The Anglo-American model is seen as increasingly dominant in European media systems, eroding the differences which characterized journalism in these societies. There has been a shift to a more 'information-oriented journalism' (Hallin and Mancini 2004: 99). Mass media associated with political parties and other organized social groups have declined. Replacing them are commercial media 'whose purpose is to make a profit by delivering information and entertainment to individual consumers and the attention of consumers to advertisers' (Hallin and Mancini 2004: 252). The result has been that the 'journalism of expression' has been displaced. Partial and polemical journalism is incompatible with the need to reach as wide an audience as possible in the effort to maximize profits. European journalism is importing Anglo-American practices, such as the separation of fact and commentary, the emphasis on information, narrative, sensation and entertainment and the commitment to objectivity and political neutrality (Hallin and Mancini 2004: 252). In some countries, such as Germany and Austria, the American approach to journalism was imposed by the Allies to ensure that Nazism and Fascism would not reappear. The separation of fact from comment was established as central to the new press system in post-war Germany (see Humphreys 1994). In other parts of Europe the Anglo-American model was disseminated through training programmes, textbooks and Hollywood films dealing with the profession (Mancini 2000: 268). The international news agencies, dominated by US and UK companies, not only provided most of the world's foreign news, but also served as vehicles to bring Anglo-American news values and news practices into newsrooms around the world (Tunstall 1977: 45–6). Hallin and Mancini (2004: 258–9) note that journalists are heavy consumers of Anglo-American media. Journalists in many parts of Europe, as elsewhere in the world, regularly tune into the BBC and CNN, as well as reading global business publications, such as *The Economist*, the *Wall Street Journal* and the *Financial Times*, and news magazines, such as *Time* and *Newsweek*. A study of Greek international news gatekeepers identified the influence of US news magazines as well as CNN International in shaping their organizations' concept of newsworthiness (Roberts and Bantimaroudis 1997). While the study found that 'European influences are not negligible', with *Le Monde* and the French TV channel TV 5 figuring prominently, American media played a central role in shaping professional judgements on foreign news.

The arrival of television is also seen as having had an impact on the practice of journalism in Europe. Broadcast journalism played a crucial part in challenging the European model by helping to weaken the political foundations on which it was based. Wigbold (1979) describes how the rise of television is associated with the 'de-pillarization' of Dutch society and the media. He argues that the introduction of a single television channel into the homes of people who had been segregated from each other previously not only introduced them to ideas, views and opinions from which they had been isolated, but also showed them that their fellow citizens were not as alien and different as they had been encouraged to believe. Television 'hastened the birth of a new unity' (Wigbold 1979: 201). It also brought into being a new broadcasting organization, TROS. Formerly broadcasting from a pirate transmitter from an offshore island, TROS eschewed politics, focusing instead on light entertainment. Its aim was to attract a large number of viewers, instead of providing a service for a particular group or community. Its success led to other broadcasting organizations emulating TROS, with the corresponding depoliticization of Dutch television. Woolton (1992) argues that journalists in France became more self-assured as a result of cultural, technological and media changes. The explosion of news in the 1980s, brought about by the rapid growth of the broadcast media, especially television, played a crucial role in helping French journalists to develop greater freedom of work and expression. The state has found it more difficult to regulate and control the private TV channels. Greater competition led to the adoption of practices as well as programmes from the USA and the UK. Bourdon (2000) outlines how European broadcasters 'consciously tried to imitate American newscasters'. Satellite technology made audiences around the world more attuned to American production values and journalistic techniques, which then increased the pressure on journalists in European television to do things the Anglo-American way. Television enabled journalists to assert their independence, but made them more open to the practices and values of US journalism. Above all, more emphasis was attached to a lack of partisanship in the collection, processing and dissemination of news and information.

Hallin and Mancini (2004: 272–3) identify several other factors that helped to break down the close connection between journalists and politics, making European journalists more similar to their Anglo-American colleagues. Rising educational levels have led to the profession incorporating into their practice more critical perspectives, drawn from the social sciences and humanities. The development of journalism schools and journalism training has improved professional standards across the continent, as well as making European journalists more aware of Anglo-American methods. Higher levels of educational attainment have increased the prestige of journalists. Commercialization has also raised the social and professional status of journalists. Papathanassopoulos (2001b: 512) describes how the rise of market-led journalism in Greece is linked to higher salaries and increased authority, and resulted in Greek journalists becoming more professional, more responsible and more detached in their reporting. The increase in the size of media organizations, as well as the development of new technologies for gathering information, has enhanced the resources at the disposal of journalists and their capacity to interrogate those in positions of power. The growth of investigative reporting in Europe is seen as another example of the demise of the European model.

Investigative journalism was only practised on a limited scale in Europe for most of the post-war period. The literary preoccupations of the European model of journalism, and the corresponding underemphasis on news gathering and reporting, are seen as having held back the development of the 'watchdog' function. Close connections between journalism and politics, and the low status of the journalist in European society, also contributed to the emergence of a journalistic environment which discouraged the uncovering of facts. Rieffel (1984) notes how the majority of French journalists were traditionally hostile to the practice of investigative reporting. Prior to the 1980s such reporting was carried out by a small numbers of news magazines. *Le Canard Enchaîné* led the way in the years following the war, breaking several political scandals, the most significant of which for the development of French journalism was the Bokassa affair, which rocked the presidency. *Le Canard Enchaîné* had revealed how President Giscard D'Estaing had accepted 'gifts' from the self-styled emperor of the Central African Republic. More crucially, the episode sparked an interest in investigation in the daily press. In the face of considerable pressure and intimidation from the government, France's most influential newspaper, *Le Monde*, allocated resources to investigating the affair. The result was that there was greater acceptance of investigative journalism, apparently sealed with the appointment of Edwy Plenel as *Le Monde's* investigative reporter. Soon most of France's major newspapers and magazines were uncovering what the powers-that-be did not want them to know. The 1980s witnessed a boom in investigative reporting, which culminated in 1991 when the weekly magazine, *L'Événement du jeudi*, revealed details of government complicity in the provision of HIV-contaminated blood to haemophiliacs.

Several factors have been put forward to account for the rise in investigative reporting in Europe. One possible explanation is the decline in the effectiveness of government censorship. Newton and Artingstall (1994, cited in Humphreys 1996 44–7) outline the form, nature and extent of censorship in several liberal democracies. State intervention and secrecy have been features of the media systems in France, Germany and Britain. Chalaby (2002b) describes how the French state under General de Gaulle intervened in the operation of the media, using a panoply of legal and illegal mechanisms to restrict what was reported. If censorship and intervention were at their height under de Gaulle's presidency, his successors have been increasingly reluctant to resort to such methods. The judiciary has become more independent of government and less willing to prevent the disclosure of information. In Germany the *Spiegel* affair in 1962 led to a change in the legal protection of the press (Humphreys 1996: 48–9). Following the publication of an article highly critical of the government's defence policy, the offices of the investigative magazine were raided, some of its journalists arrested and its printing presses seized. Public outcry resulted in the freeing of the reporters and the resignation of the minister responsible for the action taken, as well as an amendment to the constitution to further safeguard the disclosure of information in the public interest. Another change which has assisted the rise of investigative journalism is the growth of individualism in European society (see chapter 1). The prevalence of collectivism underpinned the view that explanations for political failings were to be found in the political system and not necessarily in the individuals who exercised power within it. The breakdown of such collectivist thinking led to people in authority being held more accountable for their actions, with a corresponding focus on the corrupt or deviant behaviour of political actors.

While such external changes were no doubt important in accounting for the emergence of investigative reporting, developments within the profession were more significant. Growing awareness of the power of journalism to bring about political change, most clearly manifest in the reporting of Watergate by the US press in the early 1970s, appear to have provided a major impetus for the growth of investigative reporting in many European countries. Woodward and Bernstein, the heroes of Watergate, became role models for journalists, not just in the Anglo-American world. Watergate coincided with a new generation of reporters entering the profession, who were more committed to investigation and disclosure. Their capacity to investigate and expose was increased by the introduction of greater competition. This meant it was no longer acceptable simply to report official statements or focus on abstract political ideas. More 'exclusives' about politicians and clashes within government and political parties were required. Scandals and misdemeanours began to feature more prominently and investigative journalism was able to develop, if not flourish.

Evidence to support the claim that European journalism is becoming less distinctive, and more like Anglo-American journalism, is found in surveys of journalists' opinions of their profession. The commitment of German journalists to the 'missionary' role is seen to have wavered in the 1990s. Schoenbach et al. (1998: 225) conclude from their survey of over 1500 journalists in West and East Germany that 'the superiority of a "missionary" self-concept over a "bloodhound" one did not reflect the reality of Germany in the early 1990s'. Weischenberg et al. (1998: 251) question the extent to which German journalists ever adopted a missionary role, concluding from their study that there has been 'a convergence in journalism in western liberal democracies'. This finding is in keeping with the work of Splichal and Sparks (1994), who, based on an examination of journalism students in 22 countries, argued that there was a universal set of professional values emerging, particularly regarding autonomy and objectivity. They dismissed the notion that there is a typical 'European' or, for that matter, any other politically or geographically defined kind of journalist. However, not all survey material points in the direction of the emergence of a common approach to the practice of journalism. The notion of common values among journalists is challenged by Weaver (1998), whose comparative analysis of journalism across national boundaries concludes that there are no common values and purposes of the profession other than bringing news to the public's attention as quickly as possible. Weaver (1998: 468) identified considerable disagreement over the importance of analysis and acting as a watchdog on government. While surveys may provide insights into what journalists think about their profession, they do not necessarily provide a reliable guide as to how they act.

Examining what journalists do raises some questions about how far the Anglo-American model of journalism has become prevalent in Europe, as well as the extent to which European journalism has been depoliticized. Cultural factors have been identified as acting as a barrier to the adoption of Anglo-American styles of journalism. Graham-Holm (1999) draws attention to the ways in which Danish journalism has resisted the style and practices of American TV news. She describes how the deep-rooted traditions of Danish society have laid down powerful cultural boundaries, which 'protect Danish TV journalism from outside influence, boundaries so powerful that penetration is a slow process'. The refusal of news reporters to 'sign off', that is to conclude their report by telling the audience who and where they are, is but one of many examples of style, content and presentation cited. Papathanassopouolos (2001b: 507) argues that political and cultural particularities make it 'difficult to develop a culture of journalistic professionalism faithful to the American model' in Greece. While most Greek journalists say they adhere to the neutral and objective model of journalism, in practice facts and comments are freely mixed together in Greek news reporting. Commercialization and a more market-oriented news media are changing Greek journalism, with the growing influence of television reporting leading the way, but at times of 'intense political contention' the political affiliations of journalism and the media are made apparent. Unabashed partisanship remains a feature of the Greek press, which is 'in some cases laced with adjectives that in most western media would be considered incompatible with fairness' (Papathanassopoulos 2001b: 511). Mancini (2000: 272–3) describes how objectivity 'has not found a comfortable abode in Italy'. Italian journalists adhere to the concept of objectivity as a 'purely external legitimation in keeping with the perceived model of professional canons', but their journalism is practised in a society which is highly politicized, from top to bottom. Politics pervades Italian society, 'dominating and influencing many social systems: economics, the judiciary system and so on'. People's level of participation in politics is high and in this situation 'journalists . . . cannot be abstracted and detached from the other social powers', as required in the Anglo-American model.

It is also the case that more European than Anglo-American journalists disapprove of and are unwilling to use many of the controversial techniques of investigative journalism – including pretending to be someone else to gain information, quoting from confidential government documents and infiltrating organizations to acquire information. German journalists are seen as particularly reluctant to deploy such tactics. A survey found that only 19 per cent of German journalists would pretend to be someone else to acquire a story, compared to 47 per cent of British reporters (cited in Kleinsteuber and Weischenberg 2001: 290). Some argue this is not an indication of the 'weak' tradition of investigative reporting in Germany, but a reflection of higher standards of ethical behaviour and greater reticence in discussing professional practices. After all, one of the best known 'heroes' of investigative journalism is the German writer and reporter Gunter Wallraff. However, Wallraff's career of infiltrating and exposing the works of a number of organizations – including Germany's leading newspaper, *Bild*, which he accused of faking stories – has been regarded as an 'undesirable' part of the profession by some journalists (Wallraff 1978). The closeness of the ties between journalists and politicians in many European countries continues to impede the development of more critical and investigative journalism. The complicity between journalists and politicians is highlighted in the case of France by leading television reporter Christine Ockrent, who speaks of the close connections between the journalistic community and the 'hermetically sealed world of politics', where 'people know each other too well, because it is the same 5,000 people who are going to do things, comment on them, react to them' (quoted in Palmer 2001: 267).

Determining the extent to which European journalism is becoming more Anglo-American in style and practice is difficult. Mancini (2000) highlights limits to the transformation of European journalism, stressing that the extent to which the Anglo-American model has taken hold in Europe depends on the peculiarities of the social structures and contexts of different European countries. He notes that, in practice, journalists conform to the traditions of their particular countries, which in most European nations emphasize the political commitment or involvement of journalism. Mancini (2000: 266) draws attention to the 'striking contradiction between a sort of theoretical wisdom diffused among most of the professionals (journalism has to be neutral and detached from power) and the real practice (journalists are advocates and close to different social powers)'. This argument finds favour in studies of journalism in various European countries (see Papathanassopoulos 2001a). It also raises questions about the Anglo-American model. While British and American journalists might not have direct ties with political parties and politicians, their commitment to objectivity and neutrality is tempered by the political orientation of the publications and organizations they work for. The highly partisan nature of the British press clearly colours the interpretation of events offered by its journalists and shapes the way in which they work.

While it is difficult to be precise about the extent to which European journalism has been influenced by Anglo-American practices, it is clear is that the profession has changed considerably in the last couple of decades. Three factors have had an immense impact on what European journalists do: technology, commercialization and the rise of public relations, especially the development of government PR. The consequence of this is that the daily experience of 'doing' journalism is becoming similar in the newsrooms and on news beats across Europe.

The end of journalism?

New media technology has resulted in an information explosion and an acceleration of the speed at which news and information circulates in society. As a result, the nature of news gathering and processing is changing rapidly. Journalists all over Europe are locked into the 24-hour news cycle. They have to file more stories and more reports, more quickly than ever before. The opportunity to check and double-check the accuracy of what they are told is increasingly restricted in an age which demands a constant flow of news into newsrooms and onto pages and screens. New sources of information, such as the internet, are changing the way in which journalists collect information. Not only does the net enable journalists to meet the requirement of regular supply, but it is also relatively cheap and cost-effective. However, technological advance does not necessarily mean the 'same old journalism but with better tools' (Koch 1991 quoted in Bardoel 1996: 295). A former CNN bureau chief in London describes the technological changes as a 'seismic shift' in the way in which broadcast news is gathered, received, watched and used (quoted in McGregor 1997: 2). Newsroom production has been revolutionized, impacting on the traditional division of labour. Journalism is no longer a one-way street, as interactive services allow readers, viewers and listeners to respond to what they see, hear and read on the screen. Interactive services have also increased the opportunity for citizens to communicate with one another. Technology has enhanced the capacity of the citizen to access information more directly. The advance of the 'information society', direct news supply through the net, the explosion of information and the increased ability of the citizen to communicate in an unmediated way seem to suggest that there is less need for journalism. Journalism is seen as becoming 'redundant' as a result of these internal and external changes brought about by new technology, 'losing its prominent place in communication between the citizen and government' (Bardoel 1996: 283). Some speak of the end of journalism (Bromley 1997).

Journalism's search for a role in the brave new media world is a matter for debate. What is the role of journalism and how far is journalism changing? Much of the rhetoric that has accompanied the emergence of the internet and other new media has emphasized their potential for the democratization of public communication as a result of more diversity, openness and accountability. However, the rhetoric seems to have outstripped the reality of the development and impact of new media. For most people working in the old and new media the discourse of democratization passes them by. A study of Irish online journalists found that, while most practitioners recognized the potential of the new media to improve public discourse, they did not share such a vision (O'Sullivan 2005). Interviews with editors of Europe's leading newspapers found that many were not convinced that the new media will be better able to inform the public (Van Dusseldorp 1998). They were concerned that the overwhelming amount of information on the internet could result in people being less well informed.

Research from several countries has found consistently that new media have not had a significant impact on the views journalists have of their profession, leaving them wedded to the ways in which journalism has been practised for the last hundred years (see Deuze 2004; Bardoel 2002). As Deuze (2004: 141) states, 'the contemporary use of multimedia projects and processes in news organizations tends to reproduce existing . . . journalistic practices and culture'. Most of the news on the internet is 'parasitic', drawn from traditional sources and practices. The features that could shape a new kind of journalism are resisted. Interactivity, for example, is regarded as a good thing, but in practice journalists are cautious about interacting with their readers, listeners and viewers. Many aspects of interactivity, such as the use of email, are accepted as part of newsroom life throughout Europe, but are seen primarily as 'an aid or add-on' to what journalists are already doing (O'Sullivan 2005: 59). Developing interactivity beyond the confines of the traditional practices of journalism is seen by many reporters as problematic. The new media have the potential to push journalists to rethink their relationship with the consumer, but in reality most cling to the view that they should decide what the public reads, sees and hears about the world (Deuze 2004: 146). As one Irish journalist puts it, 'the notion that readers and other net users get the same sort of platform as the original news story would obviously be very dangerous ground' (quoted in O'Sullivan 2005: 58). The reluctance of journalists to embrace new media is highlighted by studies of online reporting of events. Research into the reporting of the September 11th attack on the World Trade Center's towers by online newspapers identified a 'lack of technological readiness to use the medium', a 'reluctance to use its interactive capabilities' and an 'editorial immaturity' in the coverage (Salaverria 2005). The recent tsunami in South-east Asia, however, forced journalists to acknowledge the importance of the web in reporting international events of such magnitude. Traditional sources failed to provide a sufficient overview of what was happening – something recognized by the general public, who went to primary sources to access information rather than relying on the traditional media.

If journalism resists seeing the new media as 'other than an extension of the old order' (O'Sullivan 2005: 65), it does not mean that they are not influenced by technology. While some research is upbeat about technology making things 'faster', 'easier' and 'better', qualitative studies have produced a more complex and contradictory picture about the ways in which journalism and news organizations are responding to technological change (Deuze 2004). Frustration, fuelled by fear and insecurity, characterize the findings of some of the research. The bringing together of media, reporters, departments and newsrooms is 'far from smooth', with 'all kinds of clashes and misunderstandings between journalists (from different beats, genres or departments)' (Deuze 2004: 144). The fusion of editorial and marketing is a particular source of tension. The creativity of news work is seen as curtailed by the limited range of options offered by pre-programmed formats, which is a source of frustration for practitioners. Online journalists also express the concern that they spend less time 'out on the streets' and more time inside the newsroom at the computer, as a result of the steep learning curve needed to become accustomed to the technology (Deuze 2004: 146). Fear is accentuated by the view that media executives regard new media as a way of downsizing, doing more with fewer people (Deuze 2004: 143). The final complication is the journalist's increasing struggle to attract public attention, as a result of competition from a range of other information and communication specialists.

Journalism and the PR state

The advance of the public relations industry has been a feature of mass communications in the late twentieth century. The industry has grown more rapidly in America and Britain than in mainland Europe, with the world's PR industry today dominated by a small number of US and British consultancies. Miller and Dinan (2000: 8) attribute the smaller size of the PR industry in Europe to the slower pace of privatization and deregulation. The dramatic expansion of PR capacity in Britain in the 1980s is attributed to the intensification of political differences following the collapse of consensus politics in the mid-1970s, and the decision to place the market at the heart of government economic policy. Increased political competition and the need to 'sell' privatization and deregulation to the public led to the growth of government and corporate propaganda and PR. In order to have their voice heard in public debate, trade unions and pressure groups also embraced PR in this period. Today PR is an essential part of the armoury of all those seeking to influence British politics and policy-making. The greater resistance to privatization and deregulation in Germany and France has impeded the growth of PR. However, government PR has been part of European politics since the Second World War. The rise of the welfare state and the needs of economic and political reconstruction following the war required the development of government communication to explain policies and promote citizenship (see Katus and Volmer 2000 for a discussion of the Netherlands). The emancipation of the press and media from the political elite encouraged this development. As the political press declined, European journalism ceased to be a conduit for politicians, becoming a more critical profession which required politicians to look for different ways to influence the public. The rise of PR and government information specialists in Europe is associated with the politicization of the flow of information in European society. What is significant for the practice of journalism is that PR and information specialists have grown in numbers more quickly than the profession of journalism, but the rate of change varies from country to country. It is estimated that in the Netherlands PR specialists outnumber journalists by a ratio of 2 to 1 (Bardoel 1996: 285). In countries such as Greece and Portugal, where journalism remains more closely linked to the political elite, the demand for PR specialists is weaker.

The demand for information specialists has been met by the arrival of spin doctors in most European countries. The spin doctors of mainland Europe lag behind their American and British counterparts. In Germany the term spin doctor was first used during the 1998 general election (Esser et al. 2000: 214), and spin-doctoring in countries such as Germany has been described as a 'low-gear' operation compared to Britain and the USA. The rise of spin-doctoring can be accounted for by the weakening of multi-party politics in Europe. Elections in Europe can be characterized today by a version of presidential politics, as political parties come together in electoral pacts to run candidates alongside each another. The 1994 elections in Italy witnessed the personalization of Italian electoral politics, as two broad party coalitions formed in the wake of the collapse of the old political system to put up their candidates for prime minister. The campaign was a 'turning point' in political communication in the country, as a 'bizarre mix of US type hoop-la and traditional Italian practices' characterized the efforts of the party coalitions (Mazzoleni 1995: 301). The emphasis on candidates is responsible for an increase in political marketing, with parties relying on advertising and PR specialists to sell their candidates and coalition. Similar developments can be seen elsewhere in Europe. Changes in the nature of the media have encouraged the growth of spin. The huge increase in news outlets has made European politicians less certain that what they say is getting through. Public service monopoly used to guarantee that what politicians wanted to say was heard. In a multi-channel world, with a variety of programmes and outlets covering politics, and a 'huge stream of fast flowing news', there is more doubt (Tunstall 2002: 228). Hence the need to employ information specialists to get the message across.

The impact of spin doctors, image consultants and PR specialists on the practice and performance of journalism is difficult to assess, given the lack of systematic research. As Esser and his colleagues (2000: 218) note of Germany, there is evidence to show that journalists 'have grown more and more dependent on spin doctors as their most important source of information', especially at election times. The process of collecting information has also changed. Traditionally, political journalists relied on national legislatures to obtain their information. The arrangements governing the interaction between legislators and reporters vary. In Britain and Germany formal arrangements have been made to determine the interaction. The German Bundes-Pressekonferenz resembles the British lobby system, in that both are professional associations of reporters working in the legislature, with a set of precise rules governing the gathering of information and mechanisms to ensure that rules are respected. This contrasts with the situation in Italy. Until the mid-1990s political news gathering was 'unstructured and informal', as a result of 'no tradition of regular press conferences by government members and officials' and 'press secretaries [who] perform no important functions' (Mancini 1993: 35). Whether through chance encounters or formal meetings, journalists acquired political information and news in this narrow and limited way. Today there is an extensive supply of political information, coming from a variety of outlets – from news agencies to government and political parties – which is updated perpetually and can be accessed at any time. It is almost as if journalists do not have to leave their offices to cover politics.

The cosy relationships that have formed the basis of political journalism in many European polities are changing. With a variety of specialists to provide the public with information, the primacy of the political correspondent no longer exists. The extent to which this has changed the nature of reporting is a matter of dispute. Some argue that PR and 'spin' is making journalists more dependent on official sources of information. European journalists, as we have seen, have always been closer to politicians and political parties than their Anglo-American counterparts. Several studies have indicated that German 'newspapers use PR information to a high degree without revealing the source and often do not research its background' (cited in Esser et al. 2000: 217). One study of political coverage in regional newspapers in the 1980s found that nearly two-thirds of the items covered by press, radio and television came from official handouts, press releases and news conferences or events (cited in Humphreys 1996: 51). A more recent study, by Donsbach and Wenzel (2002), of reporting by newspapers in Saxony of their state assembly found that fewer than one in three reports could be traced back to PR reports. What cannot be denied is that journalism is increasingly more deskbound and source-dependent than previously.

Journalism as entertainment

Increased competition within the media has had an impact on the practice and performance of journalism. The search for ratings is seen as making journalists part of the entertainment industry, shifting their focus from the serious to the appealing. There has never been a strong tradition of tabloid newspapers in Europe – hence the debate about 'tabloidization' focuses more on television than the press. However, since the 1980s, the impact of tabloid reporting on journalism has become a matter of concern, with critics highlighting 'falling standards' in the profession, as scandal, infotainment, celebrities and triviality become more prevalent in the output of Europe's press and broadcasting media. Neveu (1999) describes a new kind of political journalism emerging on French television, characterized by the trivialization and personalization of information. The culmination of the 1995 presidential elections was the spectacle of Jacques Chirac riding his Citroen car through the streets of Paris, followed by a cavalcade of reporters and camera crews on motorcycles. Broadcast live by CNN, many journalists saw this as a 'painful' episode, as it showed them 'belonging to a profession capable of exaltation for so little' (quoted in Neveu 1999: 381). The shift from analytical depth to superficial gimmicks and spectacles is illustrated, according to Neveu, by three trends in the framing of political programmes (see also Maarek 1997). The 'psychologization' of political coverage refers to the increasing emphasis on disclosing details of the private lives of politicians. Dedicated to the personality, lifestyle and moral values of candidates and political figures, including a visit to their homes, such programming represented a 'peep show' into politicians' private lives. 'Watering down' describes the use of celebrities as opposed to experts and politicians to explore the political topics of the day. The final trend is the increased use of interactivity, through phone-ins and similar audience feedback, to assess and rank the performance of politicians. While there were differences between the TV channels in their coverage of the 1995 elections, the overall effect was a delegitimization of political journalism on French television. The existence of the expert position of the political journalist is weakened by generalist reporters, talk show hosts, celebrities and the public becoming the primary interrogators of the political elite.

The so-called 'dumbing down' in the content and practice of journalism is perceived across the television schedule. Ornebring (2003) traces the development of current affairs debate programmes on Swedish television between 1956 and 1996, identifying a shift from a 'courteous' form of journalism, 'focusing on objectivity and a certain deference towards authority', to a 'popular' form, which emphasizes criticism and conflict and locates the journalist as a representative of the 'common man and woman'. Topics of discussion have moved from public issues to subjects traditionally associated with the private sphere, such as relationships and sexuality, as excitement has become as important as enlightenment. Current affairs programming in general throughout Europe, in spite of a variety of approaches to the genre, is described by one Spanish TV producer as changing from being 'long, slow and analytical' to 'short, punchy items with lots of quick cuts' (quoted in Pritchard 1990). At the centre of the 'dumbing down' debate have been the news media, in particular TV news, which have been blamed for growing public cynicism, disenchantment and apathy in relation to government and the political process. The 'panic over tabloid news' varies across Europe, figuring more prominently in discussions about the nature and future of the mass media and journalism in Britain, Germany and Scandinavia (Sparks 2000: 5). Perhaps the most trenchant and influential criticism of the changing content of the news media has come from France. Sociologist Pierre Bourdieu created a stir when he published his book *Sur La Television* in 1996. Marshalling evidence about the commercial, technological and professional changes in the practice of journalism, he denounced the general dullness, and the homogenization and depoliticization of journalism and television (Bourdieu 1998; see Marlière 1998 for discussion).

The lack of any systematic cross-cultural content analysis of the news media in Europe means it is difficult to come to any definitive conclusion about the extent to which the media has 'dumbed down' (Sparks and Tulloch 2000). The research that has taken place does not show clearly a continuous decline of serious news and programming and the rise of tabloid news and infotainment. Djerf-Pierre (2000) concludes, from her evaluation of Swedish TV news from the 1950s to the 1990s, that reporting has gone through different phases, characterized by specific practices of news selection and modes of representation. Studies identify national differences between the content of popular tabloid newspapers. Some titles, such as *VG* in Norway, contain a lot of serious material alongside their diet of sport, scandal and human interest (Eide 1997), while others, such as the *Sun* and the *Mirror* in the UK, contain 'relatively little' (Rooney 2000). A study of Germany's *Bild-Zeitung* found an emphasis on drama, conflict, personalities and emotions in the coverage of politics, but this existed alongside 'political education and advice', as 'readers are offered guidance in understanding a complex political world as journalists are asking and answering elementary political questions touching on the everyday political reality of ordinary people' (Klein 1998: 91). Popularization in this sense is enhancing broader public understanding of the political process and assisting civic engagement. Several studies have found a correlation between attention to the news media and a higher level of knowledge and understanding of politics (Norris 2000a; Holtz-Bacha 1990). Historians of the press point out that charges of trivialization are long standing. Wieten (1998) identifies a strong resemblance between the concerns expressed about tabloidization in Europe today and the criticisms voiced against the US press in the 1940s that led to the establishment of the Hutchins Commission which reproached newspapers for their sensational reporting and made recommendations, laying down the basis for greater social responsibility in the press and journalism.

While there are doubts about the extent to which serious journalism is disappearing, it is clear that the balance between the serious and the sensational is changing at the present time. This is not happening in the same way across the whole of the media. For example, public service television is different from commercial television. It is also far from clear what the effect of this change is on audiences. Journalists should not be treated as a single, homogeneous group, as implied by critics such as Bourdieu. Finally, the changing relationship between journalism and the public is not solely influenced by commercial factors. The vast socio-economic changes in European society have had as much of an impact on journalism, which, despite all that has happened to the profession in the post-war period, still emphasizes the importance of responding to the interests and preferences of their viewers, readers and listeners. However, journalists' relations with their public have changed considerably in the last 20 years or so. Surveys conducted by the EU have found that public trust in the media across Europe is declining. In 2001 62 per cent of respondents stated that they tended to trust radio and television, while only 46 per cent said they trusted the press (Eurobarometer 2002), so perhaps the major handicap that confronts journalists, especially those working in the press, is that their audience no longer trusts them to the extent it used to.

Conclusion

European and Anglo-American journalism have different roots, traditions and histories. Gradually, European journalism has started to conform to the styles and practices of the Anglo-American press. However, there are still sufficient differences to distinguish journalism in Europe. Most crucially, European journalism still has a close attachment to politics and political actors, and an ideological and interpretative approach to the practice of the profession. A simpler division of labour characterizes European newsrooms, perhaps providing journalists with more freedom than their Anglo-American counterparts. Nevertheless, European journalism is being buffeted by major forces for change in the form of technology, commercialization and the rise of public relations. These factors are beginning to make the daily working routines of journalism similar the world over.

chapter five

European film – Hollywood, GATT and all that

In 1995 the European film industry celebrated its centenary. Pioneered by the Lumière brothers in Paris, the Skladanowskys and their Bioscope in Berlin and Robert Paul in London, the cinema thrived in Europe prior to the First World War. Businessmen, such as Leon Gaumont and Charles Pathé, expanded their activities across Europe and North America, opening studios and distributing their films. Their success was short-lived. War destroyed the industry and paved the way for US dominance of the European film business. By the 1920s film production, distribution and exhibition in nearly every European country was controlled by Hollywood, thereby establishing the relationship that has shaped European film ever since. Europe's screens today exhibit many more Hollywood films than European ones, which are more usually seen at film festivals or in art-house cinemas. Resisting the stranglehold of Hollywood is the major concern of European cinema. This chapter examines how this struggle has shaped the development of the industry in Europe. It looks at the national and supranational efforts to resist US influence and cultivate a 'European cinema', which reached a high point in the early 1990s with negotiations over the renewal of the General Agreement on Tariffs and Trade (GATT), which promotes free trade between nations. During these negotiations Europeans fought for, and eventually won, a 'cultural exception' for the audio-visual sector. While this struggle was being waged, the film industry underwent considerable changes, resulting in European cinema becoming more dependent on its small-screen rival for its economic survival and aesthetic appeal.

Some history

Prior to the First World War the cinema industry in France was the 'most important in the world', with its closest competitors found in Italy and Denmark (Forbes and Street 2000: 3). The ravages of war diverted resources away from the industry and destroyed domestic production. In France 80 per cent of the films screened before the war were produced domestically; by 1917 this had dropped to 37 per cent, with American films making up one-third of foreign films shown on French cinema screens (Forbes and Street 2000: 4). By the end of the war, America dominated the European film market. Hollywood's success was not only the result of the structural and organizational changes wrought by the war. Changes in the style and content of American films, apparent before the outbreak of war, produced a distinctive product, combining a 'peculiar mixture of savagery and sentimentality' which made American films more popular with European audiences (Tunstall 1977: 72). The American film industry had also become highly adept at marketing (Jarvie 1998: 35). The glamour of movie stars was used to promote films, the economic importance of which was highlighted by the huge salaries paid to big box office stars by 1918. Exclusive agreements were entered into with local subsidiaries to ensure Hollywood films got the same attention and promotion abroad as they did at home. Publicity and public relations were as important – if not more so – than the quality of the film in selling Hollywood's product. While the US industry benefited from a range of commercial advantages, many in Europe believed there was something 'unnatural' about Hollywood's export success, suspecting it to be a consequence of Europe's plight after the war. Hollywood's rapid domination of a medium which had taken control of the leisure time of most Europeans sparked a response. European movie moguls travelled to Hollywood to investigate America's successful formula (Nowell-Smith 1998: 12). European governments attempted to protect their film industries. European film-makers cooperated in the 1920s to distribute and exhibit their films in each other's countries. The coming of sound to the cinema ended such collaboration. It also temporarily stymied Hollywood's expansion into Europe, until dubbing was developed in 1933.

The popularity of cinema expanded enormously during the interwar years. By the eve of the Second World War, the historian A.J.P. Taylor could describe cinema-going as the 'essential social habit of the age' (quoted in Williams 1998: 81). In many countries the cinema played an important role in the war effort, maintaining morale at home by acting as the major conduit for propaganda and escapism. Following the war Europeans flocked to the cinema to escape hunger and boredom and satisfy their desire for a bit of fun after years of misery and deprivation. They went to see American films in the main. Even in France, a country perceived as a stronghold of domestic production, 'the demand for American films was enormous, covering all strata of society and all political tendencies' (Jeancolas 1998: 48). The strength of demand is explained by the denial of access to American films during the war and the popular perception that the ability to view these films was an indication that Europe was free again. The Second World War, like its predecessor, had strengthened the position of the American film industry in Europe. Film production in the USA had proceeded without interruption during the conflict (Jarvie 1998: 36). On the cessation of hostilities, Hollywood had a huge stockpile of films to release to the newly liberated countries of Europe. The desire to 'dump films in the European markets' was hidden by associating the export of American films with the rhetoric of democracy and freedom (Forbes and Street 2000: 17). In the occupied countries, primarily Germany and Italy, Hollywood had a fairly easy time in ensuring trading arrangements were in its favour. Elsewhere there was a struggle, but the conditions of austerity, public demand for American films, the need to provide people with relief from the hardships of the war years and the threat of a dispute over film imports preventing aid for reconstruction enabled Hollywood to prevail. As Janet Wasko (1994: 225) puts it, 'the cataclysmic events of World War II were especially effective in cementing Hollywood's grip on the European celluloid market'.

The late 1940s were the heyday of the cinema in Europe. Audiences across Europe went to the cinema in record numbers. Attendance figures in Britain reached an all-time peak in

1946, with 1635 million admissions to the cinema. The boom was relatively short-lived. Attendance started to fall in the 1950s as a result of competition from television and other leisure activities that were now within the reach of many more working people, as a result of growing prosperity and technological advances. The consumer boom drew people away from the cinema. From the 1960s, the fall in cinema attendance in Western Europe accelerated. Numbers going to the cinema fell by 60 per cent between 1960 and 1990, with total admissions plummeting from 2.9 billion to 564 million (Miller et al. 2001: 159). The rate of decline varied. Britain and Germany experienced a rapid decline as television spread more quickly in these countries than elsewhere in Europe. It was not until the 1970s that Italy, Spain, France and the Soviet Union experienced a substantial drop (Forbes and Street 2000: 21). The general trend of declining audiences hides some national differences. Hayward (1993: 48–9) notes that cinema attendances in Britain and Germany (then West Germany) peaked in the early and mid-1950s respectively, much sooner than in France. However, audience levels in these two countries were still much higher than in France until the 1970s.

Despite having the leading cinema industry in Europe, the French have never been dedicated film-goers. When Europeans were flocking back to the cinema after the war, the French lagged behind. In 1948 the average French person went to the cinema 9 times a year, compared to 29 times for the average Briton (Tunstall 1977: 256). It is a misnomer that the French love the cinema more than their European neighbours. If cinema matters to the French, it is to the elite, the intellectuals and government policy-makers, who have supported the industry through good and bad times. Such support has meant that French cinema attendances fell less quickly than in other European countries, from 400 million in 1955 to 175 million in 1990, compared to decreases of 1200 million to 145 million in the UK, 810 million to 155 million in Italy and 790 million to 160 million in Germany for the same years (Hayward 1993: 49). Even though French audiences held up better than elsewhere, the 1970s and 1980s saw a significant decline in cinema-going in Europe. Cinema audiences in Spain declined by two-thirds between 1971 and 1985 (Forbes and Street 2000: 21). Smaller European nations experienced similar declines and the nadir was reached in the early 1990s, the 'worst ever years' for national film industries around Europe (Tunstall and Machin 1999: 224). In 1997 annual admissions fell to below 150 million in France, Germany and Britain, with Italy just scraping over the 100 million mark.

The popularity of American films grew as the cinema-going audience fell away. The American share of the European film market rose from just under 50 per cent in the early 1980s to just over 70 per cent in 1994 (Nowell-Smith 1998: 3). In 1986 French cinema-goers went to see more American films than French for the first time (Powrie 2003: 120). The most significant change was in Europe's primary film-producing nations, France and Italy; in 1994 the share of the French market held by indigenous film-makers had dropped to 32 per cent, and in Italy to 15 per cent – the lowest figure since 1945. Only Britain seemed to buck the trend, with a small increase over the period between the 1960s and early 1990s, from 15 to 20 per cent. The last decade has seen the USA maintain, and in some cases extend, its dominance of domestic film markets in Europe. By 2002 the US share of this market, based on data for 12 EU countries, was estimated at 70 per cent (European Observatory 2003). In smaller European nations the hold American films exert over the cinema-going public is almost complete. In the Netherlands, American films accounted for 80 per cent of the market, with only 6 per cent of the audience going to see Dutch movies in 1999 (Brants 2004: 151). But even in larger markets US films have increased their popularity: in 2000 their share of the German market rose to over 80 per cent (Kleinsteuber 2004: 84). In 2002 only two European films made the list of the top 20 films at the box office: *Asterix & Obelix* and *Die Another Day*, both of which were co-produced with American money. The familiar pattern established in the European film market since the 1960s is that national markets are dominated by US productions, with national productions the only other significant presence. The output of other European countries receives a very small market share. American influence is also felt in relation to the other ways in which people watch films: video sales and rentals and DVDs. In both the rental and purchasing markets US film products account for 50 per cent of the total expenditure by Europeans, and by adding US TV material on video the total rises to well above half of all European video expenditure (Tunstall and Machin 1999: 225). European cinema had by the 1990s become a relatively minor player in the vast audio-visual industry that had developed across the continent.

In response to declining audiences, the European film industry sought ways to make their product more appealing. Technological developments were seized on to make films appear more spectacular. In the 1950s 'cinemascope' was introduced, quickly followed by an array of widescreen formats, such as Cinerama, Vistavision and Kinopanorama. In the 1980s it was the turn of sound, with the advent of Dolby sound, followed in the 1990s by THX and digital sound. Directors and film-makers experimented with form and style. In the 1960s 'new cinema' flourished (Forbes and Street 2000: 21–2). The most celebrated manifestation of new cinema came in France. When François Truffaut won the best director award at the 1959 Cannes Film Festival, for his *Les Quatre Cents Coups*, it inaugurated the *Nouvelle Vague* of young directors, including Jean-Luc Godard, Claude Chabrol, Jacques Rivette and Eric Rohmer. In Britain 'free cinema' represented the introduction of new directors, such as Lindsay Anderson, Karol Reisz and Tony Richardson. Italy chipped in, providing cinema directors of the calibre of Federico Fellini and Michelangelo Antonioni, and Spain had Carlos Saura. Later the German new cinema of the 1970s threw up directors such as Wim Wenders, Werner Herzog and Rainer Werner Fassbinder. The critical acclaim these directors and their films attracted was not matched by box office success. Technological innovation, new directors and aesthetic experimentation failed to prevent the decline.

The decline in cinema-going was only reversed in the late 1990s. By 2002 admissions in France had risen to 185 million, in Germany to 164 million, in Britain to 176 million and in Italy to 112 million (European Observatory 2003). The return to the cinema is partly a response to developments in cinema infrastructure. New multiplex cinemas, with several screens, were built to make going to the cinema easier and more pleasurable. If offering cheaper and better facilities helped attract Europeans back to cinema theatres, reviving the fortunes of European film production was a greater challenge. Film-making has become an enormously expensive business: the average cost of releasing a Hollywood film in 1997 was $75.6 million (Miller et al. 2001: 83). Increased investment was essential simply to maintain (let alone develop) European film-making. The 1990s saw a significant restructuring of film financing in Europe, with a resurgence in film co-productions, as national producers turned away from nationally financed films to collaborate in making 'Euro-films', assisted in many cases by EU money, as well as support from the private sector.

Protectionism

The precarious nature of the effort to raise such vast sums of money for cultural production – as well as the cultural value attached to film by Europeans – has ensured that European governments regularly intervene in the film industry. Supporting the film industry by ensuring that domestic films have preferential treatment has been a feature of European cinema almost since Charles Pathé recommended in 1918 that a law should be passed to make French exhibitors screen 25 per cent of films of French origin in their programmes (Jeancolas 1998: 54). Europeans have provided a variety of subsidies, quotas, levies, taxes, tax concessions, trading agreements and restrictions to finance the production of national films. Protection began in Germany, which in 1921 introduced measures to restrict the import of films (Forbes and Street 2000: 7). Quotas were also introduced in Britain, Italy and France. Such measures were reintroduced after the Second World War. In Britain the Dalton Duty of 1947, National Film Finance Corporation (NFFC) and the Eady levy were examples of the ways in which governments attempted to finance the rebuilding of the British film industry (Dickinson and Street 1985). The Centre National de la Cinématographie (CNC) was established in 1946 to oversee the financing of French films, using a support fund, or *compte de soutien*, drawn from a compulsory levy on box office receipts and, since 1984, a tax on the profits of television companies (Jeancolas 1998: 56; Hayward 1993: 46). In Italy the Andreotti Act of July 1949 set up 'a system of taxing imports to support local production by means of the so-called "dubbing certificate"' (Forbes and Street 2000: 19). Wherever we look in Europe there is a national body charged with supporting indigenous film-making. Whether it is the Danish Film Institute, set up in 1972, or Italy's National Board for Cinema, which came into existence in 1958, or the Greek Film Centre, inaugurated in 1979, European governments have emphasized the importance of supporting financially the development, production, distribution and marketing of national films and protecting their market from external competition.

State intervention reflects the economic realities of the marketplace for film. European film has for a long time had difficulty in competing with Hollywood. Tunstall and Machin (1999) outline a variety of inadequacies and difficulties that have confronted the European film industry. One crucial problem is the difference in scale between Hollywood and the national cinemas of Europe. The example of Italy, one of the world's most respected film-making nations, is cited. In the 1990s Hollywood was able to outspend the Italian industry in making films by margins of between 25 and 30 to 1 (Tunstall and Machin 1999: 215). Hollywood's competitive advantage has not been due to business acumen alone. Skill, luck and events have all intervened to provide commercial success. As important has been the ways in which successive US governments from the 1920s have provided assistance to their film industry. Claims that Hollywood is purely free enterprise are problematic. A vast array of hidden subsidies, state and local government provision, tax credit schemes and state and commerce department representation have been deployed to back one of America's major exporters (Miller et al. 2001: 46–7). The importance attached to the industry by the US government is highlighted in official reports and statements over the years (see Jarvie 1988, 1990, 1992). In the 1920s Commerce Secretary Herbert Hoover, later to become president of the United States, praised the industry, not just for its export earnings, but also for the way in which it acted as 'a powerful influence on behalf of American goods' (quoted in Miller et al. 2001: 26). The part Hollywood played in selling the American way of life to Europeans was a critical component of US trade policy (see Schiller 1969), and to this end 'the US government has devoted massive resources to generate and sustain its "private sector" film industry in the interests of ideology and money' (Miller et al. 2001: 25).

Hollywood's increasing dominance of the international film industry has drawn European governments into regulatory and legislative actions to support local production initiatives. Safeguarding local employment and protecting capital investment is part of the motive for these actions, but traditionally Europeans have attached great significance to the cultural value of film. Throughout Europe, to a greater or lesser degree, film has been seen as a form of collective expression and artistic endeavour. A former secretary of state for information in the French government (quoted in Jeancolas 1998: 53) summed up this position most clearly when she wrote in 1953:

> Cinema is something very different from industry. It is a means of expression through the image, a means of expression for a collectivity. The image which a country, a society offers of themselves. That is why a politico-economic offensive which seeks to stifle this means of expression in a given country can only be compared to the forcible means which conquerors sometimes use to deprive the vanquished of their language.

Usually the collectivity most referred to in the debate about Hollywood and the European film industry is the nation, and what Europeans are seeking to protect are their national cultures. The French have been the most articulate in defending their national culture from the onslaught of Hollywood films. President François Mitterrand, speaking in 1993, (quoted in Jeancolas 1998: 59) was clear in articulating the threat posed by Hollywood:

> What is at stake is the cultural identity of all our nations. It is the right of all peoples to their own culture. It is the freedom to create and choose our own images. A society which abandons to others the way of showing itself, that is to say the way of presenting itself to itself, is a society enslaved.

If Europeans considered film as 'art of the twentieth century', and a matter of national importance justifying government intervention, it did not mean that protectionism was welcomed everywhere. Exhibitors have usually resented the loss of freedom to show the films they believe the public want to see and thereby maximize their profits (Nowell-Smith 1998: 5). This was most acutely expressed in France, Italy and, above all, Britain. British exhibitors felt they were being penalized for the failure of British film producers to make a product audiences wanted. The liberalization and deregulation agenda of the 1980s also saw a retreat in some countries from the commitment to state intervention in the industry. In Britain Mrs Thatcher's government did away with the Eady levy and the NFFC, replacing them with a private company, British Screen, whose responsibility was to make loans to the industry. The aim was make the film industry prosper without government assistance, with British Screen becoming a self-supporting, profit-making enterprise by the end of the 1980s (Hill 1996). This never happened. Mrs Thatcher initiated only a partial retreat from government financing. Britain, like some other countries, may have reduced its support for the industry, but most European governments continued to offer economic protection for their film industry. In some cases, governments pursued contradictory policies in relation to film and television. Protection of the film sector occurred alongside the liberalization and privatization of television. The result was that differences over film policy, particularly between France and Britain, which, between them, accounted for three-fifths of EU film production expenditure, undermined the ability of Europe to present a united front in their negotiations with Hollywood (Tunstall and Machin 1999: 216).

Intervention in the industry, forcing the industry to show a certain number of 'national' films, requires governments to define what is meant by a national film. This is not easy. Forbes and Street (2000: 27) reveal how ineffective the early efforts to identify a 'national' film were. Location was initially emphasized, but where a film is made is no indication of who invests in it, who owns the product or who benefits from its distribution. Many of the quota films made in Italy in the 1920s were shot with American money. The British Quota Act of 1927 defined a British film in terms of the 'proportion of labour costs paid to British nationals'. Such a loose definition meant a film produced by Americans, using American directors, actors and scriptwriters could be defined as British if a certain percentage of the production costs were paid to British technicians (Mattelart 2000: 41). Ownership further complicated matters, as many of the 'quota quickies' were made by British subsidiaries of American companies. The co-production of films by different European countries – a feature of the industry since the 1920s – also makes the notion of a national film problematic in economic terms. In spite of the difficulties, legislation has typically used purely economic criteria, such as the nature of the production company and the proportion of labour from indigenous sources, to define a national film. While governments have emphasized the 'economic', film producers and directors have often seen themselves as 'being in business to make films which stood or fell by their national cultural content' (Nowell-Smith 1998: 5). Whether a film promotes national or any other cultural objectives has rarely figured in legislation to protect the film industry, with the exception of France, where language has been used, among other criteria, as a qualification for subsidy. Thus the cultural rhetoric which dominates the expressions of European concern about Hollywood's influence – whether it is about the right to national self-expression or resistance to alien culture – is not translated into regulatory detail. The protection of the European film industry on either economic or cultural grounds has to confront the problem of defining what is being protected. The rhetoric on both sides of the Atlantic Ocean concerning the 'Americanization' or 'Hollywoodization' of Europe rests on an assumption that there is a clear distinction to be made between the European cinema and Hollywood. But what exactly distinguishes European cinema?

Is there such a thing as European film?

Making a distinction between Hollywood and European cinema is problematic on several grounds. First, the relationship between Hollywood and Europe historically can be seen as a 'productive example of cross-fertilisation' (Forbes and Street 2000: 43). Hollywood owes much of its success to European émigrés of one sort or another. The American film industry has employed – and today continues to employ – Europeans in large numbers. Many of the great names of Hollywood have been European migrants, such as Alfred Hitchcock, Fritz Lang, Charlie Chaplin, Ernst Lubitsch, Otto Preminger and Greta Garbo (Forbes and Street 2000: 28; Nowell-Smith 1998: 1). Many of the great European stars, including France's iconic star of the 1930s, Jean Gabin, were forced into exile in the USA during the Second World War. East European directors, such as Roman Polanski and Milos Forman, emigrated to America during the communist period. Today European directors, such as Ridley Scott, Paul Verhoeven and Luc Besson, as well as stars such as Jean-Claude Van Damme and Arnold Schwarzenegger, ply their trade in the USA. Leading US directors of contemporary Hollywood, including Martin Scorsese and Quentin Tarantino, acknowledge their debt to European cinema culture. Many of the techniques of contemporary Hollywood were imported from Europe. One example is German expressionist cinema of the 1920s, which influenced the *film noir* genre that characterized Hollywood in the 1940s. European cinema has continually adapted and reworked US genres, such as the Italian spaghetti western, the French crime film or the German road movies (Forbes and Street 2000: 41), while many of Hollywood's box office successes have often been remakes of European films. Britain's foremost director of the 1930s, the Hungarian Alexander Korda, teamed up with United Artists to release his film *The Private Life of Henry VIII*; in 1949 he produced *The Third Man* with one of Hollywood's great movie moguls, David O. Selznick (Nowell-Smith 1998: 8–9). Thus there is not a rigid divide between film-making in Hollywood and Europe.

Within Europe there is a variety of national cinemas, which have very different ways of representing and expressing themselves. 'European cinema is not a monolith, but a series of expressions of different ways of questioning and portraying itself and the world' (Everett 1996, quoted in Forbes and Street 2000: 48). However, faced with the challenge from Hollywood, European cinema has chosen to emphasize its common characteristics – in some instances more successfully than others. Three of these in particular are often identified in the rhetoric of national governments and the writings of European film-makers and scholars as distinguishing European national cinemas from Hollywood: the 'auteur' doctrine, film as an art form and realism. Debate often reduces the difference to one of art versus commerce. If European cinema is about artistic endeavour, Hollywood is about money and business. Implicit in the distinction is that 'cinema as art' is something to be valued, while 'cinema as commerce' is valueless (Mulvey 1998: 119). Auteurism, art and realism are packaged to prove that European cinema has a value that Hollywood lacks. The concept of film-maker as auteur owes its origins to French theorizing about the nature of cinema. In the 1950s, film clubs were set up across France to educate people to interpret films critically. These clubs were serviced by film magazines, such as *Cahiers du Cinéma*, which argued that the cultural worth of a motion picture rested with its director, just as a book's value rested with its author. The focus on the director as the artist-author of the film contrasted with the factory system of the Hollywood studios. Auteur films 'bear the imprint of a particular director's artistic vision', in contrast to Hollywood, 'where scripts are usually written by committee and where producers generally maintain control of the finished product' (Ezra 2004: 16). The result was that European national cinemas became synonymous with the personal and subjective vision of leading directors. In France, under President Mitterrand, auteur theory became official state doctrine, which made it easier for ministers to justify directing subsidies to particular individuals (Tunstall and Machin 1999: 219). The emphasis placed on the auteur is not without its consequences for the European film industry. According to Tunstall and Machin (1999), singling out the director 'atrophied the key film skill of scriptwriting' and taught film-makers to emphasize 'artistic merit' above box office success and, subsequently, television ratings.

Auteurism is tied intimately to the view that the cinema is an art form. Historically, European cinema has been associated with a variety of artistic and cultural movements, including surrealism, Dadaism, expressionism and the avant-garde (see Kuenzli 2004). Art cinema is seen as concerned with an 'existential quest, the interrogation of subjectivity and experiment with narrative form' (Forbes and Street 2000: 38). Unlike the classic Hollywood film with a beginning and an end, where cause and effect are used to organize the narrative and filmic devices, such as sound, editing and cinematography, are deployed to advance that narrative, art films are ambiguous, subjective, complicated and not clearly driven by any explicit narrative. In labelling Antonioni's *L'Avventura* (1960) as a 'typical art film', Forbes and Street (2000: 37) identify 'its apparent inconsequential narrative, unexplained shifts of focus and characters who are engaged in a compelling but unresolved quest' as the components that make it typical. Articulation of film as a work of art thrived in the late 1950s and the 1960s, when film-makers, particularly in France, were actively involved in educating their audiences to understand and appreciate films as art. Yet to characterize European cinema as solely about art films neglects the tradition of popular cinema that has flourished almost unnoticed in European film criticism and academic scholarship. Sorlin (1999) refers to film series such as the *Heimatfilme* in Germany and Austria, melodramas in Italy and the *Carry On* films in Britain, which were so popular with their audiences that the formula was repeated on numerous occasions to satisfy the demand. Some of these formulas, such as the Bond movies, acquired universal acclaim. Usually they were parochial, satisfying particular national needs with little or no accessibility to audiences outside the country. It was these films – not art films – that made up the majority of what was produced in most European countries in the heyday of European cinema in the 1950s and 1960s.

The final characteristic applied to European cinema is 'realism'. European films are seen as engaging with daily life in all its gritty detail. An 'authentic' portrayal of everyday situations is emphasized, with ordinary people located in 'settings not obviously glamorised', hence the label 'kitchen sink' dramas to describe British cinema of the 1960s (Forbes and Street 2000: 38). While 'realism' had a modest place in European cinema prior to 1945, this approach to film-making came to dominate art cinema in the post-war period. The beginnings of the post-war revival came with what has been labelled as 'Italian neo-realism'. Born out of practical necessity, Italian directors such as Vittorio de Sica, Roberto Rossellini and Luchino

Visconti were forced to shoot on location in the war-ravaged streets of Rome, using ordinary people and low-grade film footage, producing the 'grainy look' which characterized such cinema (Ezra 2004: 118; Wagstaff 1996: 220, 226). Social themes, such as unemployment, the effects of the war on society, politics, class warfare and deprivation, were common in Italian neo-realist cinema, which thrived in the 1950s and 1960s, gaining international acclaim for its directors (see Bondanella 2004). European art cinema was influenced by this movement and national cinemas throughout Europe developed their own take on 'social realism'. Scandinavian cinema became associated with the psychological realism of directors such as Ingmar Bergman, while British directors focused on the frustrations of young working men and women in their efforts to escape the emotional and physical constraints imposed by their social class (see Schepelern 2004; Street 2004). If 'realism' became a part of every national cinema in Europe, its appeal was limited. While finding favour with critics, artists, intellectuals, academics, government policy-makers and the industry in general, it was rarely successful at the box office. Ordinary people did not show much interest in seeing themselves on screen, preferring the escapism of Hollywood and more popular offerings from their own country.

Pan-European cinema

Cooperation between film-makers has been a feature of European cinema. The initial influx of Hollywood films in the 1920s led to attempts by European studios and directors to cooperate to defend their industry. New thinking about the cinema and cultural industries in general emerged from Germany in the period immediately following the First World War (Forbes and Street 2000: 8–9). Motivated by the need to break down anti-German feeling in Europe in the aftermath of the war, and by an awareness of the economic potential of the medium, the German film industry advocated pan-European cooperation. Erich Pommer, head of UFA, a holding company that controlled most of the German film industry, called for the production of 'European films that were no longer French, English, Italian or German films but continental', and which could be 'distributed throughout all of Europe, thereby recouping their enormous costs of production' (de Grazia 1998: 22; Forbes and Street 2000: 9). UFA made a number of agreements with Russian, French, Italian and British companies that they would distribute each other's films. Financial problems, which led to US investors buying into the company, prevented UFA from developing co-productions. However, other German companies did so. Westi Films cooperated with Pathé, investing in one of the most celebrated films of the decade, Abel Gance's *Napoleon* (1927). Such partnerships were encouraged by the League of Nations, which advocated film as a means to promote international understanding. Efforts at pan-European film cooperation were facilitated by the silent cinema. The introduction of sound accentuated national rivalries and ultimately stifled the cooperation that had developed in the 1920s.

Under the Nazis there was renewed interest in developing a European-wide film industry. This interest was driven by very different considerations, as the Nazis sought to extend their influence across Europe. Not only did they value cinema as a means of propaganda, but also 'for its capacity to express creatively Germany's superiority as a *kulturnation*' (de Grazia 1998:

23). The German film industry invested in and entered into partnerships with other national cinemas, and in 1935 attempted to set up an international body to challenge Hollywood. Its potential market of 80 million German speakers across the continent made this a viable proposition. The Fascist vision of Europe which took hold in the 1930s helped diminish doubts about whether a single European brand of the same quality as that of Hollywood could be produced out of the mish-mash of national cinemas. Coercion and invasion ultimately resulted in most of Europe's local film industries coming under Nazi control. Motivated by political imperatives, a massive infusion of capital was put into local film production, helping to revive national cinemas; for example, the French film industry is seen as undergoing a 'cultural blossoming', with higher quality products and wider circulation through the German distribution system (de Grazia 1998: 25). The system imposed by the Nazis was ultimately artificial, disappearing with the collapse of the Third Reich. While the circumstances of the period were out of the ordinary, Josef Goebbels, the Reich's minister of propaganda and public enlightenment, recognized the importance of entertainment values and commercial organization in the development of cinema, and the structures he established assisted the development of national cinemas.

In the post-war years a new vision galvanized attempts to develop a pan-European cinema. There was optimism that what was to become the EU was building a European value system, which would increase the appeal of films with a European theme. The role of film in developing European unity was recognized by intra-governmental bodies, such as the Western European Union (WEU) and the Council of Europe (COE), set up in the late 1940s. The WEU's cultural arm established a cinema subcommittee in the 1950s, to promote cooperation and produce films illustrating Europe's common heritage, while the COE set up a committee in the 1960s to bring together European film-makers and establish a film prize (Hainsworth 1994: 13–14). Piecemeal activities such as these were replaced in the 1990s by a more concerted policy to develop mechanisms to support the financing of the industry. MEDIA (Measures to Encourage the Development of the Audio-visual Industry) was set up by the European Commission in 1989, to provide aid and encourage initiatives to further the audio-visual sector; the EURIMAGES project had been launched a year earlier, establishing a pan-European fund to support the co-production of fiction and documentary films (see chapter 7).

The growth of film production in the 1990s was not only a result of increased supranational support for the industry. Bilateral and multilateral collaboration between European nations increased enormously. Confronted by rapidly declining audiences and escalating production costs, every European country 'felt the need to spread the financial burden of film production, and by the mid 1990s, the search for more co-production partners had become a necessity' (Jackel 2002: 154). Co-production has become a way of life in contemporary European cinema. Subsidizing the film industry at the national level, especially in smaller European nations, has become increasingly onerous. Nations have looked to cooperate more closely with one another. Without co-production there would be no film industry in some of the smaller European countries (Jackel 2002: 152). The importance of putting together co-production agreements was recognized in the immediate aftermath of the war. France and Italy signed an agreement in 1949, which had resulted in the production of well over 1500 films by the 1990s (Jackel 1996: 87). France was a strong advocate of co-production, entering into agreements with more than 40 countries, including some outside Europe. It was also the driving force behind setting up EURIMAGES and MEDIA. Britain, the other major film-producing country in Europe, was more reluctant to cooperate with European partners. A Franco-British agreement in 1965 produced only a handful of films, on average one per year in its first 25 years (Jackel, 1996, 87). Britain joined the EURIMAGES project in 1993, only to quit two years later, much to the disappointment and opposition of British film-makers. The government's decision to leave was described as 'incomprehensible' by the industry, which had received £14.5 million from the fund, to which the government had contributed just £2 million annually (Jackel 1999: 188). The success of the Franco-Italian agreement represents the cultural, institutional and industrial affinities between the two countries, while linguistic and cultural differences proved to be obstacles to Franco-British cooperation. However, it was differences over film policy which really created difficulties between the two countries.

French film policy traditionally has been firmly directed towards preserving national culture and identity through a highly developed system of subsidies. British film policy, particularly since the early 1980s, has been more laissez-faire, focused on film as a sector of the economy. If the government in Britain has virtually ignored the film industry in the last 25 years, French governments since the late 1950s have had a close and committed relationship with the industry through the ministry of culture (Jackel 1999: 177). The status of the industry also differs in the two countries: French actors, directors, writers and technicians look down on working in television, seeing it as 'minor if not degrading work', while their British counterparts have long gravitated to television drama and entertainment departments (Jackel 1999: 176).

The rapidly deteriorating economic position of the industry and fundamental changes in the political economy of Europe ensured that change took place in both countries, encouraging greater cooperation. In 1994 a new agreement was signed between the UK and France, which sanctioned not only tripartite film production, but also financial involvement in other co-productions. This acknowledged a state of affairs that had begun to develop in the late 1980s and early 1990s. France was moving towards a policy geared to commercial success at the international level. French directors with an international reputation were increasingly willing to film in English. French companies such as Bouygues and Canal Plus launched ventures to enter the US market. Commercial success became part of the objectives of the French government. The 'internationalization' of French film policy was accompanied by the 'Europeanization' of British film policy. The contraction of national sources of finance meant that Europe was increasingly an attractive prospect for film finance. Many British companies also had US investors who were looking for new ways to enter the highly lucrative European market (Jackel 1996: 88). The result was that from the late 1980s there was a high degree of cooperation between Britain and France in the production of large-scale, big-budget movies, often with American stars, aimed at the international market.

Franco-British collaboration, supranational finance and co-production unleashed the European blockbuster onto cinema audiences around the world. Some of these films attempted to engage with European culture and identity. Films such as Claude Berri's

Germinal, Jean-Paul Rappeneau's *The Horseman on the Roof* and Ridley Scott's *1492* drew on Europe's history and high culture to appeal to worldwide audiences (Jackel 2002: 152). Changes in legislation in France, particularly new tax incentives for high-budget films, assisted the dramatic rise in this kind of production, from 3 in 1988 to 22 in 1997 (Danan 2000: 356). Public reaction to these films was not particularly positive and critics dismissed them as bland and lacking distinctiveness. Only three of the 'big pictures' identified in France as 'blockbusters' secured healthy export revenues: Milos Forman's *Valmont* (1989), Jean-Jacques Annaud's *L'Amant* (1992) and Luc Bresson's *The Fifth Element* (1997). These films have been labelled 'Euro-puddings' or 'films for the bureaucrats'.

Jaco van Dormael's *Toto les Heros* (1991) was supported by a financial package that included money from the Belgian government, Belgian and French public television, Canal Plus, MEDIA, EURIMAGES and the European Script Fund. The director spent three years negotiating where the film should be shot and in what language. It is seen as a classic example of a 'Euro-pudding' (Thompson and Bordwell 2003: 609). MEDIA and EURIMAGES are criticized by academic commentators such as Colin McCabe for 'making sure it's possible to see more bad European films' (quoted in Hainsworth 1994: 20). The focus on blockbusters was regarded by many as detrimental to the development of national cinema and the European film tradition. As a result, the French government introduced legislation in 1999 to reduce the trend and, according to France's film board, 'refine the balance between an opening up to international projects and the defence of nationally-based productions' (quoted in Danan 2000: 357). Similarly, EURIMAGES drew a distinction between two different schemes for financial assistance, projects with 'circulation potential' and films of 'artistic value' (Jackel 2004: 155).

Not everyone agrees that the efforts of public and private finance have been a failure. Co-productions have helped some films to reach audiences they would not have done otherwise. Some smaller budget films, such as Matthieu Kassovitz's *La Haine*, not only won prizes at film festivals and engaged with pressing social issues, but also attracted large audiences. Some observers believe whatever the quality of these 'Euro-films', they have to be the way forward, as distinctive national cinemas have no future. The money is simply not there. According to one European film producer, 'unless all European producers work together then we will have zero per cent of the market' (quoted in Thompson and Bordwell 2003: 609). This view is supported by the failure of private capital in the 1990s. The private sector in the 1990s had attempted to develop cooperative ventures and pan-European operations. Most significantly, Polygram built up Europe's largest film enterprise during this decade. Owned by the multinational company Philips, Polygram Filmed Entertainment (PFE) brought together a collection of subsidiaries, including British companies such as Working Title (Tunstall and Machin 1999: 223). It produced a number of box office hits, including *Four Weddings and a Funeral*, a quintessentially British film, as well as much admired low-budget 'American films', such as *Fargo* and *Dead Man Walking*. This enterprise was basically an effort to establish a European major to compete with Hollywood in making products for both the big and small screen. It was never really able to match Hollywood, in spite of its box office successes and its access to Philips/Polygram offices across the world. In 1998, having lost nearly $1 billion on PFE, Philips sold the company to a Hollywood major, MCA-Universal (Tunstall and Machin 1999: 138).

Cooperation and co-production has resulted in an increase in the number of films produced in Europe. However, as Jackel (2002: 155) points out, 'the growth in production has not been matched with a greater cross border appeal of European films'. Only 8 per cent of European films were screened in other European countries in 2002 (European Observatory 2003). Many of the films made in the 1990s failed to make it onto the big screen, receiving only limited release or no release at all. Film distribution in Europe is dominated by the Americans. It has been estimated that 60 per cent of the European film distribution industry is owned by American companies (Wasko 1994: 222). They decide which films are released, when and where. The greater capacity for US companies to promote and market their films, and the hold US interests have over the distribution of European films, are major barriers to the success of European films with global and European audiences. The industry has undergone another radical change in the last couple of decades, as more and more people are watching films on the small screen.

Film and television

The advent of television has had a profound impact on the film industry. Video rental sales have grown vigorously over the last 15 years and now exceed box office sales by a 'considerable margin' (Scott 2004: 53). All the major US companies have established a specialized division to distribute their films in video and DVD formats. The boom in new pay-TV channels has made an even more important contribution to the nature of the industry. Movie channels have become a common feature of the new TV landscape created in Europe in the last couple of decades. Classic movie channels – sometimes called library channels – broadcast old films, while other channels, such as CineCinemas, broadcast more recent films. Crucially, films – along with sport – are considered 'a driving force' for the development of digital television (Papathanassopoulos 2002: 154). In an increasingly competitive television market, films are a staple feature of the output of terrestrial and satellite channels. The extent to which movies can be used to bulk up the TV schedules was highlighted in the early days of deregulated television in Italy, when 400 local stations broadcast 2000 films per week (Thompson and Bordwell 2003: 607). What is apparent is that TV is the main outlet for the film industry today. Pay TV spending, as a proportion of total film expenditure in the EU, is now greater than video rentals, sales and box office receipts (Miller et al. 2001: 100). As a result, television companies are investing heavily in the film industry.

German TV was the first to support film-making in a systematic way when it produced the Film and TV Agreement in 1974, offering financial support for joint productions (Thompson and Bordwell 2003: 606). The efforts of public service broadcasters were superseded by commercial companies following deregulation. As competition increased, commercial companies needed more new films to air and they started to fund production. In Italy, by the end of the 1980s, 80 per cent of feature films were financed by television companies (Forbes and Street 2000: 23). In Britain Channel Four paved the way, backing 130 films between 1990 and 1996, many of which gained international acclaim, including Neil Jordan's *The Crying Game*, Mike Leigh's *Secrets and Lies* and Ken Loach's *Carla's Song* (Jackel

1999: 180). One of its most notable successes was *Trainspotting*, a film financed solely by the channel for a negligible amount in film terms – £2 million – which earned over $12 million at the US box office in its first eight weeks (see Street 2000). The financing arrangements for *Trainspotting* were not typical, as Channel Four usually entered into partnership with a number of private and public concerns, as they did with Polygram, for example, to back *Four Weddings and a Funeral*. The channel did not take a purely commercial view of film production, but sought as far as possible to commission young or first-time directors (Jackel 1999: 181). It launched a digital service, Film Four in 1998, and where Channel Four has led, BBC and ITV have followed reluctantly. However, the European TV network most associated with film production is the French channel, Canal Plus.

Canal Plus was established by the government in 1984 as a terrestrial pay-TV channel. It has developed into Europe's largest pay-TV channel, with subscribers in France, Belgium, Germany, Spain, French-speaking North Africa, Poland, Italy and the Netherlands (Miller et al. 2001: 102). Films and sport are the main components of its output, with an emphasis on first-run movies. Until 1997 Canal Plus was the only outlet for new French films. By the end of the 1990s it is estimated that the channel was involved in financing 80 per cent of all current French films, broadcasting nearly 100 new films every year (Miller et al. 2001: 103; Tunstall and Machin 1999: 220). The channel also established a major European film studio, as well as a distribution network. This involvement is the consequence of the system of regulation in France, where the relationship between TV and cinema is carefully policed. TV channels are prevented from showing films – any films – at certain hours on certain days, to encourage people to visit the cinema, and advertising movies on TV is banned, the intention being to stop the heavy marketing of US films (Tunstall and Machin 1999: 220; Mazdon 1999: 75). All the country's major TV channels, TF 1, France 2, France 3, M 6 and Arte are legally required to operate a film subsidy system. In setting up Canal Plus, the government partly conceived the channel as a 'saviour of the French film industry' (Tunstall and Machin 1999: 196), and by 2001 it was estimated to have helped finance over 700 films around the world (Thompson and Bordwell 2003: 608).

If the French regulatory environment assists the cooperation between film and television, in most European countries television has become the main source of finance for the film industry. As European audiences increasingly watch movies on TV and video, television companies have invested more and more in the production of European films. By the mid-1990s, television financed the making of more than half the films produced in Europe, with television having a stake in all the films made in some countries, such as Belgium and Portugal (Hill 1996: 152). Public service broadcasters have been more supportive of European film-making than their commercial rivals, primarily as a consequence of legal obligations to cooperate. By the beginning of the new millennium the television interests of most of Europe's media empires had led them to invest in film. While TV finance may have helped to save the European film industry, television is seen by some film-makers as having had a negative impact on the aesthetics of film. Directors such as Britain's Alan Parker charge that television '"boxes-in" the cinematic imagination of film makers and the cinematic experience of the audience' (cited in McLoone 1996: 78). They see TV as a 'talking-heads' medium, which works against producing the 'epic dramas' that characterize the big screen. As a result of making films for the small screen, Europe's new generation of directors are accused of losing the ability to direct for the big screen, thereby furthering Hollywood's dominance of the movie industry. The influence of television can be seen in the development of European cinema from the 1990s onwards. In France slick images, chic fashion, hi-tech gadgetry and the conventions of TV advertising dominated the films of a new generation of directors such as Jean-Jacques Beineix and Leos Carax. Dubbed the 'Cinema du Look', these films 'privileged a sleek visual aesthetic over any overt social or political content' (Ezra 2004: 14; Harris 2004). However, to see European film as boxed in by television is to ignore the tradition of European film-making, which has emphasized social realism and naturalism, thereby bringing it closer to the fare of television than that of Hollywood epics. Europe's directors also offer 'images of scale and intensity not found on television', but less in the form of the 'hyper kinetic spectacles of chases, explosions and special effects' that characterize Hollywood epics, than as 'beautiful and startling images' that 'absorb the spectator in rapt contemplation' (Thompson and Bordwell 2003: 619).

GATT

The clearest manifestation of the differences between Hollywood and the European film industry was during the GATT negotiations of the early 1990s. GATT was the predecessor of the World Trade Organization (WTO). Charged with the responsibility of promoting 'free trade' between nations, GATT was established in 1947 to negotiate regular adjustments to tariff provisions. The Uruguay round, the eighth and final readjustment of international tariffs, began in 1986 and eventually came to a successful conclusion in December 1993. However, this outcome was not before a titanic struggle had taken place between the USA and the EU over the audio-visual trade and tariff conditions. The USA demanded that European film and television markets should be open to the unrestricted circulation of 'goods'. This demand was in response to the system of quotas and restrictions that had been put in place to protect the European audio-visual sector, in particular the European film industry. The Television without Frontiers directive, along with the MEDIA and EURIMAGES programmes, were regarded as restrictions on free trade (see chapter 7). The European argument was that film and television, along with the rest of the so-called cultural industries, were not comparable with other economic goods, and therefore the audio-visual industries, film and television, should be excluded from the GATT negotiations. The call for the 'cultural exception' resulted in a battle between the Europeans and the Americans in which the film industry was central.

On one level the battle was articulated as a clash of principles. For the Americans, 'cultural exception' represented placing limitations on the rights of Europeans to see what they wished and denying artists and producers the financial rewards they deserved (see Collins 2002). It was about 'freedom'; any attempt to 'meddle with the mass media was both a form of censorship and economically unwise because it deprived consumers of the power to decide for themselves' (Pells 1997: 276). For the Europeans it was matter of 'cultural rights'. This was most clearly expressed by the French government, whose minister of culture, Jack Lang, caused most offence, with a sustained attack on US cultural imperialism. European film directors joined the fray, expressing the view that a free market in film and television would create a 'world hegemony of American films', which would result in 'a dreadful monoculture, a kind of cultural totalitarianism' (quoted in Pells 1997: 274). Behind these lofty principles were baser economic and political concerns. Film and television were second only to the aerospace industry in producing a positive balance of trade for the USA. The comparative advantage the Americans enjoyed in the audio-visual market ensured they would benefit from freer trade. The Clinton administration, indebted to Hollywood for political and financial support, was highly responsive to the lobbying efforts of the US film industry (Miller 1996: 80). Americans argued that the Europeans were using the principle of cultural rights to shore up ailing and inefficient film and television industries. The 'Cola versus Zola' war in the early 1990s was far more antagonistic than previous arguments between film industries on either side of the Atlantic Ocean. Pells (1997: 273) accounts for the bitterness of the battle for GATT in terms of Europeans being more apprehensive than at any other time in the twentieth century about the survival of their industry. Perhaps what was – and what continues to be – more pertinent was the growing profitability of the global media industries in the late twentieth century. The EU and Hollywood were in a struggle to secure a share of the profits of one of the world's most successful sectors of the global economy.

The impressive mobilization of European politicians, bureaucrats, intellectuals and film-makers – although Europe was by no means unanimous in presenting a united and fully committed front in the GATT negotiations – did result in a victory. Over 40 countries exempted their audio-visual industries from the final agreement. Winning this battle, however, represented only a brief respite in the war against Hollywood. Since its creation in 1995 WTO has been more aggressive in asserting the role of the market in the audio-visual sector. The activities of the organization have been described as aiming to 'entrench privatisation and de-regulation worldwide' and 'rein in democratic controls over corporations across a broad swathe of business activities' (Miller et al. 2001: 38). Central to its operation is the effort to break down quotas on Hollywood.

Conclusion

The history of the European film industry is dominated by the struggle to resist Hollywood's invasion of European screens. The popularity of Hollywood films with European audiences has resulted in Europe's governments, film producers and supranational bodies seeking ways to support and develop the industry. These efforts have resulted in clashes between Hollywood and Europe, culminating in the acrimonious dispute surrounding the negotiation of the eighth round of the GATT agreement in the early 1990s. The intensity of this dispute is explained by the clash of two different views of cinema. European film-makers, intellectuals and policy-makers have a conception of the role and function of the medium that is distinct from that of their American counterparts. For Europe, film is more than a commercial enterprise and more than an art form; it is a matter of cultural expression. More so, perhaps, with than any other medium of mass communication, film in Europe is intimately tied up with matters of national and cultural identity. The decline of cinema-going and the increasing amount of American material on screen is not simply a commercial problem – it is a matter of the survival of national cultures. In the last decade, fundamental shifts in the industry are seen as threatening the survival of the European film industry. Technological advances have changed the ways in which most people watch films. The growing influence of television on the film industry reflects the fact that more people are watching films today on the small screen. Deregulation of the international marketplace has increased competition, forcing Europe's film-makers to address matters of commercial viability as much as forms of cultural expression. The increasing costs of production have forced national film industries in Europe to cooperate more closely, and to turn to the EU and other supranational bodies for finance and resources, with consequences for the kind of films that are produced.

chapter six

The media in Eastern Europe

The collapse of communism in the late 1980s was a momentous event. It represented a fundamental shift in European society. The cold war, with its rivalry between East and West, melted and washed away the divide that had characterized post-war Europe. For many the media played a crucial role. Some argue that television was responsible for the rapid collapse of the Soviet-styled regimes in Eastern Europe by empowering the peoples of these societies to get out onto the streets and demonstrate. It showed people they were not isolated in their struggle for freedom and helped to mobilize opposition against the communist regimes. Western television was crucial in this respect. Technological developments increasingly made it impossible for communist regimes to control the flow of information into their countries. Showing the peoples of Eastern Europe that their counterparts in the West enjoyed better lifestyles is seen as having a 'corrosive effect' on political and social stability, which ultimately undermined communism. This chapter explores the role played by the media – in particular, the Western European media – in regime change in Eastern Europe in the late 1980s. It will also examine the emergence of new media structures in Eastern Europe since the demise of communism, focusing on the extent to which these new media are capable of building democracy in Eastern Europe. How far the involvement of western media interests is contributing to, or detracting from, the development of citizenship and political democracy is also discussed.

The media and the collapse of communism

The events in Eastern Europe in the late 1980s have been described as 'the stuff of great reporting' (Giles et al. 2001: xiii). Demonstrations throughout the region saw people in huge numbers pouring onto the streets of cities such as Prague, Leipzig, Warsaw and Bucharest, calling for freedom and their basic human rights. Some of the protests were peaceful. Some involved struggles between police, soldiers and special forces and angry protestors. Elsewhere radio and television stations were seized so that news could be broadcast of the proclaimed 'revolution'. Serious violent conflict broke out in only a few places; for example, in Romania, where the loss of life culminated in the execution of the country's former dictator. All these upheavals reached their high point with the dismantling of the Berlin Wall, the symbol of the post-war divide between West and East Europe, in 1989. The pictures of men and women standing on top of the wall, tearing it down stone by stone, represented the end of the Soviet bloc and its oppression of Eastern Europe. Such was the speed with which the old regimes fell apart that many argue that the media 'played a fundamental role in the collapse of the communist regimes of eastern Europe' (Horvath 1997). The media, in particular television, were 'decisive' in determining the outcome of events; not only did they satisfy the need for day-to-day information in a rapidly unfolding situation, but they also played a crucial role over a longer period of time in weakening communism and the regimes it sustained.

The then deputy editor of *Channel 4 News* singled out television as 'one of the catalysts to change in Eastern Europe' (Baines 1990). In the short term, television 'accelerated events' by broadcasting the street demonstrations and protests happening in countries undergoing change across Eastern Europe. The medium produced a 'role model on how to challenge the state apparatus'. Romanians, for example, were emboldened to come out onto the streets as a result of seeing on their TV screens what was happening in Poland, East Germany and Czechoslovakia. The importance of television was emphasized by demonstrators in Romania seizing the TV station to assist their efforts to organize the so-called revolution. The new regime 'actually governed from the TV station', and the pictures shown of military defectors, the trial and – after his execution – the body of former dictator, Nicolae Ceausescu, and crowds standing up to machine-gun fire are deemed crucial in mobilizing and maintaining popular support for change (Alter 1990; Baines 1990). In addition, radio stations such as Voice of America, Radio Free Europe and the BBC 'beamed in reports of the tumultuous events elsewhere in Eastern Europe', which gave Romanians hope. Similarly, pictures of the increasingly large demonstrations in Leipzig broadcast by western TV stations into East Germany encouraged more than half a million people to come out into the streets to call for an end to the old regime. The broadcast media brought to the attention of the public events that were unfolding and turned the small-scale activities of newly born political actors into a social and political phenomenon.

In the longer run, television is seen as having 'acted as a corrosive force on the political superstructure of Eastern Europe' by broadcasting pictures of 'a superior lifestyle and higher standard of living across the wall' (Baines 1990). The receptivity of East European audiences to the images and reports from the West was accentuated by the 'decades of doublespeak' on their television screens (Alter 1990). An unrelenting stream of propaganda had driven people away from the communist broadcast media and undermined their believability. Foreign broadcasters, such as the BBC, taught its listeners in Eastern Europe to 'judge critically' what was happening in their own society, thereby playing a role in undermining the foundations of these societies (Tusa, J. 2001: 15–16). East Germany's leading news programme was watched by only 7 per cent of households (Alter 1990). It is estimated that 85 per cent of East Germans regularly tuned in to programmes from West Germany or Austria, many 'for the pop music, visions of laden supermarket shelves and scenes of faraway places' (Tusa, A. 2001: 30). The communist authorities recognized the threat posed by television. As far back as 1961, East German Party boss, Walter Ulbricht, said that the 'enemy of the people stands on the roof'. Controlling where those aerials and antennae pointed became more and more difficult as technology advanced.

Television – an instrument of revolution?

Assessing the part played by television in the fall of communism is far from easy. The short-and long-term impact of western television on social and political change in Eastern Europe is a matter of conjecture. It is possible to argue that the significance of western television in the events of 1989 was exaggerated at the time, as a result of the prevailing view that the end of the cold war represented the 'triumph of the West'. Believing 'we had won the cold war' there was a tendency to place too much emphasis on what the West in general, and in this case western television and media, had done. The reality was that for many years leading up to the collapse of communism the western media and western society were reluctant to believe that political change was taking place in the Soviet Union and Eastern Europe. There was resistance to the view that a fundamental change was happening behind the Iron Curtain. This was the consequence of our reporting and interpreting of events in Eastern Europe being dominated by a particular framework of understanding (Halliday et al. 1992). Western reporting had been determined throughout the post-war period by what has been labelled a cold-war ideology.

Noam Chomsky (1989) describes 'Cold War Ideology' in his book *Necessary Illusions.* It is based on the West's profound and deep-seated suspicion of the Soviet Union, which characterized the conflict between West and East not as a struggle for political advantage but as a struggle between hope and despair, between workable capitalism and unworkable communism, between good and evil. American presidents of different political persuasions shared the view of the USSR as an 'evil empire' (Reagan) and a 'ruthless and monolithic conspiracy' (Kennedy) that was likely to go to war at any time due to its single-minded commitment to global conquest. Central to the mythology of the evil empire was the 'communist plot', 'conspiracy' or 'master plan' for world domination (Halliday et al. 1992: 69). The result was that the West had to be in a permanent state of military readiness to respond to Soviet interventions throughout the world. Attempts to explain Soviet actions in other ways tended to be marginalized by this official mindset, which was triggered by the response to the Russian Revolution in 1917 and cemented in the anti-communist hysteria of the late 1950s. For Chomsky and others, western journalism and entertainment had largely absorbed these assumptions (Chomsky 1989; Herman and Chomsky 1988; Parenti 1986, 1992; McNair 1988). The result was double standards in the reporting and representation of Soviet and American global actions. The USSR was motivated by the 'darkest possible intentions', while the USA was seen as providing a necessary response to Soviet perfidy. The reporting of USA–USSR summits and arms control negotiations were typical: Soviet proposals were reported and interpreted as 'ploys' and 'propaganda', while American proposals represented 'new initiatives' or an 'attempt to break the deadlock'. This was described as zero-sum journalism. Global events were reported as either a loss for the USA and a gain for the USSR or vice versa, and occurrences in the so-called Third World were only explicable in terms of the cold war game and nothing to do with domestic conditions in those countries. This view was reinforced by the behaviour of the USSR, a country whose history had made it deeply suspicious of the West and of western reporters. Limitations were placed on information, expression and the practice of journalism within its borders. Inept news management meant that little or nothing was said about certain events. This helped to reinforce the negative view of its actions in the West. As a result of the cold-war conditioning and the 'endless series of distortions and oversimplifications' in the media coverage, the picture of what was happening in Eastern Europe and the Soviet Union was extremely limited.

Cold-war conditioning meant that the western media did not attach sufficient significance to Gorbachev's attainment of power in the early 1980s. He was seen initially by many in the West as a clever operator whose reforms were not part of a process of freeing up the Soviet system, but a new tactic for winning people's hearts and minds in the Soviet propaganda campaign to shape global public opinion. Gorbachev's policies of glasnost and perestroika, which helped to open up Soviet society, were dismissed as a process of change in the Soviet Union by much of the western media. A BBC memorandum in 1989 warned of giving too much prominence to Gorbachev, who was labelled a highly efficient PR operator. It was only when the Berlin Wall came down that the media began to see Gorbachev differently. This event came as something as a surprise to the western media. The initial demonstrations of people power in Eastern Europe took place in East Germany in June 1988. Street protests in East Berlin were reported in news magazines such as *Newsweek* as 'rock riots', a reflection of what was perceived as a growing drug culture in the city. As a result of attitudes entrenched during the cold war, there was a reluctance to accept that these events represented change taking place through popular dissent. It did not fit the frame. The realization that fundamental political change was happening led to a shift in coverage, but again it was rooted in the preconceptions of the cold war.

The focus of the new reporting in the Anglo-American media shifted to the theme of how the West had won the cold war. The tumbling of the regimes in Eastern Europe was seen as confirmation of a victory for freedom and western values. Freedom was often reported in material terms. East Germans who streamed into the West were portrayed as leaving the country in order to buy consumer goods. The impression was that with the fight for freedom over, economic prosperity for the former communist regimes of Eastern Europe was just around the corner, with the 'free' market and privatization as guarantors. Similarly, the political forces that had helped to overthrow these regimes were represented within the frame of the cold war. Coverage concentrated on their anti-communist credentials and western dispositions, as well as their commitment to western democracy and the free market. Groupings that did not fit the frame, such as the New Forum – the main opposition in East Germany – which combined social democracy and environment politics in an effort to define an alternative to capitalism and communism, were not reported fully. Groupings such as the National Salvation Front in Romania, whose anti-communist credentials were open to doubt were reported more critically. Former communists winning power at the ballot box, as happened in Bulgaria in 1995, were ignored. The nature of the political and social movements that toppled communism was never fully explored, as the complexities of political change across Eastern Europe were located within the simplistic framework of the cold war. It is not surprising that such coverage placed too much emphasis on the role of the western media and journalism in the political transformation that took place. What western audiences were left with was a set of comforting illusions, which hid many of the difficult questions about how democracy would develop in the wreckage that accompanied the fall of communism. This focus on winning the cold war and triumphing over communism meant that the nationalistic fervours which were to erupt in bitter ethnic conflict in the Balkans and other parts of Eastern Europe in the 1990s came as a surprise not only to western audiences but also to western reporters (Johnson 2001: 218).

Development of the post-communist media

Following the collapse of the Soviet Empire, it was assumed that the mass media in Eastern Europe would rapidly assume the form of their counterparts in the West. Democracy and the market economy would be accompanied by media systems that stressed the core practices of western journalism, including objectivity and balance, as well as independence from the state and critical scrutiny of the powers that be. The 'westernization' or 'Europeanization' of the former communist media of Eastern Europe was regarded by many commentators in the West as a formality. This was not shared by many leading intellectuals in the East who had been at the forefront of the movements for democratic change. They had envisaged the development of a 'third way', neither capitalist nor communist, East nor West. The power attributed to the media, particularly television, in the downfall of the old regimes, ensured that they would be at the centre of the process of transition. This process has not been easy or straightforward.

The countries of the former Soviet bloc have emerged from communism at different rates and in different ways. Some countries, such as the Czech Republic and Hungary, have embraced western-style media systems more smoothly than others. Other countries have remained attached to the media practices and processes that characterized the communist regimes, including the Russian Federation, where the media have had to struggle to establish their freedom from both the government and business oligarchies. In many of the post-communist societies of Eastern Europe the 'transition' to western media practices and structures is proving more slow and more problematic than envisaged in the heady days following the collapse of the Berlin Wall. For one commentator, the media situation in Eastern Europe is summed up as 'business as usual' (Jakubowicz 2001: 68). Another sees the media in Eastern Europe becoming 'a copy of those in the West'; not in terms of the idealized version which emphasizes the social role of journalism and the media in creating citizenship and a public sphere through critical, objective and informative reporting, but in the extent to which they operate as commercial entities, geared to making private profit by the provision of cheap, sensational entertainment formats (Sparks 1991, 1998). Others say that it is far too early to make any assessment of the media operations, the media still being in an early stage of transition. While each country has developed its media system in a unique set of circumstances and at different speeds, there are some common features.

New media systems

The collapse of communism initially led to a flourishing of the mass media and journalism in Eastern Europe and the former Soviet Union. Johnson (1998: 184) describes how the 'last days of communism were glory days for journalism' in Eastern Europe. The decline of the influence of the Communist Party freed the media and journalism from the shackles of political control. Horvath (1997) describes how 'newsstands throughout eastern Europe became choked with a myriad of publications, ranging from political analysis to alternative lifestyles and . . . pornography'. The rapid development of new titles happened everywhere. In Hungary alone it is estimated that around 600 new newspapers came into being (Sparks 1991: 11). A similar number of newspapers were established in Poland after Solidarity came to power in 1989, and between 1990 and 1992 nearly 100 new titles were being registered every month (Horvath 1997; Sparks 1998: 102). The early 1990s witnessed rapid growth in the print media in Russia. Between 1993 and 1997 there was a 45 per cent growth in the number of publications, with the establishment for the first time of business newspapers and glossy magazines (Vartanova 2002: 14). Even in smaller nations, such as Slovenia, the number of daily newspaper titles doubled (Sparks 1998: 102). New press forms developed. Tabloid or boulevard newspapers had not existed prior to the collapse of communism. In Hungary their readership had reached more than 786,000 by 2000 (Gulyas 2003: 103). Similarly, lifestyle magazines saw a surge in their readership. Women's magazines and leisure/hobby publications experienced rising circulation throughout the 1990s. In Hungary weekly women's magazines increased their sales threefold from the mid-1980s, only to fall off in 2001 with increased competition from other kinds of material, such as television magazines and celebrity kiss-and-tell publications, such as *Story*, which is estimated to sell 479,000 copies every week (Gulyas 2003: 91; Kiss 2004: 105). Business newspapers also emerged. Some of these newspapers were new; others were the result of established newspapers trying to adjust to the changing circumstances. In Russia *Izvestia* entered into an agreement with the *Financial Times* to produce a Russian publication based on the latter, targeted at the newly emerging private entrepreneurs (McNair 2001: 275). In the immediate aftermath of the change of regime, the most common types of publications to be founded were political. The newly established political parties and factions wanted to have their own official organ or mouthpiece. The flourishing of the newspaper scene in Eastern Europe was set into motion primarily by the process of political pluralization that followed the collapse of one-party rule.

Broadcasting also grew, if not quite so rapidly. By the mid-1990s new, private television and radio channels were emerging. As in the West, these channels began to attract large audiences and the state broadcasters suffered. In Russia major shifts took place in the 1990s, with the birth of private stations, such as NTV and TV-6, which challenged the state broadcasters, ORT (Public Russian TV) and RTR (Russian TV), at the national level; similar developments were taking place at the regional level, where more than 1000 channels existed by the beginning of the new millennium (Vartanova 2002: 14). These private channels – which today include one all-national federal channel (NTV), four federal networks (TVS, which replaced TV-6, Ren-TV, CTC and TNT) and two regional channels with national distribution (Kultura and TVC) – have eaten into the audiences of the former state broadcasters. Nowadays 41 per cent of Russians prefer to watch ORT, while only 13 per cent choose RTR (Vartanova 2004: 196). More spectacular has been the success of private TV in the Czech Republic. In 1994 a new commercial channel, TV Nova, was launched. In its first year it attracted 70 per cent of the viewing audience and in its third year of operation posted a staggering profit of $45 million, on the basis of a turnover of $109 million (Culik 2004: 35). Recent figures show that TV Nova and the Republic's other private national TV station, Prima TV, attract nearly two-thirds of the TV audience, with the two channels of the public service broadcaster reaching only 32 per cent (Culik 2004: 39; Druker 2001: 83).

The expansion in the media industries was facilitated by changes in government policy. New laws and regulations were introduced, aimed at securing media freedom, and previous control mechanisms were rescinded. Democratization demanded political changes and at the forefront of these changes were the removal of censorship and the guarantee of freedom of expression. All the post-communist states moved quickly to undo the subordination of the media to the political authorities which had characterized the Soviet media systems. The new legal and regulatory frameworks guaranteed editorial independence. Political change was accompanied by economic change, with market reforms and privatization the flavour of the month. The free market was embraced with alacrity, as many saw it as a necessary prerequisite for political democracy. State enterprises, including the media, were sold off with almost undue haste. Fuelled by the revival of official belief in the efficiency of the market in the West, substantial voices offering alternatives to the market were non-existent in the newly emerging governments in Eastern Europe. A foreign investor buying into the Czech press compared the situation to the 'Wild West of America in the last century' (Sparks 1998: 143). Embracing open media markets was not matched by an enlightened form of regulation (Molnar 2001: 109). As Sparks (1998: 119) notes, 'there was no attempt to ensure that the newly freed press was an embodiment of diversity either internally or externally'. Alternatives to the market and private ownership arrangements were not considered. The press, as Sparks says, was 'simply passed over to the market and moderated only by the political interests of the government'. Thus in Hungary the sale of the newspaper *Magyar Nemzet* (Hungarian Nation) to a Swedish investor was blocked by the government, who considered the potential buyer too politically liberal (Splichal 1994: 39). Rather than addressing the problems of building citizenship and pluralism, the governments formed in the immediate aftermath of the political changes of 1989 were driven by an ideological commitment to the free market and 'guided by the political agenda of the New Right in the West' (Splichal 1994: 34).

Privatization and free market economics were applied to the print media more quickly and more completely than to broadcasting. There was never a process of negotiation and some newspapers were privatized or sold off without any reference to legal considerations and with no effort to regulate the process (Sparks 1998: 103). The privatization of newspapers was often questionable. One controversial example occurred in Hungary, where the Axel Springer group from Germany purchased a large chain of local newspapers. Culik (2004) describes how means were found to close down newspapers to ensure no compensation was paid to the state and then to relaunch them as new, private newspapers, with virtually the same name, to be sold eventually to foreign companies. If the press was 'left to its own resources and to the marketplace almost overnight' (Splichal 1994: 36), politicians from across the political spectrum were reluctant to establish broadcasting institutions free from their control (see Bakardjieva 1995; Sparks 1998; Splichal 1994). The perception of the importance played by television and radio in the process of political change, along with the jockeying between the newly emerging political parties over the structure of broadcasting in a post-communist society, held back the development of broadcasting in Eastern Europe.

The growth in the print and broadcast media was not long-lived and, ultimately, the events of the early 1990s resulted in a realignment in the media industries. The influence of television in post-communist Eastern Europe increased as a result of two developments: changing media consumption patterns and the decline in the print media. Television viewing has become more popular. Take Hungary as an example: Hungarians are now watching more TV. The average number of hours spent every day in front of their TV screens increased from 2 in the mid-1980s to 3.5 by 1995 (Gulyas 2002: 35). Vartanova (2002: 13) describes the same phenomenon in Russia, where newspapers were superseded by television at the top of the media hierarchy, partly as a result of the greater trust people placed in the medium; while 36 per cent of Russians found TV the most reliable media, only 13 per cent selected the press. Increased television viewing and greater trust in the medium has corresponded with the rapid demise of the press. The initial blossoming of new newspapers and titles in the early 1990s was followed by their decrease in the latter part of the decade (Gulyas 2003: 90). Closures and declining circulation, as in the West, became the norm. In countries such as Hungary, Poland and the Czech Republic sales of the national dailies almost halved between the mid-1980s and the end of the 1990s (Gulyas 2003: 97). Sparks (1991) identifies a variety of problems that make it difficult for the press to survive. Years of political and economic protection insulated the press in Eastern Europe from the political and financial realities of selling newspapers. The end of state subsidies led to widespread difficulties in raising revenue to keep the press going. Raising cover prices tended to deflate newspaper circulation, but newspapers did become more expensive. In Hungary the average price of a daily newspaper was 21 times more in 1996 than in 1990 (Gulyas 2003: 88). Such increases did not go very far in covering the costs of newspaper production, which, Gulyas points out, were similar in Poland, Hungary and the Czech Republic to Western Europe. The problem was that the cover price was on average four times lower. Advertising revenue was not always available to cover these costs, given the depressed state of many of the economies of the region. Matters were worsened by the desperate need to invest in new equipment. The technology of newspaper production under the communist system was poor, and underdeveloped by western standards. Investing in new plant and machinery added to the costs of production. It was also unfortunate that the explosion of publications, all of which could only command small circulations, coincided with a crisis in the economies of Eastern Europe in 1990 to 1991, with inflation rising, average incomes falling and demand slumping as a result. The consequence was a marked drop in newspaper circulation. In Hungary, readership dropped by 10 per cent and 100 newspapers closed (Splichal 1994: 39). Of the 80 local newspapers founded in East Germany after the wall came down, only 14 were still operating by the end of 1993 (Hagen 1997: 10). Very soon the newspaper markets of Eastern Europe began to resemble the gradual fading away of the press that has characterized Western Europe.

The fate of the press is indicative of the general problem of adapting to a new form of media economics in Eastern Europe. Structural changes in the financing of the media have meant that newspapers and television stations now have to operate in a more competitive world, driven by ratings and advertising. The influence of advertising and advertisers has become significant. It has been calculated that by the early 1990s 60 per cent of the Hungarian press was funded by advertising, compared to 25 per cent under the old regime (Gulyas 2002). In broadcasting, advertising has been allowed onto public service television, as well as acting as the driving force for commercial channels. Public service channels, such as MTV in Hungary, Czech TV (CT) and Polish Television (TVP), struggle to stave off financial shortfalls and possible bankruptcy, which seem to recur regularly as a consequence of the inadequate funding arrangements developed by the government. Turning to advertising as a source of revenue has, as in the West, resulted in a significant change in programming, with an increase in entertainment fare at the expense of more serious material. Commercial stations, such as TV Nova, TV Markiza in Slovakia and TV2 in Hungary, often supported by western finance and know-how, have led the way. Competition has seen the audience share of the public broadcasters fall way behind that of their commercial rivals in most cases. Those working in the media industries are not sufficiently knowledgeable about how to operate in a more competitive, market-driven system. Economic realities have quickly punctuated the initial wave of enthusiasm that greeted the events of 1989. As a former editor of *Komsomolskaya Pravda* noted: 'We used to have one profession – journalism. Now we have to be managers and economists' (quoted in Horvath 1997).

The effort to attain financial stability is increasingly the most important activity of those working in the media. Sparks (1991) identifies some of the revenue-raising options the media have examined. They could turn back to the state to obtain a grant, which many found unacceptable, given the recent past. They could take out a commercial loan, which, given the precarious state of their business operation, was fraught with problems. They could align themselves with a political party or faction, hoping to fund their operation from political funds, but at the expense of their independence. Or they could enter into a partnership with western commercial operations. If there was some degree of interest shown by western media industries in their country, most of the new media – and some of the established media – chose the last option.

Thus western media interests quickly moved in to take control of the media. Foreign ownership soon became a feature of the development of the media in Eastern Europe. Large sectors of press and broadcasting industries fell into the hands of foreign capital. Hungary was one of the first countries to sell off its media. By 1990, a majority of the country's newspapers were in the hands of multinational media companies, including Bertelsmann, Springer, Maxwell's Mirror Newspapers, Hersant and Murdoch (Splichal 1994: 38). Outright acquisition and direct ownership were common. Agreements were made, with the former communist newspaper *Nepszabadsag* signing a deal with Bertelsmann when it was privatized in 1990. Similarly, Robert Maxwell signed a deal in the same year to take a 40 per cent interest in the Budapest evening paper, *Esti Hirlap*. By 1999, it was estimated that foreign ownership of the Hungarian press accounted for over 80 per cent of newspaper circulation (Gulyas 2002: 37). Elsewhere in Eastern Europe western interests moved into the newspaper industry. In East Germany the larger newspapers were taken over by West German interests: 31 of the 34 daily newspapers found West German partners (Splichal 1994: 34). Most of the old East German magazines were bought up and then closed down; ultimately, the print market of the former GDR was controlled by the 12 largest West German publishers, who owned more than 85 per cent of the former East German press (Hagen 1997: 9; Splichal 1994: 35). Not that every country in the region was equally appealing to western media conglomerates. Few companies showed any interest in buying into the press in smaller or more troubled nations, such as Bulgaria or Romania or the former Soviet Republics. But even in these countries western interventions did occur: the Swiss publishing house, Ringier, launched a business weekly in Sofia, and Maxwell donated 1000 tonnes of newsprint to the country (Bakardjieva 1995; Sparks 1991). The primary interest of foreign media concerns was in the larger and more developed media markets of Hungary, Russia, Poland and East Germany, which promised greater profits.

Foreign involvement in broadcasting took a slightly different form, as a result of greater political and cultural sensitivity about direct ownership of television (Sparks 1991: 12). Television, in particular, was identified as a political and cultural asset that new governments were unwilling to allow to pass completely into foreign hands. Partnership and joint ownership were more common: today both of Hungary's most watched channels, RTL Klub and TV 2, are co-owned by Hungarian and western interests, including Sweden's SBS and the Pearson Group from the UK (Gulyas 2002: 37). Programme purchasing agreements with western broadcasters developed rapidly. The latter years of communist rule had seen a considerable increase in the amount of western programming appearing on Eastern European television screens. In 1986 Hungary's state broadcaster, MTV, purchased 601 programmes from western sources, including Britain and West Germany, representing almost 70 per cent of its total acquisitions (Sparks and Reading 1994: 251). Hungary was the most open television system, but others, including Poland and Czechoslovakia, were major importers from the West. Following the collapse of communism, this kind of arrangement was entered into more throughout the region. Bulgarian TV established relations with Central TV in the UK – partly owned by Maxwell – America's Worldvision and Turner to explore programme purchasing agreements (Sparks 1991: 12). Even in countries where there were greater efforts to resist foreign intervention, state or state-protected channels were forced to buy from western companies because they offered the cheapest programmes. Western programmes also became highly popular. In Poland, for example, the American soap opera *Dynasty* drew an audience of 16 million viewers every night, Monday to Friday. Relations between local and foreign interests were not necessarily comfortable. TV Nova started as a partnership between a group of former dissidents, led by Vladimir Zelezny, and Central European Media Enterprises (CME), an American company run by Ronald Lauder, the heir to the Estée Lauder Cosmetics empire, and a former diplomat, Mark Palmer, both of whom had served as ambassadors in Eastern Europe (Druker 2001: 82). The success of the channel, which by 2001 had amassed three-quarters of the Czech advertising market, coincided with an increasingly fraught dispute between the partners, which saw Zelezny go on TV news in 1999 to explain his side of the argument in a 9-minute item, while CME received only 30 seconds (Druker 2001: 84). At the heart of the dispute was the nature of the agreement between the parties, which led to Zelezny taking the station off-air, replacing it with his own Nova TV 2 in August 1999. The outcome of this act was a legal dispute which saw CME win substantial damages from the Czech government, estimated at $500 million, and Zelezny repaying $28 million (Culik 2004: 35). Zelezny left the channel and CME continued to expand into other countries, including Slovenia and Slovakia, furthering what one commentator has called Lauder's wish to 'become the Murdoch of the former communist countries' (Sparks 1998: 171).

The consequences of foreign companies playing a leading role in the development of Eastern European media should be a matter for close examination. European companies have been more active than their US counterparts. Many of the US firms that have intervened have done so as a result of historical and personal factors as much as financial. The Lauder family's interest in CME is the consequence of their Hungarian-Jewish background as much as the potential they see in making money in Eastern Europe. Only in the former Soviet Union do US firms seem to be playing a leading role. There seems to be a division inside Eastern European societies over the role of foreign investors and conglomerates. The hold these companies are exerting over media markets is tightening, as it has in Western Europe. For example, the press throughout the region is increasingly owned by outside interests. Thus two-thirds of the national newspaper market in Hungary is controlled by the Swiss media company, Ringier (Kaposi 2004), which also holds considerable interests in the press and magazine business in the Czech Republic (Culik 2004). Of the 90 leading publishing houses in Poland in 1998 nearly half were totally or partly owned by foreigners (Jakubowicz 2004: 170).

In addition, foreign ownership has coincided with the increasing concentration of ownership. The market share of the leading companies has increased year on year. The worry expressed by an Estonian editor about the concentration of ownership on the development of pluralism in his country reflects the views of many media workers in Eastern Europe. 'Plurality, which was so hard won, is still very fragile. In Estonia we have markets where radio, television, the weekly paper, the morning paper and the evening paper are all from the same group. It's very easy to manipulate the political agenda in such a situation' (quoted in Nelson 2001: 174). Others do not share this concern, seeing the main threat to media freedom coming from political forces rather than large private owners, who are not seen as a threat to democracy in same way as the state (Gulyas 2002: 37; Kaposi 2004). There appears to be little public uproar about foreign media ownership. Some argue foreign funding is preferable to the situation in Russia, where many newspapers have fallen into the hands of a small number of wealthy 'oligarchs', who use the press to promote their own narrow political agendas (Nelson 2001: 172). Perhaps of more concern is the strength and extent of the commitment of such companies to long-term development of Eastern European media. The rapid disappearance of these companies, whether for financial or political reasons, has highlighted the fragility of their involvement. The lure of higher profits elsewhere or a failure to perform to expectations have seen western media interests pull out of Eastern European media markets.

New media outlets and the changing economic structure of the media industries have been accompanied by adjustments in media content. New economic realities, as we have seen, resulted in a huge increase in the amount of western programming on Eastern European TV screens. The most significant change is the growth of entertainment material, particularly on the commercial and cable channels. For example, in the Ukraine 29 private channels were launched, all of which were devoted to entertainment, in particular cartoons and B films imported from the West. TV Nova's success was put down partly to its purchase of the rights to dozens of US sitcoms, soaps and dramas, such as *Dallas, Beverley Hills 90210* and *Days of*

Our Lives (Druker 2001: 82). Nudity, sensationalist and glossy news coverage and crime also feature prominently. *Pocasicko*, the late evening weather forecast, is usually presented by a stripping female forecaster. Gruesome pictures of accident victims and celebrity gossip are regular items on news programmes. Quiz and game shows, associated directly with the spread of consumerism, became a staple feature of television. The Soviet version of *Wheel of Fortune*, even with its creaky sets and cheap prizes, such as an old vacuum cleaner, was very popular. Similar changes in the content of newspapers are apparent. After the initial flourishing of the political press, newspapers went downmarket. The rise in sensational papers corresponded with a decline in the political and quality press. After years of boring copy, focusing on the comings and goings of the party faithful, people demanded something different, and sensationalism, celebrities, scandal, gossip and titillation seemed to fit the bill. The new economic need to tailor media products to reach audiences willing to pay forced newspapers to change their content. The huge surge in sex and sensationalism is a reflection of the new economic structures.

One medium of mass communication that did not thrive in the wake of the events of 1989 was the cinema (Horvath 1997). Under the communist regimes, the film industry had received considerable subsidies from the state. Massive cuts, the withdrawal of secure funding and falling audiences contributed to 'volatile structural changes' in the industry, which resulted in rapid decline (Iordanova 1999). Without experience of western fundraising techniques, and with many leading film-makers moving into the more lucrative world of advertising, the industry basically imploded. Hungary's capital city, Budapest, saw a fall in cinema attendance from a yearly average of 17 million prior to 1989 to 5 million by 1995. Ticket prices had risen in this period by over 500 per cent, as desperate attempts were made to cover the inflationary costs of making a new film and respond to the need to overhaul the poor state of the city's theatres (Horvath 1997). The film industry in the former Soviet Union had, in the era of perestroika, established a reputation for energy and achievement, producing over 300 films in 1990, the merits of which were acknowledged by the regularity with which these films won prizes at international film festivals (Graffy 1998: 188). However, the changes in the industry which accelerated after the collapse of communism set the stage for the destruction of the cinema. The loosening of the production and exhibition systems resulted in a huge influx of foreign films into the country. These films were highly popular, and the ending of state subsidies and the privatization of the studios meant that Russian film-makers struggled to finance their productions. Matters were worsened further by the rise of cable TV, which showed more and more films on the small screen, and the growth of the video industry, which saw video saloons being set up to show often pirated copies of films not yet released in the cinema (Graffy 1998: 189). Cinema attendance fell drastically and the production of films plummeted; while 300 films were produced in 1990, the number of Russian films made in 1995 had slumped to 46 (Graffy 1998: 190). Some high-quality films were still being made, but Russian directors and actors were increasingly working and filming abroad and cinema screens at home were showing more and more American movies or cheap Russian imitations. Elsewhere a similar picture emerges: state funding disappearing and audiences falling drastically. In some countries complete meltdown has been averted only by the intervention of television. In the Czech Republic, film-making would have disappeared completely without the support of Czech Television (Culik 2004: 37). Without an economically strong television system, other countries have presided over the demise of their film industry. Hungarian films, which had gained an international reputation, virtually ceased their production in the 1990s. Public television, with its financial difficulties, could not step in. In 2001 the industry went through a limited revival. The basis for this revival was a return to state subsidies, which, while sparking a debate about politically biased cinema, has at least enabled a significant number of Hungarian films to be made again.

The new journalism?

Journalism has also been changing since the upheavals of 1989. The old Leninist model, which ensured journalists served the propaganda needs of the party (see Altschull 1995), disappeared. The journalism that replaced it was modelled on that of the West. Post-communist journalists dressed like their western counterparts and introduced western ways of doing things. Presentation and camera styles are examples of this. Soviet television and film work used to be of a high standard. In fact, many of the key developments in the history of cinematography are the result of innovations pioneered in Soviet cinema. Much of the camerawork on Russian and Eastern European television today conforms to western ways of doing things. Western styles of political reporting have been copied, with gladiatorial and inquisitorial styles used to interview politicians and ministers becoming more prominent in news and current affairs programmes. Western concepts of journalism have also been introduced. Objectivity, critical scrutiny, independent comment and balance and fairness are some of the new skills that have had to be learned. Investigative reporting has also made an appearance in the East European media. TV Nova launched investigative shows that exposed government corruption and uncovered some of the excesses of the new capitalist system (Druker 2001: 86). Poland's leading newspaper, *Gazeta Wyborcza*, has played its part in toppling cabinet ministers guilty of corruption or other offences (Jakubowicz 2001: 66). Some reporters have embraced these imports eagerly, while others have resisted, seeing them, at best, as inappropriate to the conditions that the media and journalism face in the post-communist world, and, at worst, as an example of cultural imperialism. Journalists, at first highly responsive to change, have become more sceptical about the new business ventures of which they have become part, realizing, in the words of one Russian journalist, that 'the free market's demands could be even harder to come to terms with than the communist censorship of the past' (quoted in McNair 2001: 275).

Establishing the independence of journalism in the post-communist societies of Eastern Europe has not been without its difficulties and there is some way to go before it is possible to see the practice of independent journalism fully accepted. Journalists continue to be harassed, jailed and murdered. In some countries – Romania, Bulgaria, Ukraine, Belarus and, most notably, the Balkans – the situation has not improved very much. In Belarus the authorities have not accepted that journalists and the media have the right to criticize the government. In the early 1990s the country's prime minister said he would 'support all the press, except publications opposing the government' (quoted in Splichal 1994: 42). There are numerous cases of journalists who have exposed the wrongdoings of government paying with their lives.

In the Ukraine the television reporter Gyorgy Gongadze was killed after investigating the activities of the president, Leonid Kucema. New laws, often promulgated in the name of media freedom, have been used or abused to restrict the ability of journalists to investigate and report. The absence of significant economic growth means that many journalists in the region are still poorly paid and open to bribery. Nelson (2001: 176) notes how journalists simply sell their services to companies who wish to promote a particular product or require good news. Perhaps the most significant obstacle to the development of independent journalism is the mindset of the journalists themselves. Years of developing their skills under a communist system has made many working in the media more comfortable with the practice of political journalism, serving the interests of their party masters and propagating a particular political line or agenda. There is still a degree of discomfort at criticizing those in power and the preference exists for commentaries, editorializing and opinion, rather than reporting (Splichal 1994: 72). McNair (2001: 281) refers to the struggle of Russian journalists to throw off their 'genetic memory' of their professional role as agitators and propagandists. He cites the example of Sergei Dorenko, who is 'biased and proud of it', in using his prime-time slots on Russia's leading public service channel to promote a particular politician or party. He was 'an unremitting propagandist for President Yeltsin' during the 2000 election campaign. As McNair (2001: 278) says, the development of independent journalism requires much more than simply putting into place legal instruments to protect practitioners from state and government interference. Effective change depends not only on building new media structures and institutions, but also on changing the culture and mindset of the people who work in these organizations, as well as the people who consume their products (Molnar 2001: 103). This depends on a much more fundamental shift in political culture and society than is so far apparent.

Continuity

One of the features of the media systems of the post-communist societies of Eastern Europe is the extent to which there has been a continuity of personnel, structures and attitudes. In the early 1990s Splichal emphasized how the emerging systems carried with them 'important characteristics of the former totalitarian model', and how the new governments operated 'in the same way as did previous communist governments', using 'communist-like means of media control' (Splichal 1994: 43, 86, 60). Sparks (1998: 175), in a detailed examination of the nature of the transformation of Eastern European societies and media, based on a study of the Visegrad countries, makes a similar assessment at the end of the decade. In spite of a shift 'towards a much more commercial media system, integrated into the world market . . . [a] . . . surprising amount of the old order survives'. The capacity of old media associated with communist regimes to survive and, in some cases, prosper, is apparent in several ways. Media from the old regimes still exist. In the print market of East Germany, West German newspapers failed to make significant headway (Russ-Mohl 2001: 126). East German regional newspapers lost nearly a third of their circulation in the 1990s, but increased their market share from 63 per cent before 1989 to 78 per cent in 1999 (Russ-Mohl 2001: 125). Gulyas (2003) reveals how the former newspaper titles of the Communist Party survived the changes in the system in Hungary, Poland and the Czech Republic and went on to prosper. *Nepszabadsag*, the former organ of the Communist Party, became Hungary's most popular quality paper in the 1990s, while its equivalent in the Czech Republic, *Pravo*, established itself as the second best political paper (Gulyas 2003: 93). Continuity is also maintained by many of the same people working in the media. While senior editors and those whose faces were closely associated with the old regimes may have gone, it is the same journalists and reporters who run the papers and the radio and TV stations as was the case under communism. Nearly 70 per cent of those working in East German newspapers today were in employment before 1989 (Russ-Mohl 2001: 125). Many of them are seen as more critical of the new political order than the old. Hence it is argued that they are associated with popular support for PDS, the old Communist Party in the East, and popular dissatisfaction with the process of transition. The failure of many West German reporters to move to the former East Germany in the wake of reunification is seen as contributing to the problem. However, by focusing on local news, identifying with the problems of surviving in the new order, the former GDR journalists have been responsible in no small part for the success of regional newspapers in East Germany (Hagen 1997; Russ-Mohl 2001). The continuation of those working in broadcasting is a result of the policy of trying to change organizations 'without a witch-hunt' (Hankiss 1994). Critics believe the failure to purge the personnel of the old regimes has led to 'the same mafia . . . still running things' in television (cited in Sparks 1998: 101). Internal restructuring of the media has happened relatively slowly: today media institutions have been left untouched in some countries. The problem is more complicated than the continuation of a discredited political ideology. Culik (2004: 32) sees the problem of rank-and-file journalists simply switching sides as inhibiting the 'courage of individuals to produce independent and critical writing because they could at any time be accused of behaving questionably in the past'. Younger people coming into the profession are less inhibited, but the continuity in media personnel has resulted in journalism that for the most part is 'timid, unenterprising, superficial and conventional' – words used by Culik to describe the Czech Republic in the 1990s, but which could apply to any Eastern European country.

More significant in terms of continuity between the old and new is that the political elite running the political systems of post-communist Eastern Europe do not depart radically from their predecessors in their attitudes and actions towards the media. In every one of these countries, even the more liberal, such as Poland, Hungary and the Czech Republic, governments have shown considerable resistance to the growth and spread of independent media, particularly broadcast media. On becoming president of Poland in 1994, Lech Walesa – former leader of the Solidarity movement, which played a leading role in the overthrow of communism in his country – intervened regularly in broadcasting to ensure that media managers who were too independent and unwilling to comply with his wishes were dismissed (Sparks 1998: 159). In doing so, he brushed aside challenges from parliament and legal rulings that declared such action outside his powers.

Another leader associated with popular resistance to communism who appears not to have been able to tolerate criticism was Boris Yeltsin. In 1996 Yeltsin dismissed Oleg Poptsov, head of public service broadcaster, RTR, for what was seen as negative and 'excessively doom-laden' coverage of events in Russia (McNair 2000: 90). Later that year, in the name of democracy, nearly the entire Russian broadcast media suspended all criticism of Yeltsin in the face of the electoral challenge he faced from nationalists and communists, neither of whose candidates were given equal time to Yeltsin on Russian TV. The lack of media criticism of Yeltsin did not represent a return to the old ways, but, according to McNair (2000: 91), it reflected the 'lingering authoritarianism and lack of democratic maturity' that characterized Russian political culture. In Romania, where the fight for freedom had resulted in the loss of life, press freedom failed to materialize fully under the National Salvation Front, which used unfavourable economic circumstances to impede the development of opposition newspapers (Splichal 1994: 41; Ruston 1991). Cronyism still exists, with the new political parties selecting their own men and women to serve in key decision-making positions in the press and broadcasting. The allocation of TV licences often depends more on political connections than on any understanding or experience of the TV business. Sparks (1999) describes the success of TV Nova, whose 'political capital' enabled it to win the first commercial TV licence in the Czech Republic. Various governments have used their control of printing facilities, ownership of the means of distribution and monopoly of newsprint to exert their influence over what the press reports. Laws have been passed in nearly every Eastern European country, providing for the punishment of those who malign or defame public officials (Ognianova and Scott 1997: 372). Political change has not necessarily meant more independence for the media. Censorship and control still exists in the new democracies, but now they take different forms.

It is not surprising, therefore, that there are doubts about the capacity of the media to assist in rebuilding democracy in Eastern Europe. Pessimists talk of a 'long night' facing the peoples of the region and a 'new media order' being established by 'riding roughshod over the interests' of the population (cited in Splichal 1994: 237; Kilborn 1993: 469). Sparks (1998) argues that the media operate as agencies of control in both capitalism and communism. On the other hand, Gross (2002) believes that, in spite of failings, the media have played a key role in the development of civil society in Eastern Europe. He argues it is impossible for the media today to ignore the non-governmental organizations that have developed, and coverage of issues such as ecology, women's rights, health, children's concerns and housing matters has increased. Non-governmental bodies have also proved adept at using the media to get their message across, importing the techniques of public relations. Gross also argues that, more recently, popular agitation has played a part in the depoliticization of broadcasting. A mass rally involving journalists and the public in the winter of 2000/1 against political interference in Czech TV played a key role in toppling the station's director, a political appointee (Gross 2002). The result was that the Czech Parliament ensured that the council that runs TV shifted from a political party base to one rooted in civic associations. Johnson (2001: 228) sees the politics and sensationalism of the media as helping to 'draw readers and viewers into the circle of political participation'. Whatever the viewpoint, the debate about the future of the media in Eastern Europe increasingly resembles that which is taking place in the West.

Conclusion

The development of the media in Eastern Europe since 1989 has been a dramatic story. Press and broadcasting structures are now radically different from the communist era. Private ownership and market economics have come to dominate the operation of media systems. Media freedom has been asserted in the passing of new laws and media practices have changed in the new environment. While these changes represent the consolidation of the anti-communist revolution, the contribution of the media to the construction of a democratic political culture remains problematic. There has been limited opportunity for the new media structures to develop their own particularities. In most cases they have become pale imitations of the structures in the West. A distinctive voice and style of journalism has not emerged. The basic continuity of those working in the media has not facilitated the growth of independent journalism and media. The end of censorship has not accompanied the growth of private and market-led media. Politics still constitute the major determinant of the ways in which the media operate, and politicians in the new democracies are just as willing to use their power and influence to control anti-government publications and broadcast stations. Private ownership is dependent on a process of accommodation with the political powers that be. Reliance on the market in a hostile economic climate is producing media that are increasingly financially unstable and politically supine. The content of the media in Eastern Europe is more and more entertainment-oriented, which ensures they are less able to play their part in the construction of democratic structures and a democratic political culture. Most of the post-communist media systems are, to a greater or lesser extent, 'free but not independent' (Jakubowicz 2001: 59).

(This chapter draws on several articles from the magazine Deadline, *which is published in New York by the Center for War, Peace and the News Media.)*

chapter seven

Media policy and the European Union

In the previous chapters we have seen how Europe's media define themselves in national terms – some more explicitly than others – and how technological, political, social and economic developments are eroding the national foundations on which broadcasting, cinema and the press have been built. This also applies to the regulation of the media, which was framed in the national context until the 1980s. This chapter examines the factors that have shaped the attempts of the EU to establish media regulation at the supranational level. At the heart of EU media policy is a conflict between the desire to use the mass media to develop European identity and the economic priorities of increasing the industrial competitiveness of Europe's media industries. This clash is represented by divisions inside the EU between two conflicting camps, the interventionists, or dirigistes, and the liberals, or free marketers. In simple terms, the former represent the cultural aims of the EU, the latter, its economic objectives. The tension between these two camps has had a major influence on the formulation of EU media policy.

Policy is not driven simply by internal factors, but also responds to external circumstances. The dream of a common European identity and the aspiration for a unified European audio-visual industry take place within the context of the process of globalization, whereby US political, economic and cultural power is extending across the world. European identity is often conceptualized as a bulwark against the threat posed by the flow of American popular culture into the continent, while a unified industry is seen as being able to mount a challenge to the USA's dominance of the international television market. The process of unification is the most visible phenomenon happening in Europe, but this should not hide the considerable developments in the last 30 years which have led to the rise of regional Europe. Addressing the rise of regional media has also formed part of the EU's regulatory activities.

The European context

The impetus behind the European ideal and the need to build a united Europe was the 'savage excess' of European nationalism, which resulted in the Second World War and the loss of life of millions of Europeans (Collins 2002: 8). The founding father of what was to become the EU – the Frenchman, Jean Monnet – hoped that a union of Europeans would prevent such a conflict taking place again. His starting point was economic integration, drawing Europeans into a single market and encouraging economic cooperation in the form of organizations such as the European Coal and Steel Community (ECSC). The ECSC was established by France, Germany, Italy and the Benelux countries in 1951 and was the first institution of what was to become the European Union. Attempts to create common defence and political communities failed, but in 1957, under the Treaty of Rome, a European Economic Community (EEC) and an energy community (Euratom) were created (Grantham 2000: 93). These bodies merged in 1965, with a single commission, council and assembly. The commission acted as a secretariat, with some executive powers; the council was composed of representatives of the member states; and the assembly (which became the parliament) acted as a quasi-legislature. The relationship between the three bodies was characterized by the commission proposing legislation, the council enacting and the parliament playing an advisory role. The powers of the union to attain a single, common market among its six member states were interpreted liberally by the European Court of Justice, set up to adjudicate between the rights of member states and the powers of the supranational body. Throughout the 1960s and 1970s the EEC grew, with new members joining, and by 1980 the supranational body had 15 members, rising to 25 in 2003. Decisions made by the EU are binding on all residents, governments and organizations of each member state. However, decision-making within the EU is shaped by its unique political architecture, which is characterized by a complex and time-consuming multi-institutional, multi-level and multi-step process (Rollet 2001: 373–4).

As economic cooperation advanced, member states ceded more economic and political decision-making power to the EU. Media and cultural matters more generally were not part of the early considerations of how to foster collaboration and build a common sense of identity among Europeans. They were not even mentioned in the Treaty of Rome. Monnet is later reported to have said that 'if we were beginning the European Community all over again, we should begin with culture' (quoted in Collins 2002: 25). As the EU grew, more importance was attached to culture and the mass media, and the Maastricht Treaty in 1992 formally acknowledged that the EU had a role to play in cultural matters. The process of 'Europeanization' advanced more quickly with the first directly elected parliament in 1979 and the appointment of a strong advocate of closer integration to head up the European Commission, the former French finance minister, Jacques Delors. Delors' efforts to propel Jean Monnet's dreams were assisted by events in Europe. The collapse of communism and the fall of the Berlin Wall freed Europe from the political and ideological shackles of the cold war and put the question of European identity at the forefront of the political agenda. The media, specifically television, were identified as potential multipliers of European community feelings by those who sought to build a united Europe. National regulations governing broadcasting and copyright laws were seen as possible barriers to this.

EU media policy was motivated, on the one hand, by the cultural imperative of fostering a European identity. European unity was seen as essential to avoid the recurrence of conflict on the continent and provide the basis for developing prosperity. Pan-European television was seen as helping to 'improve mutual knowledge amongst the peoples of Europe' and 'increase their consciousness of the values and the destiny they have in common' (Robins 1993: 81). As one commission document put it: 'European unification will only be achieved if Europeans want it. Europeans will only want it if there is such a thing as European identity. A European identity will only develop if Europeans are adequately informed. At present information via the mass media is controlled at the national level' (quoted in Bakir 1996: 178). Fostering European identity and consciousness was not the only, or even the most important, imperative behind the development of EU media policy. Economic reconstruction and development was the primary motivation of the EU. Improving economic competitiveness through the creation of an economically integrated Europe was considered central to this. Broadcasting and the audio-visual industry were seen not only as cultural actors, but also as drivers of economic growth and creators of employment opportunities. Globalization and technological change enhanced the potential of the media industries. However, Europe's media industries faced problems in realizing their potential. They were fragmented into a range of small national units, subjected to a variety of forms of national regulation and had run up a huge audio-visual deficit with the USA, amounting to a staggering total of $8.2 billion in 2000 (Steemers 2004: 36). Underpinning the development of EU media policy was the goal of liberalizing or freeing broadcasting and the audio-visual industries from myriad rules governing their operation, thereby improving their competitiveness to face the challenge from US broadcasters and film-makers, and increasing their size in order to do so.

An important year in the evolution of the EU's media policy came in 1982, with the European Parliament passing its first resolution on broadcasting, and the launch of the first European satellite service. Politics and technology came together to provide the impetus for the development of policy. Satellite technology made pan-European broadcasting possible and was welcomed as an instrument to foster greater European unity. The European Parliament passed the Hahn resolution, which stressed information as a 'decisive factor' in European integration, advocating television as the most important audio-visual means of communication. As a result, media policy at the European level began to focus primarily on film and television, with little or no attention paid to radio and the print media. The lack of press regulation at EU level also reflects the traditional weakness of national press legislation and the reliance that most EU commissioners have on their own domestic newspapers to operate effectively in Brussels (Tunstall and Machin 1999: 207). It also put the EU on a collision course with national broadcasters, which were mainly public service organizations at this time, and seen as a major impediment to building a common identity among member states. Breaking down national broadcasting regulations was seen as an essential prerequisite for the development of pan-European broadcasting and building European unity. How to do this was a matter of contention.

Divisions inside the EU

Hahn did not see broadcasting as a market that could be treated like any other. His report warned against deregulation, stressing the dangers of broadcasting becoming 'an article of merchandise' (Collins 2002: 13). The parliament, in adopting his report, agreed that some form of intervention was a better way of promoting European unity than the free market and commercialization. It advocated a 'combination of prohibitory regulation and facilitating subsidies' as the way forward. This decision meant the parliament sided with the dirigistes, or interventionists, against the liberalizers, or deregulators, inside the commission. The dirigistes believe in the necessity of political intervention in markets in order to produce specific outcomes, while liberals advocate the creation of conditions in which free, competitive markets can thrive without intervention, thereby ensuring the efficient allocation of resources (Collins 1997: 332). In broad terms, dirigistes are associated with 'the desire to maintain the principles of European cultural identity', supporting public service broadcasting and advocating quotas and subsidies for films and television, while liberals emphasize 'the economic priorities of industrial competitiveness', advocating the paramount importance of consumers' interests and the beneficial consequences this brings to the broadcasting and audio-visual market (Wheeler 2004: 350). These conflicting camps resulted in differences between parliament, council and commission, between the directorates within the commission and between the member states.

Policy making inside the EU is an outcome of the interaction between commission, council and parliament. Differences of opinion between these bodies have to be resolved in the formulation of policy. However, the relationship between these bodies is not one of equality. The powers of the European Parliament, the only democratically elected institution inside the EU, are limited. Since the election of parliament in the late 1970s, the body has extended its powers so that today it has influence over amending and adopting legislation, with parliamentary assent now required for crucial legislation (Sarikakis 2005; Kevin 2003: chapter 1). The commission plays the main role in the decision-making process and it is the 'policies and practices of the Commission that have decisively shaped European broadcasting' (Collins 2002: 14). But the commission is also divided, further complicating the policy-making process. The commission is composed of a number of 'directorates', with responsibility for different aspects of EU policy. These directorates can and do clash. On audio-visual and broadcasting issues there have been clashes between the directorates of Competition (DG IV) and Internal Markets and Industrial Affairs (DG III), which are liberalizers, and Education and Culture (DG X), which is interventionist, with Information Industries and Innovation (DG VIII) somewhere in between. Their struggles have shaped the policy that has emerged from the commission. Finally, there are differences between the member states. The UK and France are seen, respectively, as the 'ideal types' of liberalizers and dirigistes. France has sought to intervene to support film, television and media in general, through quotas, subsidies, education and training programmes, such as MEDIA, and the protection of the audio-visual sector in peripheral EU states. Britain, on the other hand, in spite of changes of government at home, has consistently sought to secure a free market in the audio-visual industries, seeking to restrict or even 'close down' operations such as the MEDIA programme (Collins 1997: 332). Inside the EU, member states divide into one of the two camps based on their own national interest on any given issue. For policy to be binding and incorporated into national laws, a 'qualified majority' is needed, which often means a long process of bargaining before any proposal becomes a binding directive. As a result, out of all the reports, documents, literature, position papers and resolutions on broadcasting and audio-visual matters, there were only 'three definitive initiatives' up to the 1990s: the Television without Frontiers Directive (1989); satellite television transmission standards directives of

1986 and 1992; and the establishment of support programmes for audio-visual production and distribution, such as MEDIA (Collins 2002: 13).

Television without frontiers

The central component, or 'backbone', of the EU's audio-visual policy is the Television without Frontiers directive, passed in 1989 (Machet 1999). It began life in 1984 as a green paper, a discussion document, which was drawn up to demonstrate the key role of broadcasting in European integration, to illustrate the importance of the Treaty of Rome for producers and broadcasters and to open discussion about member states' national broadcasting and copyright laws (Grantham 2000: 94). The ultimate objective of the EU, as stated in the green paper, was the 'step-by-step establishment of a common market for broadcasters and audiences' (Grantham 2000: 94). To achieve this objective, the revision and harmonization of national broadcasting and copyright laws would be required. Article 2 of the directive abolished the sovereignty of member states over their national broadcasting systems, facilitating the free movement of television services across EU frontiers (Wheeler 2004: 355). Proponents of the directive argued that it would provide the EU with a home market equivalent in size to that of the USA and would enable television viewers to see programmes from other member states, thereby helping to promote a shared European consciousness and culture (Collins 1999a: 200). The directive had been introduced by DG III as part of a liberalizing agenda, but in the period between the publication of the green paper and the final directive, a 'considerable tugging and hauling between various interests groups' took place (Humphreys 1996: 267).

The most influential lobbying group, as we have seen, was the coalition of European press owners and advertisers, who promoted the deregulation and liberalization of the broadcasting market for their own commercial reasons (see chapter 3). The advertising lobby organized themselves at the European level through the European Advertising Tripartite (EAT), which had represented the industry at Brussels from 1980. This gave them an advantage over many of their opponents, who were still organized at the national level (Tunstall and Palmer 1991: 95). The extent of their influence is illustrated by the dependency of DG III on the data supplied by the advertising lobby in compiling its case for the directive. Press owners saw the opportunity of developing their businesses by being able to buy into a deregulated television market. Finally, independent producers were keen to break the monopoly position most public service broadcasters had in Europe, thereby opening up the industry to their talent and entrepreneurship. The directive responded to the advertising lobby, providing for 'the unrestricted flow of programmes carrying advertising across borders' and harmonizing the amount of advertising that could appear on television – no more than 15 per cent of daily airtime, 20 per cent of prime time (Wheeler 2004: 355). The provision for independent production was less favourable, limited to 10 per cent of transmission time.

The dirigistes ensured that the liberalizing tone of the green paper was tempered by the introduction of certain forms of intervention to ensure the directive would apply to cultural as well as economic matters. Within six weeks of the publication of the green paper, France's culture minister, Jack Lang, made sure that the issue of quotas was put on the agenda

(Grantham 2000: 95). The French government was sceptical that an unfettered single market would assist the development of the European television industries or promote European consciousness. One advisor to President Mitterrand stated that 'its straightforward application to the audio-visual sector would be economically unjustified, culturally damaging and undemocratic' (quoted in Collins 1999a: 201). With their traditional concern about US cultural power, the French believed that the single market would benefit American film and television producers by opening up national markets to their products. Lang and the French government supported the introduction of quotas, guaranteeing the amount of European material to be broadcast on European television. Quotas became the main matter of dispute regarding the directive, threatening to deadlock the whole process (Grantham 2000: chapter 3). Even a change of government in France did not see a weakening of French commitment. Lang's right-wing successor, Toubon, was equally assertive in promoting quotas.

The French, supported by their dirigiste counterparts in DG X, succeeded in adding quota regulations to the directive. Article 4 requires that member states ensure that broadcasters reserve at least half their transmission time for European works, excluding news, advertising and sporting events (Wheeler 2004: 356). A quota for European works was only included after a watering down of the requirements, without which the directive would have been unlikely to receive enough votes to bind all member states to its legislation provisions. The compromise agreed on quotas qualified their application by broadcasters with the words 'where practicable' and 'by appropriate means', and by allowing the introduction of quotas be 'achieved progressively' and according to 'suitable criteria'. The attempts of the French and the European Parliament to toughen up the wording were to no avail, and the quota requirements that ended up in the directive were 'non-specific, non-binding and non-enforceable' (Grantham 2000: 110). Quotas were further undermined by the definition of what constitutes 'European' as 'any legal or natural person domiciled in any of the member states of the Council of Europe', which, in practice, meant that US companies based in Europe could be described as European (Wheeler 2004: 356). The result was that throughout the 1990s quotas were more an expression of intent than an actual attempt to develop European material. Quota provisions were never rigorously enforced and infringement proceedings have only taken place in the most extreme of cases (Machet 1999). The final version of the directive was a victory for those seeking to liberalize the television market.

Supporting and subsidizing EU media

Fears about the impact of the single market led to additional efforts by dirigistes to intervene in the audio-visual industry. Inside the industry and the commission many believed that the Americans would reap the benefits of the single market, as their dominant place in the global television market made them more competitive. They could undercut their European competitors by selling their programmes at lower costs. To offset this competitive advantage, the dirigistes, led by the French government and DG X, explored ways to increase the productive capacity of the European audio-visual industries. A range of mechanisms to support audio-visual distribution and production were launched, the most significant being MEDIA and EURIMAGES, which were established to service the needs of the entire audio-visual sector and not aimed solely at the ailing European film industry (see chapter 5). MEDIA, set up by the commission through its own discretionary resources, was designed to provide programmes for training, research and development, finance, distribution and encouraging the use of minority languages. EURIMAGES was an initiative of the council to create a pan-European fund for the co-production of films and documentaries and their distribution (Humphreys 1996: 280–1; Hirsch and Petersen 1991: 50–1).

MEDIA I and II ran though the 1990s, and MEDIA Plus, the current programme runs until 2007, with negotiations already taking place to implement a successor to 2013. MEDIA I and II operated with fairly modest resources. The basic aim of MEDIA was to strengthen the European film and television industries, with a special focus on small and medium-sized enterprises, emphasizing the cultural value of the industries. Economic and cultural criteria both played a part in the selection of projects to fund. The first tranche of financing (200 million euros) was spent between 1990 and 1995 on a wide array of projects. Some of these were related to film, such as the European Script Fund, which supported 800 scripts, while other projects related to archives, film education, cartoons and animation (Tunstall and Machin 1999: 222). The programme suffered from a number of failings. Operational control was handed over to 19 different organizations, which not only meant high administration costs, but also presented huge challenges in terms of managing projects (Henning and Alpar 2005: 233). The most significant problem was the lack of sufficient funding to have a major impact on building synergies and boosting production, although an audit report found that, in spite of limited budgetary allocation, MEDIA I had made a contribution to networking and understanding between European producers.

The second tranche (310 million euros) focused on training and distribution, but, again, was spread thinly across a number of projects. By this time the programme had been incorporated into the EU's core activities, but still lacked serious funding. Tunstall and Machin (1999) are highly critical of the 'think small' approach adopted by the MEDIA initiative, arguing there is little value in providing finance for small independent companies from small European countries, and noting that only 20 of the 800 scripts supported achieved commercial or critical success. The 'scatter-gun' approach is commonly seen as a weakness of the initiative (Finney 1996: 3). It is generally accepted that it failed to bring about a strong European audio-visual structure, but the MEDIA initiative has not been without value. Some see its contribution as 'significant', while others applaud the 'breadth of its vision' (Jackel 2002: 154; Humphreys 1996: 280). One example is the key role it played in increasing the output of Europe's animation industry (Papathanassopoulos 2002: 239). However, given the modest resources at its disposal, the impact could only be minimal.

MEDIA Plus, the third stage of the programme, was launched in 2001, with an increase in resources – an estimated 513 million euros for the following five years (DCMS 2004). The objective of the programme remains unchanged, with more money allocated for development and distribution (Henning and Alpar 2005: 239). In practice, MEDIA Plus appears to be attempting to 'widen its scope' by increasing the number of companies allocated funding for development. This has reduced the scale of support for applicants, something which is also apparent in distribution support, where there has been a sharp drop in the average amount given for individual films (Henning and Alpar 2005: 242). Critics see this change as 'a big step in the wrong direction', as the 'programme's good intentions are partially rendered meaningless by its actions' (Henning and Alpar 2005: 241, 248). The enlargement of the EU, with new members seeking support for their film and television industries from the programme, is likely to lead to a further dilution of funding. Funding smaller projects and companies may support cultural heritage and diversity, but will not necessarily produce internationally competitive films, programmes and enterprises, nor challenge the US domination of the market.

The EURIMAGES project is more central to the film industry. Bringing together nations from Eastern and Western Europe, the fund grew from its 12 founding members to 25 by 2002, a third of which are from the former communist bloc. The basic objective of the fund is to stimulate European television and film production and exhibition, by providing financial support to co-production. EURIMAGES is supposed to support films that 'uphold values that are part and parcel of European identity' (cited in Jackel 2002: 155). No specific definition of such an identity was ever attempted and what constitutes 'European cinema' remains unclear. The lack of specificity means a broad range of films have been funded. Between 1989 and 1998 support had been provided to around 627 feature films and documentaries co-produced by more than 1000 European companies (Henning and Alpar 2005: 234). The main criterion is that in order to gain support, a project must involve independent producers from at least three member countries. EURIMAGES has supported large-scale productions as well as low-budget films and new directors, many from smaller European nations. The fund has assisted collaborations between Western and Eastern Europe, with many directors from the former Soviet bloc countries benefiting from its support (Jackel 1997). Following the collapse of communism, many film-makers were faced with the reality of raising capital in the marketplace instead of the highly developed subsidy system that had supported them previously. State-run political censorship had given way to economic censorship of the producer. Disappointment and disillusionment set in, as many directors expressed their doubts about local entrepreneurs and what they saw as 'foreign exploitation of their national film industries' (Jackel 1997: 113). EURIMAGES, together with other pan-European institutions, as well as national bodies, such as British Screen and France's Centre National de la Cinématographie (CNC), provides a source of funding for Eastern European film-makers that has enabled them to maintain their artistic integrity and creative autonomy. Besides contributing substantially to the development of networks of cooperation and exchange across Europe, EURIMAGES has made an important contribution to the increase in film production (Jackel 1997: 112). By the end of the decade the fund was providing finance for more than 50 per cent of films co-produced in Europe. In spite of the support it has provided, EURIMAGES has been criticized for not achieving its objectives. Distribution of the films has not been as wide and certainly much less international than anticipated (Henning and Alpar 2005: 234).

The final area of intervention is not concerned with software, which was the focus of the Television without Frontiers directive and the MEDIA programmes, but with hardware. The danger of US domination of the content of European television was matched by the threat posed by Japanese and Asian manufacturers to the domestic European television receivers market. An EU official spoke of the 'serious risk of European viewers watching only American series on Japanese television sets' (quoted in Collins 2002: 47). To protect the European television hardware industry and to further the goal of establishing the single audio-visual market, in 1986 the EU introduced a directive on satellite television transmission standards (the MAC Directive). It hoped to establish the MAC standard as the norm throughout the EU, thereby avoiding the situation that had developed in terrestrial television, with separate markets emerging based on different and incompatible transmission systems, PAL and SECAM. The attempt to impose MAC proved 'ill-fated' as it proved impossible to reach an agreement (Hirsch and Petersen 1991: 54). In actual fact, the Astra system, based in Luxembourg and supplying services to a range of commercial channels, including Sky, had established itself using PAL standard equipment. Cheaper and more reliable than the MAC-based systems, broadcasters who had already committed themselves to using Astra were reluctant to give up what was known for a leap into the dark. Sections of the electronics industry had a vested interest in opposing the imposition of one system, and Hollywood lobbied against MAC in order to maintain the continued compartmentalization of the European market. As a result, the directive expired in 1991 without any progress (Collins 1997: 337). Agreement was reached on a new draft directive in 1992, which would have allowed established PAL and SECAM channels to continue, but mandate new channels to operate MAC. This was not acceptable to certain member states, and after revision it was agreed that channels coming into being after 1995 would use MAC, but would be allowed to simulcast PAL and/or SECAM, which can be seen as an abandonment of the search for a common standard (Collins 1997: 338). Subsidies to support the introduction of MAC were watered down, thereby making the directive weaker than the dirigistes would have liked.

EU media policy saw intervention from Brussels in film and television through initiatives such as the MEDIA programme. However, intervention was, and continues to be, anchored firmly within 'a framework of thinking dominated by market economics' (Schlesinger 1993: 10). European integration is seen primarily in terms of the creation of a single market, as reflected in the Television without Frontiers directive, which – in spite of references to communication helping to build collective identity and the importance of intervention to support Europe's audio-visual industries – placed overwhelming emphasis on the principles of deregulation and liberalization to enlarge the European television marketplace and stimulate audio-visual production (Wheeler 2004: 366). Some argue that circumstances from the 1980s onwards have made 'liberalisation an obligatory step in the evolution of European communications policy' (Rollet 2001: 376). Globalization, with the trend to corporate concentration, consolidation and expansion, which first manifested itself in the corporations of Europe's main rivals – the USA and Japan – put pressure on European business to follow suit. Technological advances, in particular the convergence of media, telecommunications and computers, called for horizontal and vertical integration and undermined the national broadcasting monopolies of the public service era. Individualism and consumerism, which, as we have seen, are a major trend in the post-war development of European society, demand that consumer choice is responded to more rapidly and more effectively.

The EU and media concentration

One of the major obstacles to the free and unfettered operation of any market is the concentration of ownership. The EU is clearly committed to an anti-monopoly position. The Treaty of Rome bans anti-competitive practices and taking advantage of a dominant market position, and states the importance of regulating mergers. In light of this position, it seems strange that the Television without Frontiers directive makes no reference to the problem of media concentration. In spite of asserting that every effort be made to ensure that competition in the common market is not distorted, one of the most commonly highlighted barriers to free competition – the tendency to monopoly – is not addressed (Humphreys 1996: 287). Some argue that the EU has adopted a minimal action approach to the question for fear of private media corporations relocating out of Europe, with the consequent loss of jobs (Rollet 2001: 379). Others argue that the commission supported the growth of large European media conglomerates that could challenge the Americans and Japanese in the global media marketplace.

Pressure to rectify this glaring omission came from European media unions and journalists' organizations, who were concerned about the threat posed to pluralism, the free flow of information and diversity of opinion and expression. They warned against the increasing concentration of market power in the hands of an ever smaller number of firms. Technological change and deregulation was rapidly accelerating media concentration at the national and European levels (see chapter 1). As a result of lobbying by these interest groups, between 1990 and 1992 the European Parliament issued ten reports specifically addressing the problem of the concentration of ownership, acknowledging that 'uncontrolled and unlimited merger activities endanger the independence of journalists and freedom of information' (Sarikakis 2005: 161). Finally, the commission sought to address the problems of media concentration in a green paper on 'Pluralism and Media Concentration in the Internal Market', introduced in 1992. The basic aim of the paper was to outline the different regulations regarding media ownership operating within the member states, and to assess whether action was needed at the European level.

In contrast to the unequivocal position taken by the European Parliament, the 1992 green paper was ambiguous, lacking in clarity and full of contradictions (Humphreys 1996: 288–93). It acknowledged that the media sector, especially the newspaper industry, indicated a 'fairly high level of concentration compared with other sectors', but this concern was tempered by the argument that state broadcasters had experienced increased pluralism as a result of the expansion of the private sector. It reported that the protection of media pluralism should be a matter for national legislation, while at the same time stating that disparities between national regulations might interfere with the operation of the single market. Out of the green paper came three possible policy options: no EU action; action to improve transparency – collecting data about who owns what had been a major obstacle to the gathering of information for the paper; and a directive to harmonize national laws. A call for consultation brought forth considerable responses. Murdoch, Berlusconi, the European Publishers Federation (representing newspaper owners) and other commercial interests, as well as many member states, supported no action. Media unions and the European

Parliament favoured the last option. Inside the commission, DG X favoured media ownership rules to safeguard pluralism, which it saw as a cultural matter; and DG IV, in pushing forward competition, argued that regulation was inappropriate and impossible in light of the rapid changes taking place in media technology. In the end, the decision to proceed with the harmonization of regulation was influenced by the publication of another report, the Bangemann Report on 'Europe and the Global Information Revolution'.

The EU's efforts to develop regulations, policies and programmes on broadcasting and the audio-visual sector had to take place in the context of rapid change in media technology. The digital revolution and convergence add complications to the framing of policy at both national and European levels (Hirsch and Petersen 1998). It was a major challenge to legislate for a new technology, the implications of which would unfold only gradually. To deal with the new services, their interaction and their promise of creating an 'information society', the commission published the Bangemann Report. This report took an extremely liberal view, stressing both the need to liberalize the telecommunications sector and the primacy of the private sector in the development of an information society (Servaes 2001: 434). It argued that the EU should place its faith in market mechanisms and reject public subsidies and intervention. Bangemann was aware of the rapid advances the USA was making in developing the 'information super highway' and argued forcefully that the EU should not be left behind. The report pointed out the structural inadequacies in the European market, in particular the 'structural and financial weakness of the European programme industry' (quoted in Humphreys 1996: 294). It also explored the problems of media ownership rules for the 'global competitiveness of Europe's media industry' and the growth of multimedia, and stated that rules at the European level were necessary to ensure that ownership would not be an obstacle (Humphreys 1996: 293). The urgent need for action advocated in the report, against a backdrop of rapid technological change, pushed the commission into publishing a green paper on options to strengthen the audio-visual industry in Europe. The document is described as 'pre-occupied' with digital technology and the need for Europe's film and television industries to 'compete on world markets', identifying the main problems facing the audio-visual sector and the possible impact of new technologies. In so doing, the green paper emphasized the importance of economic consolidation in the sector. One contributor to the thinking behind the paper stated that 'concentration of production is necessary' (cited in Venturelli 1998: 214). Unlike Bangemann, the audio-visual green paper did not concur with the need for some form of intervention to achieve its aims. Both the report and the green paper brought the EU back to questions of ownership regulations.

Bangemann's view of the need to overhaul media ownership regulations across Europe was framed by the argument that convergence would lead inevitably to merger activity and the desire to see the emergence of strong, European-wide media conglomerates, which could compete effectively with other global media players. This contrasts with the parliament's desire to regulate in the name of pluralism and diversity. A draft directive was introduced in 1996, which included measures identifying upper limits on ownership in national broadcasting and multimedia markets. These proposals were rejected as member states disagreed over what was an appropriate limit. Compromise between the member states based on a more flexible interpretation of limits was rejected by the European Parliament, and in

1998 the draft directive was set aside. Following this impasse, the parliament became more proactive, calling on the commission to submit new proposals in response to the 1997 green paper, 'Convergence of Telecommunications, Media and Information Technology and the Implications for Regulation', which endorsed media consolidation in the converging information environment (Wheeler 2004: 359–60). Nothing was forthcoming. At the end of 2002 the parliament challenged the commission to consider media concentration again by launching a comprehensive consultation process to assess how corporate mergers had influenced the single market. The European Federation of Journalists drew attention to the growing involvement of Europe's large media conglomerates in buying up the newly freed media of Eastern and Central Europe (see chapter 6). In 2004, in a resolution on breaches of freedom of information, the parliament expressed strong concerns about the state of media ownership in the EU and the lack of policy to deal with increasing media concentration and the abuse of media power (Sarikakis 2005: 163). So far, EU attempts to develop policy on media concentration have come to nothing, as a result of the difficulty of achieving consensus among the main parties. There is no binding European law on media concentration and the commission has no specific instruments to ensure that pluralism and diversity of opinion are maintained in the face of growing media concentration. Some argue that this is inevitable given the power of transnational media firms and their owners, who are seen as exerting considerable influence over national governments.

Characteristics of EU media policy

The debate around the adoption or non-adoption of supranational legislation highlights several general characteristics about EU media policy. First, in the power struggle between dirigistes and liberals, the latter have the upper hand in the policy-making process. Collins (1997, 1999a, 1999b) concludes, from his detailed account of the debates around EU media policy-making, that the achievements of the dirigistes were of 'lesser consequence than those of the liberals' and that intervention and protection have been subordinate to the dominant ideology of liberalization.

Second, there has been, at best, neglect of, and at worst, hostility towards, public service broadcasting in the framing of EU media policy. This is surprising given the centrality of public service broadcasting to the development of national broadcasting systems in EU member states. However, the competition provisions of the European treaties are incompatible with the primary means by which public service broadcasters are financed. The licence fee is seen as interfering with the workings of the free market, in contravention of the competition laws. As Collins (1999b: 162) states, it is 'aberrant and offensive' in terms of the liberal philosophy that underpins the Treaty of Rome. Commercial, private broadcasters have complained about the unfair advantages that accrue to public service broadcasters as a result of public subsidies. The dual funding system that has supported public service channels in France, Spain, Italy, Germany and Denmark are seen as disadvantageous to commercial broadcasting (Wheeler 2004: 353).

Liberals within DG IV and DG XIII, headed in the mid-1990s by Martin Bangemann, became implacable opponents of public service broadcasting. DG IV intervened in several cases concerning issues such as the acquisition of sports and film rights by television, to shift the 'balance of advantage . . . further away from public service broadcasters and to commercial broadcasters' (Collins 2002: 18). In response, the European Parliament sought to shore up public service broadcasting, successfully campaigning for the inclusion of a protocol in the Amsterdam Treaty of 1997 making a specific commitment to public service broadcasting (Sarikakis 2005: 162). The extent to which the EU, in particular the commission, is antipathetic to public service broadcasting is challenged by some commentators. Ward (2003) argues that scholarship in support of the view that there has been a steady retreat from public service in the EU's media policy is 'crude and simplistic'. His examination of the cases made by commercial operators against public service broadcasters, in which the competition directorate has had to adjudicate, shows that the commission has 'overwhelmingly stated that public service broadcasting is something that is acceptable within the competition rules and the terms of EC Treaty' (Ward 2003: 233). Rejecting the claims of commercial broadcasters, and, in the majority of cases, finding in favour of state subsidy to public service broadcasters not distorting the market, does not necessarily mean that the EU's commitment to encouraging competition in media markets has not worsened the situation of public service broadcasting (Wheeler 2004: 361–5).

Third, the framing of EU media policy is problematic as a result of the relationship between economic and cultural objectives. It was assumed initially that using the media to foster a common culture was compatible with developing the economic muscle of the media industries to compete with US media conglomerates and reduce the trade deficit in television programming. A single market appeared to correspond with the unified culture. Creating a common market and a common culture went hand in hand. In practice, the goals often clashed. Liberalization and deregulation favoured larger and more competitive firms, most of which were American. The increase in US products in European national markets has not assisted efforts to build a common European consciousness – just the opposite. Similarly, the development of large European media conglomerates could also work against the objective of a common culture. These firms would be motivated by a strong desire to compete in global markets rather than any sense of building 'Europeanness'. This is illustrated by companies such as Vivendi and Bertelsmann buying into the US domestic market. They wanted to produce European consumers not citizens. Standardizing what people bought rather than what they thought was more important. An increasingly commercialized environment has implications for the kind of content that the media produce. The operation of unrestricted market forces creates an imbalance in the output of the media, favouring products that realize maximum profits. We have seen how national TV markets have been skewed by the increase of particular kinds of programmes, quiz shows, chat shows, low-cost production and more entertainment-oriented material, and how newspapers across Europe have become more 'tabloid' in their content, focusing on human interest and entertainment stories. This has been at the expense of 'serious' or informational programming and content. Building collective identity in an environment in which a diversity of representation is compromised and entertainment thrives is a challenge. As Harrison and Woods (2000: 483) state, 'market forces act against the creation of the conditions whereby rational critical discourse can be conducted'.

Fourth, there is a clash between the development of pan-European culture and the protection of individual national cultures in the framing of EU media policy. This stems from a lack of clarity as regards the nature of the European identity to be developed. For those intimately involved in the supranational enterprise of the European Union, the driving force was the notion of bringing together the peoples of Europe on the basis of what they had in common. They believed there was a set of 'core' values that were universal for all nations, societies and cultures in Europe, even though they had difficulties defining what these values are. However, building this common culture could not be at the expense of, but in connection with, national culture. Television without Frontiers recognized that television reflected the 'richness' of European culture, in the sense of its diversity, while aspiring to achieve the goal of a common European culture. Television should be an expression of diversity as well as means to develop unity. However, the integrative effects of a single broadcasting market were advocated more strongly by EU policy-makers: 'The goal of unity rather than diversity was uppermost' (Collins 1997: 336).

The directive has struggled to achieve its primary aim to establish a single European television market. Integration has taken place between states using the same language – primarily German and French – but otherwise the result has been modest. Markets have remained divided on national and linguistic lines, reflecting the strength of national patterns of media consumption. Many factors, including the rapidly changing technological environment, have been identified to account for this lack of success. The realization of the difficulties of establishing pan-European channels (see chapter 8) and increasing awareness that building a common identity would require not simply a common culture, but also a common language, to survive was crucial. If a common language was necessary then English was the clear favourite. English was spoken more widely across Europe, and anglophone media services and production were highly developed. Clearly this posed a threat to other national media industries and language blocs. A spokesperson of DG X spoke for many in the commission when he said, 'we don't want to leave the audio-visual to the English language media' (quoted in Collins 1997: 341). As a result, the 'melting-pot' approach began to give way to an acceptance that Europe was a 'mosaic'. Supporting and protecting cultural diversity became the theme of intervention in the 1990s, as much as building a common identity (Collins 1997: 346).

Finally, there is an assumption within EU policy-making circles that a close, if not causal, link exists between the media and the creation of identity (Schlesinger 1993: 10). Underlying the EU's approach is the view that the media, particularly television, are a powerful and potent force in constructing the European imagined community, acting 'as social glue, pulling together the disparate parts of the European Union into a common understanding' (Harrison and Woods 2001: 479). Such thinking is anchored in a simplistic view of media power, which is highly contested in academic analysis. EU policy documents tend to cast television as an instrument for change, having a decisive impact on its audience and, if its content is packaged properly, increasing European consciousness and community values. This viewpoint is seen as problematic. Schlesinger (1993) argues that the EU should be asking how collective identities are constructed before examining the involvement of the media in their construction. Setting aside the problem of whether it is possible to distribute the same cultural product across

Europe, the supposition that consuming the same product leads to similar interpretation is fallacious. As Schlesinger points out, it is crude determinism to believe that people operating through different cultural and linguistic frameworks make sense of audio-visual texts in the same way.

Bakir (1996) points out that the media do not create the symbols which bring the national community together 'out of thin air'. They have to draw on existing symbols or exploit established rituals in order to unite people in sufficient numbers to forge a feeling of national unity. In the case of Europe, Bakir contends that 'there are few EU symbols to choose from which are relevant to all people'. National identities across Europe still benefit from considerable advantages in that they can draw on 'vivid, accessible, well-established, long-popularised and . . . widely-believed' forms of symbolic expression. Europe is 'deficient as an idea and as a process'. The shared history, traditions and cultural heritages of Europeans make it difficult to find common symbols that 'would mean something to everyone' (Bakir 1996: 193). Without such common points of symbolic and ritual reference, it is difficult to see how the media can promote European identity. Of course, identities are not immutable; they are continually being re-formed and reconstituted in light of social and cultural change. Today it is possible to see a gradual coming together of habits of consumption and lifestyles in European nations (Kleinsteuber et al. 1993: 179). Yet national and regional identities remain strong, something reflected in the media, which are still centred on the nation and the region, reflecting the priorities of their viewing public.

The pan-European dream had to confront the reality of the diversity of nations, languages and cultures in Europe. At the most basic level, the fact that more than 70 different languages are spoken within Europe emphasizes the extent to which Europe is fragmented. The mission to create a unified European culture has had to be moderated as the EU has developed its media policy. Recognizing the obstacles and responding to the growing dissatisfaction of many Europeans about the European project, the EU has amended and developed media policy to acknowledge the complexities of building a unified Europe, something made more difficult with enlargement in 2003. The central plank of EU policy – the Television without Frontiers directive – has been the subject of criticism since its inception, and in 1997 it was amended by the parliament and council so that public access to free-to-air television coverage of major events of social value could be guaranteed. In 2003 a review of the directive called for further amendment to take account of technological changes brought about by the digital revolution. Supported by the European Parliament, this call has been resisted by the commission (Sarikakis 2005: 163). The basic liberal tone of the legislation remains intact, but there is greater recognition by the EU of the strength of national feelings, the diversity of Europe and the loyalty of national audience to national products. The EU has also begun to address another problem that confronts European integration – the growth of regional Europe.

The rise of regional media

Regional policy has always been a part of the European project (Harvie 1994). Between 1957 and 1973, the regions were defined as areas with ailing industries, in need of investment and economic development in order to make the transition to a modern industrial economy. In 1973 the regional activities of the EU were formalized with the adoption of a Community Regional Policy and the identification of particular regions. In the 1980s 'regionalism' not only grew rapidly, but also underwent revolutionary change. There was a conscious re-emergence of local politics, styles and cultures, which challenged the nation states of Europe. The new regional actors took many forms, from the new 'motor-regions', such as Baden-Wurttenberg, which owed their expansion to economic growth, cooperation and development, to the rediscovery of older identities, as in Wales, the Basque country and Scotland. The 'ethnic revival' was accelerated by the collapse of communism, which witnessed the revival of ethnic identities with more tragic consequences. The growth of regionalism was recognized by the EU when the Europe of the Regions committee was formally instituted by the Maastricht Treaty as a formal component of the union in 1992.

The regional media have been a central part of this revival. Local television channels are rapidly increasing across Europe (see de Moragas Spa et al. 1999). In some countries – Germany, for example – locality has been the basis for the development of the television system since 1945; while in others it is only a recent arrival on the scene – the establishment of Sianel Pedwar Cymru (S4C) in the United Kingdom, for example. However, the growth of regional and local television has been a feature of most Western European broadcasting systems since 1980s. In Spain, for example, it is not possible simply to talk in terms of public and private television while the 'autonomic' regional channels command nearly 17 per cent of Spanish viewers (Lopez et al. 1999: 353). These channels are a mixture of private, community and public services, but all with a strong commitment to local news and information. Satellite technology, the 'digital revolution' and the growth of the community broadcasting movement have encouraged the regionalization of the broadcast media. These channels, as well as other kinds of regional media, are not uninterested in European issues, often covering Europe 'in a way which would make national media blush' (Gilson 2002). The relationship between deregulation and decentralization is problematic, but the growth of small-scale local television and radio services is partly a response to the changes that have taken place in the European audio-visual market.

EU media policy has been slow to acknowledge the rise of the regional media, and their growth was not an intended consequence of the process of liberalization. Television without Frontiers does not include any provision for regional cultures or languages. In breaking down the barriers to EU media production, the problems of particular regions, cultures and languages, as well as minority groups, have been ignored for the most part. The revival of minority cultures and media in Europe is often seen as a response to globalization and moves to European integration. Many regionalists saw integration as an attempt to reproduce the nation state at the European level, reacting with hostility to the perceived process of centralization. Language proved a particularly sensitive issue. The European project emphasized the promotion of the nine official languages of Europe and the need to break through linguistic barriers, through subtitling, dubbing and technologies such as teletext, which conflicted with the efforts to protect Europe's lesser used languages. Pressure finally led to change as the pan-European model for a unitary, coherent and collective Europe lost momentum in the late 1980s, giving way to more emphasis on diversity. Findahl (1989) also points out that the increasing threat of English has forced speakers of the major European languages to articulate arguments deployed initially by the minority language groups. Regional cultures and lesser-used languages became recognized as part of this diversity. Measures such as BABEL (Broadcasting Across the Barriers of European Languages) – part of the MEDIA initiative – were established to encourage multilingualism in the production, post-production and distribution of European film and television products (Gifreu 1996). BABEL has financed the dubbing and subtitling of programmes into minority languages. Regional broadcasters and film-makers have also benefited from MEDIA, taking advantage of projects and schemes to develop regional production and distribution.

Most of the initiatives in regional and local television have been taken and developed by the public sector. S4C in Wales was established as a public service broadcaster, funded by a levy on the commercial TV companies, and provided with a certain amount of free programming from the BBC. TVE in Spain, RAI in Italy and FR 3 in France are all public service enterprises involved in regional broadcasting. The activities of FR 3 highlight the extent of the ambitions of Europe's regional broadcasters. Created in 1975, FR 3 is a national channel that promotes the regions and emphasizes their underlying values through news and fictional programming. Giving prominence to the regional identity, FR3, according to a senior executive of French Television, seeks to integrate the regions 'more effectively into France as a whole' (quoted in Scriven and Roberts 2001: 592). The seriousness of the channel's commitment is illustrated by its employment of 1100 journalists to produce its news output. The private sector was initially reticent about the commercial potential of regional and local television. However, in the 1990s commercial interest in local metropolitan television increased as city and regional television stations offered niche opportunities in a broadcasting sector that is dominated nationally by large public service and private conglomerates. Technology and changing forms of regulation have also made such stations more viable. Private stations, such as Télé Toulouse and Télé Lyon Métropole, in France, and Hamburg 1, are now established as an integral part of Europe's audio-visual landscape. Regional broadcasting has profited from the changing audio-visual environment, even though EU media policy has not supported its growth actively. For some, regionalization is at odds with national and European interests, while others see the local and regional TV stations – because of their close proximity to the citizens of Europe – as reinvigorating the European project by 'being asked to stick the pieces back together again' (Gilson 2002).

Conclusion

The attempt to build a supranational entity called the European Union is bringing European peoples, institutions and societies together as never before. What was an effort to develop economic cooperation and integration has been transformed in recent years into political and cultural cooperation and integration. The scale of the efforts has expanded since 1989, with the collapse of communism – which freed the East European countries to rediscover their European identities – and the 1992 decision to incorporate 'culture' as a remit of the commission in the Maastricht Treaty. The media are seen by the EU not only as a potentially profitable industry, but also as a means to build a new collective European identity. In framing media policy, the EU and its member states are receptive to seeing media products as both market commodities and social goods. The struggle between those who emphasize the social and cultural value of the media and those who focus on their economic and commercial value shapes EU media policy.

EU media policy-making takes place in the context of rapid technological change, which not only increases the speed and delivery of media, but also holds out the possibility of furthering the interconnectedness of the peoples and nations of Europe. The new media technologies operate outside national boundaries, posing unprecedented problems and challenges to policy-makers. National legislation and action is no longer possible to regulate the evolving media, as government and media companies have to think and act across national boundaries. The primary goals of EU media policy – of constructing a single European broadcasting market and using television to help foster a common culture – have proved difficult to realize. Divisions inside the EU, contradictions between economic and cultural objectives and the clash between building pan-European and protecting national cultures have undermined the EU's efforts. Finally, the re-emergence of sub-national identities has added to the complexity of the policy-making environment. The extent to which EU media policy has contributed to the development of a more European-oriented media and the fostering of Europeanness is examined in the next and final chapter.

chapter eight

The 'Europeanization' of the media?

This chapter examines the consequences of unprecedented socio-economic, political, ideological and technological changes, which characterize the growth of Europe's media since 1980. It explores these consequences in two broad, but related, ways. First, it examines the extent to which the 'Europeanization' of the output, practices, performance and structures of national media systems is occurring. How far is what is happening in Europe reported in national media systems? To what extent are the activities of the EU covered in Europe's media? Is there a 'European perspective' on the issues and events of the day? Is it possible to see a commonality in the practice and performance of European media and journalism emerging?

Second, the chapter asks whether the media are contributing to the development of a greater sense of 'Europeanness' among the peoples of Europe. The possibility of 'a new kind of European awareness capable of extending beyond national frontiers' may exist as a result of new forms of media, the greater availability of information and growing awareness of what is happening elsewhere on the continent (Weymouth and Lamizet 1996: 203). These questions are often explored through the theoretical prism of the 'public sphere'. Using the work of the German philosopher, Jurgen Habermas (1989 [1962]), scholars have speculated as to whether a 'European public sphere' is developing which is different from the national, but there has been little empirical research on the subject. The absence of research into the reporting and representation of European affairs in the various media of Europe has been commented on (see Semetko et al. 2000; de Vreese 2003; Kevin 2003). Bearing in mind this limitation, this chapter summarizes some of the material that is available to assess the extent to which a European dimension exists to the operation, structure and output of national media, and the impact on social and cultural identity.

Media structures

The emergence of pan-European media structures would be one indication of the extent to which the media are becoming more European. Print, the oldest media of mass communication, appears to be the least European. Newspapers are 'deeply rooted in national traditions' and have a 'close identification with their countries of origin' (Kleinstuber et al. 1993: 151). Language acts as a major barrier, confining newspaper reading to specific circulation areas, and the variety of entrenched consumer habits across the continent further undermines any effort to produce a pan-European circulation. Attempts to publish newspapers on foreign soil have usually ended in failure, as was the case when the French newspaper *Libération* and Germany's *Bild* tried to publish in Spain in the 1990s. This is not to say that newspapers with a European-wide circulation have not existed. In the 1980s the late British media tycoon, Robert Maxwell, launched the *European*, which was published weekly in 15 European countries and attained a circulation of around 350,000 in its heyday. Written in English, its content did not differ significantly from that of any national newspaper in Europe, with the exception of the larger amount of space it devoted to Europe and EU affairs. The *European* did not survive the death of its founder, and after being sold to the Barclay Brothers it was closed in 1998. Other English-language newspapers with a European circulation survived. European editions of American publications, such as the *International Herald Tribune*, and news magazines, such as *Newsweek* and *Time*, circulate widely throughout Europe, as do business newspapers, such as the *Financial Times*.

In recent years national newspapers across Europe have extended their European activities. The *Guardian* prints international editions in London, Frankfurt and Marseilles, while Spain's *El País* is also printed in France (Vilches 1996: 199). European newspapers with similar editorial outlooks and readership have set up mechanisms to cooperate in the exchange of news. There is also growing cooperation between newspapers in the exchange of articles. *El Mundo* in Spain swaps articles with Italy's *Il Corriere de la Sera* and the *Guardian* in Britain, while cultural articles are shared on a monthly basis between the *Guardian*, *Le Monde Diplomatique* and Sweden's *Aftonbladet* (Kevin 2003: 129). Such cooperation has been furthered by the internet. Several major, quality newspapers share stories via their websites. Readers are able to access stories from *El País*, *Le Monde*, *Suddeutsch Zeitung*, the *Guardian*, *Le Soir* and *Aftonbladet*, via a link entitled 'European Perspective', which has an automatic translation programme (Kevin 2003: 131). In contrast to the press, the magazine sector — so important across the continent – has experienced the successful development of European-wide publications. Magazines such as *Reader's Digest*, and especially women's magazines, such as, *Hello!*, *Elle*, *Prima*, *Marie Claire*, *Vogue* and *Cosmopolitan*, are read in most European countries, through the production of national editions to serve different target audiences. It seems that fashion, pictures and advertising do not manifest strong national differences.

Pan-European television has a long history. TV became established in Europe at roughly the same time that the institutional foundations for the EU were laid down (Bondebjerg 2004: 67). In 1950, the European Broadcasting Union (EBU) was created as a consortium of European broadcasters, with the primary aim of exchanging programmes free of charge through Eurovision (Hjarvard 1993). More than 60 members belong to the organization today – mostly public service broadcasters from East and West Europe. In 1954 a series of European Television Weeks initiated cooperation; since then, this has centred on news exchange and coverage of media and cultural events in sport, drama and music, including European football and, more famously, since 1956, the Eurovision Song Contest (Bondebjerg 2004: 67). Some of the events exchanged have been watched by large audiences and even today the Eurovision Song Contest is a major media event. By 1981 the EBU accounted for around 5 per cent of the total programming output in an average European country, much of it same-day coverage of news and sporting events (Tunstall and Palmer 1991: 14). While the EBU's contribution to the development of pan-European television has been long-standing, it has also been minimal, and since the arrival of commercial TV the organization has concentrated its efforts mainly on safeguarding public television in Europe.

Pan-European broadcasting received a fillip in the early 1980s, when the arrival of satellite technology resulted in the considerable growth of pan-European television channels. Early ventures in pan-European broadcasting, such as Lifestyle, Screensport, Super Channel and Europa TV, did not survive for more than a few years (Chalaby 2003). Europa TV was launched in 1986 through the cooperation of several national broadcasters – ARD (Germany), NOS (Netherlands), RTE (Ireland), RAI (Italy) and RTP (Portugal) – with the aim of sharing national programming, with programmes specifically related to EU issues (Hjarvard 1993: 79). As a result of financial difficulties, limited transmission possibilities, the failure to develop a European-wide audience and the reluctance of larger public service broadcasters to become involved, the channel was unsuccessful, being on-air for just over a year (Kevin 2003: 39). Pan-European channels broadcasting sport and music have been more successful. Eurosport started in 1989 as a consortium of EBU members and Rupert Murdoch's company, News International (see Collins 2002: chapter 8). Following a court case brought against the channel by its competitor, Screensport, which saw the partnership as anti-competitive, Murdoch's share was bought up by the French broadcaster, TF 1, and in 1993 the channel was merged with the European Sports Network, owned by Canal Plus and Disney. In 2000 Disney was bought out by its partners (Papathanassopoulos 2002: 190). The channel is available in 85 million cable and satellite households in Europe, offering a service which initially broadcast identical pictures with 14 separate language commentaries. Germany accounts for one-third of Eurosport homes, and the channel has been very successful in Central and Eastern Europe (Tunstall and Machin 1999: 244).

Eurosport has struggled in the more competitive market of Western Europe, which saw a huge expansion of dedicated sports channels and the growth of sports programming on terrestrial television in the 1990s. As a result, Eurosport started to tailor its output to local markets, offering devolved services for Scandinavia, France and Britain (Chalaby 2002a: 194; Tunstall and Machin 1999: 245). These services cater for the particular needs of the Nordic, British and French audiences. British Eurosport markets itself as a British channel, banning foreign advertising and concentrating on sports such as cricket, football and rugby, which have particular appeal for the British audience. Sports, such as Nordic skiing, which are part of the European output and are of little interest to UK sports fans, are replaced in the schedule. Opting out of the common European feed to emphasize British sports and British competitors is central to the channel's operation, resulting in it producing its own news bulletins and buying up rights to UK sporting events (Chalaby 2002a: 194–5). These developments have enabled the channel to compete with domestic sports channels. In the longer run, Eurosport faces an uncertain future. Sports programming is at the forefront of the digital revolution. As channels multiply, sport plays a prominent part in their schedules. The result is the spiralling costs of acquiring the rights to live sporting events and tournaments and increased competition from US sports networks, such as Disney's Entertainment and Sports Network (ESPN), and domestic operations, such as Murdoch's Sky.

Music television channels have expanded rapidly in Europe. The most famous channel is America's MTV, which pioneered music television when it first appeared on US cable television on 21 August 1981. Introduced into Western Europe in 1987, MTV Europe was the fastest growing cable and satellite channel in Europe in the 1990s (Burnett 1996: 96) and by the middle of the decade it was distributed to 56 million households (Roe and Meyer 2000: 143). Its expansion into Eastern Europe was more dramatic. MTV began broadcasting to Poland, Hungary, Czechoslovakia and East Germany only months before the collapse of the Berlin Wall (Sturmer 1993: 60). Entry into the countries of the former Soviet bloc was facilitated by authorized and unauthorized means. Cable systems carried MTV to a number of households, but most people in Eastern Europe watched the channel 'by directly pirating the unscrambled program signal carried on the European Astra satellite' (Banks 1996: 95). By 1992 more than 2 million households in Eastern Europe were officially plugged into the channel (Sturmer 1993: 60). Unofficially, it was many more. The images of rebellion, individuality and anti-authoritarianism in the channel's output resonated with the thirst for freedom among the newly liberated peoples of Eastern Europe, as well as serving the interests of big business by facilitating access to potentially huge and lucrative markets (Sturmer 1993: 61).

MTV's operation in Europe initially sought to reproduce what the American station did at home. However, the linguistic, technological, cultural and musical diversity of the continent forced the channel to adapt its style and content to the European market (Roe and Meyer 2000: 143). It was transformed 'from a one-for-all formula of American tunes and trends into a regionalised operation with more local music, live events and national news' (Papathanassopoulos 2002: 219). In 1996 three separate services were created. MTV Central served Austria, Germany and Switzerland; MTV South served Italy; and MTV North served the rest of Europe (Roe and Meyer 2000: 150). In 1997 MTV-UK and Ireland was launched, and MTV North divided into MTV Nordic, covering Scandinavia, and MTV Europe, servicing the remaining 22 territories without a dedicated service (Chalaby 2002a: 196). Further regionalization took place in 2000, with the setting up of MTV Poland, MTV Spain, MTVf – covering France and French-speaking Switzerland – and MTV NL in the Netherlands. By 1999 MTV was reaching 85 million households around Europe, with a product adapted to local conditions (Papathanassopoulos 2002: 221).

This growth of local programming was partly the product of increased competition from European music channels. Today it is estimated that there are more than 100 domestic music TV stations in Europe, with several more in development (Chalaby 2003: 465). One of the first European channels was VIVA, a German-language music channel, which by 1997 was reaching 22 million homes in Germany, Austria and Switzerland, becoming more popular than MTV in Germany (Roe and Meyer 2000: 149). Several other European broadcasters have started their own domestic channels to challenge MTV, including Videomusic in Italy, MCM in France, S-Plus in Switzerland, Z-TV in Sweden and The Music Factory in the Netherlands (Papathanassopoulos 2002: 218). The Music Factory emulated VIVA's success, displacing MTV as the most popular music TV station in its domestic market (Roe and Meyer 2000: 149). The success of these channels was based on a formula of having a certain percentage of music drawn from local artists, as well as ensuring presenters use the national language instead of English. In Britain the magazine publisher EMAP launched several channels, including Smash Hits and the Box, which have overtaken MTV in their popularity with young Britons (Cassy 2002).

Efforts to develop pan-European news have been less successful. Euronews was launched in 1993 by EBU members, in response to CNN's domination of the reporting of the first Gulf War (Chalaby 2002a: 186; Machill 1998: 429). From the outset it did not use on-screen presenters, relying on airing unbroken footage of events voiced over in five languages (Papathanassopoulos 2002: 168). By the end of its first year of operation the channel was losing money and in 1994 sold 49 per cent of its holdings to the electronic giant Alcatel, which in 1998 was acquired by Britain's ITN. Since its launch, the Lyon-based channel has undergone at least two makeovers, to attract more viewers and advertisers. Not only have these changed the content, introducing a magazine format and a more human-interest approach to the news, but they have also produced a more European image for the channel. The aim is to present Europe 'through a unity of images and the diversity of languages' (Papathanassopoulos 2002: 169). Management's resistance to using presenters is seen by critics as an obstacle to the audience being able to identify with the channel. Without 'anchors' – regarded by many as essential to any TV news programme – and correspondents reporting live from major news events, such as summits and elections, the impersonal approach of Euronews makes it difficult for it to challenge CNN and become a major player in the international news market (Papathanassopoulos 2002: 170). It also faces strong competition from within Europe. Sky News has a European news service reaching 33 countries in Europe, while BBC World offers a separate European feed with regional elements. Both are broadcast in English and are more successful in audience terms. Nevertheless, Euronews now reaches 70 million terrestrial and 32 million cable households in Europe, as well as being available in Africa, North America and Asia. Yet this reach is not sufficient for Euronews to do anything more than cover its operating costs.

European news collaboration has not only been at the pan-European level. *Eurosud*, a news magazine, was made by TV stations from several European countries (Laborde and Perrot 2000). It lasted from 1988 to 1994 and brought together the regional operations of three public service channels: the Bordeaux region of FR 3, TVE Bilbao in the Basque region of Spain and RTP Porto in northern Portugal. It was not co-production in the sense of the pooling of finance and resources, but collaboration funded by each of the individual organizations out of their own budgets and operated editorially by joint meetings. It attempted to exploit the economic and cultural affinities between the regions. Focusing on everyday life in the regions, *Eurosud* examined how non-controversial changes impacted on the regions. Politically sensitive matters, however, were kept off the news agenda for fear of offending sensibilities. Cautious and uncontroversial in its news reporting, the channel soon dropped its plans for partners to film reports in one another's countries on the grounds of cost, in favour of the exchange of domestically produced items. As Wieten et al. (2000: 63) point out the result was 'a juxtaposition of national productions rather than a collision of "crossed looks" which explored similarities and differences in an innovative way', with the programme thus failing to 'break out of the framework established by national ways of looking'.

A public service collaboration which met with greater success is the cultural channel, Arte. Launched in 1992, Arte can be accessed via cable, satellite or digital packages by 70 per cent of German households and via terrestrial signal for 90 per cent of French households, as well as being available on cable in Belgium, Switzerland, Austria and the Netherlands (Kevin 2003: 41). Based in Strasbourg, the channel is managed jointly by France and Germany and transmits simultaneously to viewers in both countries, with all its programming dubbed into German and French (Bondebjerg 2004: 69). Funding is provided by the governments of the two countries, in support of the aim of producing programmes of a 'cultural and international nature', which will 'promote mutual understanding and unity amongst the peoples of Europe' (quoted in Jackel 1999: 183). Broadcast between 7 p.m. and 3 a.m., the channel's output concentrates on drama, documentary, opera and musical performance and film. Arte pioneered thematic programming on specific evenings, which has become a feature of TV in Europe in recent years. Some see the channel as taking up the slack in arts programming left by the decline in coverage by traditional broadcasters (Bakke 2000). It is described as making a major contribution to the development of European talent and 'quality programming', but without sustained public financial support it is clear that Arte would not survive in the competitive environment of European broadcasting (Jackel 1999: 185).

Pan-European channels such as Euronews, Eurosport and MTV have grown in the late twentieth century and consolidated their position in the European TV market. It is estimated that pan-European channels are distributed to one-fifth of households in Western, Eastern and Central Europe (Chalaby 2003: 440). However, the audience for these channels is 'extremely small', accounted for 'in the tens of thousands of viewers rather than in the millions who watch national television every day' (Chalaby 2002a: 188). While pan-European TV channels constitute only a small number of the transnational channels that broadcast in Europe, their emergence is significant as national broadcasters are no longer the only players on the European television landscape. However, to fulfil their European vision, these channels have had to either localize their services or rely on public subsidy. Localization is not undertaken in the same way by these services. News channels are 'less localised than those that are purely entertainment driven', which is explained by news being 'less deeply rooted in one culture' (Chalaby 2002a: 198). Public service broadcasters are less inclined to localize. By localizing, these channels are not becoming local in their perspective. They are simply adapting their product to local tastes to maximize their audience and, in commercial terms, realize higher profits. MTV, as Chalaby (2002a: 200) points out, retains its American identity and flavour in its local channels, with a fair proportion of its music still Anglo-American. It is simply that its playlist has greater diversity, incorporating more local artists. Localization is a device to sell more, rather than a way of truly embracing local culture.

Europe in the news

Studies of media coverage of Europe and European affairs have been described as 'scattered' (de Vreese 2003: 79). What is apparent is the difficulty of generalizing about the coverage across national boundaries and between different media. Certain countries appear to report Europe and European affairs more than others. Kevin's (2003) cross-national study of the media coverage of Europe in eight EU countries found that, quantitatively, Germany 'heavily dominated' what was counted as European news, while Italy accounted for the least. Norris (2000a: 189) found that the 'pattern of newspaper coverage . . . varied substantially' between the 15 member states, with 'by far the highest proportion of stories in the German and British press, whereas there were relatively few stories in smaller member states like Greece, Luxembourg and Ireland'. De Vreese (2003) identified some differences in the TV news reporting of European affairs in Britain, Denmark and the Netherlands. The limited amount of comparative research means that 'little is known about how European issues are covered in the news in a longitudinal perspective . . . or about the ways in which news coverage may differ or share similarities between different European countries' (de Vreese 2003: 80). Similarly, making comparisons between types of media is subject to the lack of research. The research that has been done is divided into two areas: reporting the EU, its institutions and events, such as summits, elections and economic developments – like the launching of the euro – and the coverage of Europe and European events in national media systems.

Coverage of the European Union

The importance of politics and economics to the process of integration has inevitably meant that most of the research into the media's coverage of the EU has focused on political and economic events and issues. European elections have been subject to enquiry since the first European parliamentary elections in 1979. A cross-national study of television coverage of the 1979 elections found that there was little or no mention of Europe before the campaign (Siune 1983, cited in de Vreese 2003). For the period of the campaign, the focus was primarily on economic matters, the novelty and nature of the elections and the problems and strategies of campaigning (Siune 1983: 226). Subsequent studies on television reporting found that the elections were given low priority and much of the coverage focused on national issues rather the European dimension of the issues in question (Leroy and Siune 1994). More recent studies have underscored the national slant of the media coverage of EU elections. Kevin (2003: 87) concluded from her comparative study of the 1999 elections that the media across Europe reflect the agenda of national politicians and treat European elections as a 'national event with by and large national party candidates and a focus on national issues'. While she found a 'lack of debate on specific EU policy issues', there were attempts in 1999 to approach the elections from a European perspective, with the quality press taking the lead in outlining the stance of particular parties on EU issues and comparing campaign developments in other European countries. In countries such as France, Spain and Sweden, more than 1 in 3 of the stories on the elections was devoted to the campaigns in other countries. Other countries, such as Britain, were far more parochial, with only 1 in 20 stories (Kevin 2003: 77).

A study of news output on television and in the press in EU countries found that routine coverage of the EU and EU affairs was fairly low in member states (Norris 2000a: 187). Coverage was found to peak around certain key issues and events, such as summits and ministerial conferences. The 'routine daily grind of European Parliament debates, European Commission business and presidential initiatives remains largely invisible to the public'

(Norris 2000a: 188). Limited coverage of Europe has also been identified as a problem in national elections. Examination of the reporting of national elections in Germany, Britain and the Netherlands throughout the 1990s 'shows that Europe was on the periphery of the campaigns' (Semetko et al. 2000: 130). When the EU and European affairs did surface as an issue, this was due mainly to national factors. The strong focus on EU affairs in the 1998 Dutch elections was partly accounted for by the struggle to appoint a Dutchman to be the first head of the European Central Bank (Semetko et al. 2000: 131).

Lack of visibility, or what some have called a 'communication deficit', is seen as characterizing the reporting of Europe. Whether this applies to all the media equally is open to debate. Research into the pattern of coverage in quality newspapers in selected EU member states found a 'considerable degree of European political communication', indicating 'an astonishingly high level of Europeanization of national newspapers, which contradicts all previous findings on the scarce visibility of Europe in the media' (Trenz 2004: 292). While there are differences between the national quality papers in the amount and focus of the coverage, the research showed that 35.2 per cent of all political stories focused on European or European-related matters. This finding is consistent with the way in which many European quality newspapers have developed their coverage. *El Mundo* in Spain not only has a designated European section, but also publishes interviews with leading political and cultural personalities from around Europe every Sunday (Kevin 2003: 127). Weymouth and Lamizet (1996: 205) highlight the increasing political commitment and an emergence of editorial policies promoting European coverage in quality newspapers, singling out the French quality newspaper *Le Monde* for 'an impressive dedication of its column space to the coverage of European issues'.

With regard to the quality press in Europe, Trenz (2004: 312) sees the emergence of a 'unified European media system', which his research indicates is 'a self-regulating and largely autonomous system that specializes in observing and selecting European political communication and that applies similar standards and selection procedures to build political news from it'. The exceptional case of the quality newspapers in Europe reflects the 'high and growing differentiation in the specialisation of the national media landscape'. National quality newspapers, regional newspapers and tabloids no longer represent one unified national media system and, while national peculiarities may still exist, convergence between different media segments is equally likely. Trenz cites the example of German tabloid papers being more inclined to emulate British tabloids – including copying their news – than the quality press in their own country. Other research does provide some support for Trenz's view (see Kevin 2003: chapter 11).

While the quality press may constitute an elite European communication space, there is less certainty about other media. De Vreese (2003) concludes that European affairs are 'modestly visible' on television news, the most important source of information, as well as the most preferred source for Europeans (Eurobarometer 2002). However, his analysis suggests that the 'European news story' is 'essentially a domestic story . . . [N]ot only is the majority of actors in "European news" from the country in which the news is broadcast, most of the news is also covered from a domestic angle and focuses on the implications of EU issues in the country of the news programme' (de Vreese 2003: 165). He comments that the 'absence of a

"European perspective" is striking'. The domestic slant to EU and European affairs in news is apparent in other research. For example, Heinderyckx (1993) found that journalists from several Western Europe news services turned to their own country's political leaders to make sense of the Maastricht summit. Some commentators argue that this national bias is on the wane. Weymouth and Lamizet identify a trend in media behaviour since the early 1980s, particularly observable in France and Germany, of growing complementarity in the reporting of the relationship between the EU and national governments. Previously the interests of Europe and national governments were represented as conflicting; 'they are now increasingly presented as complementary, possessing their own operational realms which are characterised by the specific requirements of a European, as opposed to a national order' (Weymouth and Lamizet 1996: 206). They argue that editors and reporters will no longer be able to ignore information related to European affairs, and the European perspective or dimension will figure more prominently in the daily routine of news selection. This argument may appear premature in light of the other obstacles faced by the news media in covering the EU and European affairs.

The trend identified by Weymouth and Lamizet is reflected by the growing resources devoted by national news organizations to covering the Brussels beat. Most European news organizations have permanent correspondents located in Brussels. The number of reporters deployed will vary according to evaluation of the political relevance of the beat; for example, Norway's decision to reject EU membership in 1994 saw a withdrawal of correspondents from Brussels (de Vreese 2003: 74). However, since the 1980s there has been a steady growth in the number of accredited correspondents in Brussels. By the early 1990s, more than 500 full-time correspondents were accredited (Morgan 1995: 324), rising to 800 by 2002, making it 'one of the biggest press corps in the world' today (Baisnée 2002: 198). This growth accompanies the increasing importance attached to news stories from Brussels. In his examination of the British press corps at Brussels, Morgan (1995: 334) records that 'most reporters claimed that Union news was being treated increasingly as important and being given the lead story position with greater frequency'. Interviews conducted in 1999 reported 'an impression that currently there are more stories about Europe and more areas of the news agenda that require a European angle' (Kevin 2003: 129). The growth of correspondents based in Brussels has ensured that pressure for the European dimension to certain news stories has grown. Nevertheless, there are many problems in obtaining EU stories or getting across a European dimension to stories in the news.

Reporting the European Union

Reporting the EU for many Brussels correspondents is a frustrating experience. British reporters have complained about the confusion in the commission's communications policy, citing the rivalries between the directorates, who are seen as having their own news policies, and between commissioners (Morgan 1995: 324). These rivalries are sometimes played out in national terms and they are promoted via the press corps of member states. While there may be greater divisions and differences of opinion within the EU, internal rivalries and internecine conflict should be seen as part of any governmental process. Where perhaps the

EU falls down compared to national governments is in its inability to get its message across. Journalists complain about the commission's weaknesses in communicating with the media. One issue is the difficulty in accessing information, with the EU labelled as a 'very closed organisation for journalists' (Kevin 2003: 122). Morgan (1995) identifies tensions between reporters and officials, particularly information officers. These may concern issues of access to the EU institutions and the quality of press officers, but as often as not they emanate from different cultural approaches to the process of communication. Reporters refer to the different national styles of handling information (Morgan 1995: 326). One correspondent compared the Irish with the Dutch, the former being inclined to leak information before major decisions, while the latter would officially give details to reporters. On the whole, press officers from the larger countries were seen as less forthcoming. Matters are further compounded by the complexity and slow pace of the EU decision-making process, which are identified as 'major obstacles to the reporting on European and EU politics' (Kevin 2003: 123). Journalists also complain about having to learn what they call 'Eurospeak', the particular terminology and language used in the EU (Morgan 1995: 332; de Vreese 2003: 66; Kevin 2003: chapter 8).

Studies of the EU's information policy identify a 'communication deficit' in dealing with the media. Tumber (1995) describes the efforts of the EU in the wake of the Maastricht Treaty to improve its media relations. The treaty itself recognized the problem of a lack of 'openness' in the working of EU institutions and made some provision for improving the dissemination of information. It also 'unleashed' reports on the future of information and communication policy, which spawned conflicting ideas about the way in which policy should develop. A code of conduct, drawn up to encourage access and bring the EU closer to the peoples of Europe, included a number of exclusion clauses which made putting it into practice problematic. Meyer (1999) highlighted this, finding the commission's public and media relations 'poor and incompetent'. He accounts for this in terms of a 'pervading technocratic mindset', 'inadequate staffing' and 'fragmented political authority'.

External obstacles to reporting Europe are mirrored by internal constraints. Studies of the Brussels press corps identify the problems the beat has with the home office. Correspondents have to struggle with home editors to get pieces accepted and then they only appear after much rewriting. One editor estimates he rejects more than three-quarters of the stories pitched to him about Europe (de Vreese 2003: 667). British reporters talk of the need in reporting the EU to 'overcome more than the normal scepticism amongst UK editors' (Morgan 1995: 325). Editors' resistance to EU news is a product of two primary factors: their perception of the audience's lack of interest in such stories and the problems of making the story interesting and comprehensible. European integration is seen as a 'dull' subject because of the difficulty in making somewhat abstract topics, such as tax harmonization, structural funds and the Common Agricultural Policy (CAP), newsworthy. Such issues 'do not supply editors with personalities, arguments and headlines' and fail to catch the public's interest (Kevin 2003: 124). Certain EU events do attract coverage. Summits are more newsworthy because of the 'heightened drama' that pervades them, with clashes between politicians attracting 'more than 3000 journalists from around the world [who] usually travel in the wake of European Council summits' (Norris 2000a: 188). Unlike much of the EU business, these summits satisfy the news media's criteria for newsworthiness by providing drama, spectacle and the ability to personalize the issues. Lack of personalization of much of what the EU does is an obstacle to gaining coverage. Declining participation in Euro-elections is one indicator that reinforces news practitioners' perception that their audience is not interested in European affairs. Sensitivity to audience tastes, particularly in broadcasting, has grown with the commercialization of Europe's media. It is central to the ratings game, and European affairs are not high on the agenda of 'sexy' subjects. Under a more public service tradition, greater emphasis could be placed by Europe's news media on educating and informing people about the EU and its activities (Semetko et al 2000: 127).

The national slant to much of the coverage of the EU and European affairs can be explained by the need to 'sell' Europe to editors and audiences. Journalists interviewed by Kevin (2003: 127) point out that 'levels of coverage are . . . dependent on the relevance for the national debate'. A similar finding emerges from de Vreese's study (2003: 71) of TV reporters, who stress the importance of 'domestic relevance' in the selection of EU news. Providing a national angle to EU issues and activities allows reporters to personalize stories by giving them a familiar face – hence the focus on the impact of policies on national institutions and activities, national members of the European Parliament and home commissioners. The extent to which there is a 'nationalization' of EU news varies from country to country. Baisnée (2002: 124–6) compares British and French news reporting. The 'national filter' appears to be more of a factor with the British press due to Europe being 'deeply embedded in national political debate', and the 'fiercest struggles between and within mainstream parties' being over European issues. The Euro-sceptic inclination of most British newspapers reinforces the national perspective. In France a greater political consensus over Europe has developed in the last couple of decades and arguments over fundamental principles about EU membership hardly occur, enabling correspondents to take a more 'European' approach to reporting the EU.

Images of the European Union

Coverage of the EU and European affairs tends to focus on certain issues and activities. The themes of the coverage vary from country to country, but there are some similarities worth stressing. Much of the reporting is on economic, financial and business affairs. Such stories are 'a fundamental part of European media coverage' (Kevin 2003: 107). Gavin (2000) found that much of the news coverage of economic matters in the United Kingdom was related to EU policies, with Europe accounting for 18 per cent of the economic news coverage on ITN and BBC. He concludes that news about Europe is 'persistent and significant' and a 'recurrent and visible' aspect of economic coverage on the main British TV news bulletins (Gavin 2000: 261). Research in Spanish news coverage in the early 1990s found that 8 per cent of the news analysed concerned economic integration, the euro and the European budget (cited in Kevin 2003: 101). Examination of Danish, British and Dutch television news found that economic topics are the main ingredient of EU news (de Vreese 2003).

'Bad news' stories also pervade EU coverage. In her study of the content of press and television coverage of the EU, Norris (2000a: chapter 9) found that overall the coverage 'proved anti-Europe'. Somewhat surprisingly, the 'tone of television news proved consistently more negative towards Europe than that of the press' (Norris 2000a: 197). However, both press and TV produced a 'steady diet of "bad news"', which in the case of the British press was supplemented by a 'series of headlines about mythical Brussels demands to introduce straight bananas, ban British bangers and outlaw Women's Institute jam' (Norris 2000a: 206, 199). De Vreese (2003: 117) identifies 'a strong presence of conflict' – 'between countries, within parties and between EU institutions' – shaping the presentation of news about European integration on Danish, Dutch and British television.

Negative news certainly typifies the British media coverage of the EU and European affairs. Gavin (2000) notes that 'negative stories' dealing with topics such as the beef wars and quota squabbles tend to outweigh 'good news', such as subsidies for ailing British industries in British television coverage of the European economy. Anderson and Weymouth (1999) found that scepticism pervades much of the British press coverage of the EU, which is exaggerated and stereotyped in its coverage, with notable exceptions, such as the *Financial Times* and the *Guardian*. Brussels bureaucrats are regularly disparaged in the tabloid press as 'faceless, boring "pen pushers"', who 'harbour dangerous views about further European integration' and are generally framed as '"dreamers" not "doers" – at best a misguided and, at worst, malign influence on Britain' (Gavin 2001: 305–6). Studies of the news coverage of specific issues also highlight an anti-EU bias and negativity towards Europe in the British press. Brookes (1999) describes how 'stereotypes of European politics and culture were easily identifiable in British press coverage of the BSE/CJD crisis', which was primarily organized around the theme of the British national community 'under threat'.

Two key European stories of the 1990s were the introduction of the euro and the war in Kosovo. These two events were European stories in that they involved a strong European dimension, had profound implications for the continent and called for action on a European-wide basis. The ways in which these major stories were reported in the European media enables some comparisons with the routine reporting of Europe in the national media, the reporting of particular events or issues and the coverage of particular institutions. The decision to withdraw national money and replace it with European banknotes and coins was a major step forward in the process of European integration. Coverage of the introduction of the euro was found to be more than simply pro- or anti-Europe. The event was of 'incontestable importance' and 'involved potentially a wide set of issues', which went beyond matters of economic development to the heart of national sovereignty as a consequence of its political impact and symbolic value (Triandafyllidou 2003). The visibility of the arrival of the European currency varied between countries and media. Coverage on television news in Denmark and Britain (which did not adopt the euro) and the Netherlands indicates that the launch of the euro was 'entirely event driven', with references to the topic 'virtually absent until a week before the introduction' and vanishing from the news within a week of the launch (de Vreese 2003: 90–1). In addition, the launch was reported primarily from a 'domestic perspective focusing on reactions in the country of the news outlet' (de Vreese 2003: 111). While national actors did appear more frequently in the coverage, some stories did contain EU actors and an exploration of the reactions of EU institutions, particularly the European Central Bank. Unlike the routine coverage of Europe, the TV reporting of the launch of the euro in these countries appeared to focus less on conflict and more on how people were affected in economic terms. This is attributed to the smooth introduction of the currency – none of the predicted stock market crashes occurred – and the lack of domestic debate in the three countries for different reasons (de Vreese 2003: 112).

British press coverage was more critical, with 45.8 per cent of the stories in the year leading up to the euro launch being negative (Werner 2002: 226). The British press carried five times as many negative stories as the German press. This can be seen in terms of the press reflecting national feelings – political and popular – about European affairs and the euro. The German press concentrated on updating their readers on the financial and economic aspects of the launch as there was less public concern with the broader implications of the new currency. The British press used the launch to engage in the broader debate about Britain's position in Europe. What is interesting in relation to the differences between Anglo-American and European journalism and news styles is that the British press was more opinionated and less fact oriented than their German counterparts. German newspapers reported the euro launch in a factual and neutral style. While the German press used the 'hard news angle 74 per cent of the time', the British covered the story with feature stories and commentaries and columns 'as much as hard news' (Werner 2002: 226). The lack of debate about the euro in the German press was not replicated in the press of other pro-Europe countries. Italian newspapers and broadcasting have been consistently pro-EU, but their coverage of the launch of the euro was 'less homogeneous than might have been expected' (Triandafyllidou 2003: 257, 260). Divisions appeared between right-wing and regionalist and centre-left media, the former emphasizing the economic development and the latter representing the euro as a 'political, historical and symbolic event that confirmed the will of the member states to form a common transnational entity' (Triandafyllidou 2003: 261). The discourse of the right-wing press and TV stations accepted that the EU and Italy were entangled in the economic realm, but separated them out in the political and social domain, while left-wing media stressed the Europeanness of Italian identity and highlighted 'the specific national contribution of Italy to European integration' (Triandafyllidou 2003: 260).

The war in Kosovo, which brought an end to 50 years of peace in Europe, was not only a major story that came to dominate news agendas in Europe's media, but also a complex crisis which provided an opportunity to examine notions of Europe and European identity. One crucial aspect was the extent to which the war was seen as a common European problem, which should be resolved by some form of unified response from the nation states of Europe. The extent to which debate about the development of a common European foreign and security policy was reported differed between national media systems. It was an 'important part of Italian news coverage' while being 'completely absent' in the UK media (Kevin 2003: 91). Grundmann et al. (2000) identified from their study of three leading quality papers that there had been a 'synchronisation' of public attention across EU member states. The quality press focused the attention of their reading public to the same issue at the same time. This was not, however, enough to produce a common public sphere for discussing the war, due to the 'marked differences in the attention and framing of issues' (Grundmann et al. 2000: 306). Difference in the content and perspectives adopted in the British, French and German newspapers that were analysed were 'dictated by national contexts and national agendas'.

Nevertheless, the coverage of the war did highlight Europe's relations with the USA. NATO, as the main body for coordinating international action against Serbia, was a site of struggle between Europe and the USA, with some newspapers and TV commentaries reporting or expressing concern about Europe's 'weakness as a coherent military force', playing 'second fiddle to the US' (quoted in Kevin 2003: 95; see also Grundmann et al. 2000). As the significant 'other' in the construction of European identity, the coverage of the USA in the Kosovo war could have been illuminating. Some news stories 'did differentiate between "Europe" . . . and the US' (Kevin 2003: 97). In one or two countries the 'Us and Them' rhetoric took on a more acute sense of difference between the two continents. The reporting of America in general in the European media is described as presenting the EU as a 'reassuring counterforce against the US' (Venturelli 2005). Coverage of the USA in the European media after the Second World War 'did not take the form of objective reporting' and since September 11th it has been given a 'new and rancorous' life. Modern European media, in particular public service television, are accused of double standards in reporting EU and US actions. 'Whereas EU actions are generally framed as rational and benign, American power is portrayed as guided by savage individualism, Darwinian capitalism, arrested cultural development and raw military force' (Venturelli 2005: 90). While there is little empirical evidence to support such claims, and the bulk of the research considered in this chapter concludes that the reporting of the EU is far from benign, the coverage of the USA in the European media would provide us with an interesting test of whether there is a common discourse that pervades the European media. Unfortunately, there is hardly any research on the subject.

Research provides us with a particular set of images of the EU and European affairs in the European media. In most national media systems there is minimal attention paid to the EU, which many see as a product of the inability of the EU to communicate effectively. Changes since Maastricht and, in particular, the shock of losing the Danish referendum in 1994 have led the union to attempt to overcome the 'communication deficit'. While there have been some improvements, and some parts of the union have become better at communicating than others – for example, the European Parliament – overcoming the deficit will not happen without change to key aspects of the EU's decision-making structure and institutional set-up. Much of the coverage of the EU is about 'bad' news, conflict and scandals. Reporting what the EU does for individuals and nation states is less apparent. Negative coverage of the EU and EU affairs is not necessarily explained by hostility to European integration or the European ideal. De Vreese (2003: 118) argues that the bias in the reporting is not necessarily 'anti-EU', but 'anti-politics'. He did not find 'any discernible differences in the pattern of evaluation' between EU actors and domestic political actors in EU coverage. It is possible to locate the reporting of European affairs in the context of the general negativity and malaise that pervades the reporting of and public attitudes towards politics.

Fictional Europe

Our picture of Europe is not only created by the news media. Fictional and entertainment media, such as film, soap operas and reality television, are intimately bound up with the way in which Europe is represented. Research highlights what is apparent in the TV schedules: that fictional programming is 'the most important category on European television', with commercial channels broadcasting twice as much fiction as public service stations (de Bens and de Smaele 2001: 54). In 2003 entertainment represented 39 per cent of the programmes with the highest ratings in Western Europe, an increase of nearly 5 per cent on the data for 2000 (Eurodata 2004). Films and series are the two main categories that make up the fictional output of European television. In recent years new formats such as 'reality television' – which include programmes such as *Pop Idol, Survivor, I'm A Celebrity: Get Me Out Of Here!* and *The Farm* – have become the driving force behind the growing popularity of entertainment.

The arrival of reality television has been a pan-European phenomenon. One programme that highlights this perhaps more than any other is *Big Brother*. *Big Brother* is labelled a 'gamedoc' as it brings together the ordinary everyday life of documentary TV with the competitive edge of a game show. The show was devised by the Dutch entertainment company Endemol and first broadcast in the Netherlands in 1999, achieving considerable ratings success (Hill 2002: 325). Within the next 18 months versions of the show were being broadcast in 12 countries: Norway, France, Portugal, Denmark, Poland, Germany, Italy, Spain, Switzerland, Britain, Belgium and the Netherlands (Tincknell and Raghuram 2002: 201). Ratings success has accompanied the introduction of the programme in every country. For example, in Germany the company that broadcast the show, RTL 2, a small TV station, increased its share of the audience from 3.9 per cent to 15 per cent for the second series, while in Portugal, TV 1, whose average share of the audience stood at 9 per cent, lifted its share to a staggering 50 per cent by broadcasting *Big Brother* (Hill 2002: 325). Only in Sweden was the ratings success not replicated. The ability of *Big Brother* to deliver large audiences was not the only factor that ensured it would be picked up by television stations across Europe and beyond. It is cheaper to produce than more traditional programming: an hour of *Big Brother* is four times cheaper than a sitcom (Sinclair 2004). It also offers 'multiplatform content', in that viewers will use other media, such as the internet and telecommunications, to interact with the programme. The reception of *Big Brother* was accompanied by similar debates about its quality and value in the countries where it was broadcast. The programme has attracted controversy, moral outrage and the charge of lowering of standards everywhere (Mathijs 2002; Bell 2001).

That Europeans are watching similar kinds of programmes in large numbers is seen as an indication of the emergence of a common European television culture. The recycling of formats such as *Big Brother* and *Who Wants To Be A Millionaire?* contributes to the construction of a common space for viewing. The same Endemol shows turn up in different guises in many European countries today (Gapper 1999). Adapting formats is not always straightforward; for example, audiences in different countries vary in their expectations about how long a programme should last. Adjusting to the local culture is vital as there is a strong demand from European audiences for products which have a local affinity. As Buonanno (2000: 25) notes of fictional programming such as serials, drama and soaps, 'unyielding local particularities . . . hinder the crossing of national frontiers on the part of the European national product'. Attempts to produce fictional material that is cross-national in its appeal have not met with much success. Pan-European cooperation to produce series such as *Eurocops* or soap operas such as *El Dorado*, which the BBC made in Spain, have not had much success. Formats for game shows, reality television and quizzes have travelled better. Research has shown a growing similarity to the fiction output produced in five leading markets for domestic fiction in Europe: Germany, Britain, Spain, France and Italy. In terms of plot, character, location and environment, there is a developing convergence which is 'rendering a part of domestic production of different European countries more open to and better accepted by the rest of Europe' (Buonanno 2000: 26).

The problem is that much of the fictional and entertainment output of European television is American-made or based on American formats. US products have always been popular in Europe. Examination of the quantity of US films and series on European television in the late 1990s found that 72 per cent of the films and series broadcast by commercial channels and 40 per cent of those broadcast by public service channels are American in origin (de Bens and de Smaele 2001: 57). In prime time, when most people watch, this proportion declines slightly, with national fiction increasing. The hold US entertainment programmes have over the schedule is more significant in smaller countries than in the larger European television markets of France, Britain, Germany and Italy, where national products account for between 12 and 27 per cent of all fiction broadcast in prime time. The dominance of US films and series corresponds with the marginal presence of material from other European countries. Non-national European material only accounts for 13.5 per cent of films and series shown on national European television. Major differences are apparent between European nations, from a total absence of series from other European countries on all British television to a third on the Walloon public channels (de Bens and de Smaele 2001: 64). In spite of the efforts of the EU to bolster national drama and comedy production, the introduction of a quota system and the growth of the amount of broadcasting hours arising from the boom in TV channels, the hold that American films and series have over the European audience has not waned in the last decade. Hollywood today not only dominates European film screens, but also European television entertainment (see chapter 5).

The omnipresence of US fiction on European television is seen as undermining cultural diversity in European programming (de Bens 1998). What has been referred to as the 'Dallasification' of television content is occurring with a consequent impact on national identities in Europe. European audiences say they want more home-grown material and Europe's broadcasters are trying to produce more of this. However, the economic reality of having to fill more airtime and the high cost of producing domestic drama and fiction means that Europe's TV channels, especially the commercial broadcasters, have to rely on cheap imported material from the US (see chapter 3). In recent years there has been an increase in European production of TV fiction, but it is the case that many of the domestic series produced are adaptations of American, or sometimes Australian, formats; for example, there are German and Dutch versions of the Australian soap *The Restless Years* (Moran 1998). National fiction is seen as playing a crucial role in the promotion of identity and culture (see, for example, Franco 2001; Koukoutsaki 2003; Dhoest 2004). American programming, it is argued, undermines such efforts through a process of cultural homogenization. As significant is the barrier it lays down to the circulation of European fiction within Europe. It is estimated that 80 per cent of television programmes made in Europe do not leave their country of origin (de Bens et al. 1992). Europeans are watching very little of what is produced in neighbouring countries, which not only prevents the development of the media industries, but also impedes the development of cultural and social awareness within Europe. There is, however, a paradox in the popularity of US shows in Europe. Many Americans would not recognize the kind of US programmes that attain ratings success in Europe. Often what makes it in Europe is not current or representative of US television culture. Popular American shows in Europe are often outdated, very old or were never widely popular in the US (Carroll 2001). Like US channels, formats and programmes are adapted to local conditions. Anglo-American television is not adopted uniformly across Europe, having to negotiate national tastes and identities which still reign supreme.

A European media sphere?

The research that has been carried out into the factual and fictional output of Europe's media indicates that national perspectives still shape what is reported and represented about Europe. While we may read, hear and see more about Europe and events that are happening across the continent, national frames of references still predominate. Sport and advertising have an increasingly distinct European feel. Major sporting events on TV offer an experience to be shared among a large number of people. It is possible to see the Champions League and the European Football Championship as an opportunity to promote European awareness. However, research shows how the coverage of such events reinforces national stereotypes, often replaying the same old national rivalries that have characterized European history (for example, see Blain, Boyle and O'Donnell 1993). TV, magazine and even newspaper advertising is appearing to conform as identical products are represented in the same or similar adverts across Europe. Even language is crossing borders; for example, car ads in French, Spanish or English can be heard in most European countries. However, in spite of the economic pressure for standardization, Snyder et al. (1991) found in their examination of the content of magazine advertisements in France, Germany, Britain and the Netherlands, between 1953 and 1989, that there was only a limited use of pan-European symbols. Like factual and fictional media, advertising and sport show the same in-built tendency to adhere to national symbols, perspectives and approaches. Changes which have seriously undermined the media's national foundations, as well as the concerted efforts of the EU to develop strategies to engineer Europeanization, have not shifted the national outlooks of Europe's media. Europe's media have only made a limited contribution to advancing European culture, promoting European understanding and fostering a European identity. While technically feasible and politically sought after, pan-European television channels have not grown significantly. There is still little sign – perhaps with the exception of the quality press – that pan-European susceptibilities are developing. It is possible to argue that EU media policy is bringing about the opposite to what it states it is trying to achieve. Rather than promoting Europeanness, the strategy of liberalization is creating more commercial channels, which are dependent on American programming. Americanization may be the unintended consequence of television without frontiers in Europe.

Bibliography

Achille, Y. and Miege, B., 1994, 'The limits to the adaptation of European public service television', *Media, Culture and Society* 16: 31–46.

Alter, J., 1990, 'Prime Time Revolution', *Newsweek*, 8 January.

Altschull, H., 1995, *Agents of Power: The Media and Public Policy*, London: Longman.

Anderson, P. and Weymouth, A., 1999, *Insulting the Public? The British press and the European Union*, London: Longman.

Arie, S., 2004, 'Furore over "junk TV" puts heat on Berlusconi', *Guardian*, 28 February.

Baines, G., 1990, 'Beams fuel the flames', *Guardian*, 8 January.

Baisnée, O., 2002, 'Can political journalism exist at the EU level?' in Kuhn, R. and Neveu, E. (eds), *Political Journalism: New Challenges, New Practices*, London: Routledge.

Bakardjieva, M., 1995, 'The new media landscape in Bulgaria', *Canadian Journal of Communications* 20 (1).

Bakir, V., 1996, 'An identity for Europe? The role of the media', in Wintle, M. (ed.), *Culture and Identity in Europe*, Aldershot: Ashgate.

Bakke, M., 2000, 'Arts television: Questions of culture' in Wieten, J., Murdock, G. and Dahlgren, P. (eds), *Television Across Europe*, London: Sage.

Bangemann, M., 1994, *Europe and the Global Information Society: Recommendations to the European Council*, Brussels: European Commission.

Banks, J., 1996, *Monopoly Television: MTV's Quest to Control Music*, Boulder, CO: Westview Press.

Bardoel, J., 2002, 'The internet, journalism and public communication policies', *Gazette* 64: 501–11.

Bardoel, J., 1996, 'Beyond journalism: A profession between information society and civil society', *European Journal of Communication* 11: 283–302.

Barnett, S., 1997, 'New media, old problems: New technology and the political process', *European Journal of Communication* 12: 193–218.

Bechelloni, G., 1980, 'The journalist as political client' in Smith, A. (ed.), *Newspapers and Democracy*, Cambridge, MA: MIT Press.

Bek, M., 2004, 'Research note: Tabloidization of news media: An analysis of television news in Turkey', *European Journal of Communication* 19: 371–86.

Bell, E., 2001, 'In search of lofty principles', *Guardian*, 21 May.

Bertrand, C., 1998, 'Media quality control in the USA and Europe' in Stephenson, H. and Bromley, M. (eds), *Sex, Lies and Democracy: The Press and the Public*, London: Longman.

Blain, N., Boyle, R. and O'Donnell, H., 1993, *Sports and National Identity*, Leicester: Leicester University Press.

Blain, N. and Cere, R., 1995, 'Dangerous television: The TV a luce rossi phenomenon', *Media, Culture and Society* 17.

Blumler, J., 1992, 'New roles for public television in Western Europe: Challenges and prospects', *Journal of Communication* 42: 20–35.

Blumler, J. and Gurevitch, M., 1995, *The Crisis of Public Communication*, London: Routledge.

Bondanella, P., 2004, 'From Italian Neorealism to the Golden Age of Cinecitta' in Ezra, E. (ed.), *European Cinema*, Oxford: Oxford University Press.

Bondebjerg, I., 2004, 'Television and the European Union' in Sinclair, J. and Turner, G. (eds), *Contemporary World Television*, London: BFI.

Bondebjerg, I., 1996, 'Modern Danish television – after the monopoly era' in Bondebjerg, I. and Bono, F. (eds), *Television in Scandinavia: History, Politics and Aesthetics*, Luton: University of Luton Press.

Bondebjerg, I. and Bono, F. (eds), 1996, *Television in Scandinavia: History, Politics and Aesthetics*, Luton: University of Luton Press.

Bourdieu, P., 1998, *On Television and Journalism*, London: Pluto Press.

Bourdon, J., 2000, 'A history of European television news: From television to journalism, and back?', *Communications* 25: 61–84.

Boyle, M., 1994, 'Building a communicative democracy: the birth and death of citizen politics in East Germany', *Media, Culture and Society* 16: 183–215.

Boyle, M., 1992, 'The revolt of the Communist journalist: East Germany', *Media, Culture and Society* 14: 133–9.

Braithwaite, B., 1998, 'Magazines' in Briggs, A. and Cobley, P. (eds), *The Media: An Introduction*, London: Longman.

Brants, K., 2004, 'The Netherlands' in Kelly, M., Mazzoleni, G. and McQuail, D. (eds), *The Media in Europe*, London: Sage.

Brants, K., 1998, 'Who's afraid of infotainment?', *European Journal of Communication* 13: 315–37.

Brants, K. and Neijens, P., 1998, 'The infotainment of politics', *Political Communication* 15: 149–65.

Brants, K. and Siune, K., 1998, 'Politicisation in decline?' in McQuail, D. and Siune, K. (eds), *Media Policy: Convergence, Concentration and Commerce*, London: Sage.

Brants, K. and Siune, K., 1992, 'Public broadcasting in a state of flux' in Siune, K. and Truetzschler, W. (eds), *Dynamics of Media Politics*, London: Sage.

Broadcasting Research Unit, 1986, *The Public Service Idea in British Broadcasting*, London: BRU.

Bromley, M., 1997, 'The end of journalism? Changes in workplace practices in the press and broadcasting in the 1990s' in Bromley, M. and O'Malley, T. (eds), *A Journalism Reader*, London: Routledge.

Brookes, R., 1999, 'Newspapers and national identity: the BSE/CJD crisis and the British press', *Media, Culture and Society* 21: 247–63.

Buonanno, M., 2000, *Continuity and Change: Television Fiction in Europe*, Luton: University of Luton Press.

Burnett, R., 1996, *The Global Jukebox*, London: Routledge.

Bustamente, E., 1989, 'TV and public service in Spain: a difficult encounter', *Media, Culture and Society* 11: 67–87.

Carroll, M., 2001, 'American television in Europe: problematizing the notion of pop cultural hegemony', *Bad Subjects* 57, October, http://bad.eserver.org/issues/2001/57/carroll.html (accessed 15 June 2005).

Cassy, J., 2002, 'SOS MTV', *Guardian*, 25 November.

Catalbas, D., 2000, 'Broadcasting deregulation in Turkey: uniformity within diversity' in Curran, J. (ed.), *Media Organisations in Society*, London: Arnold.

Chalaby, J., 2003, 'Television for a new global order', *Gazette* 65 (6): 457–72.

Chalaby, J., 2002a, 'Transnational television in Europe: The role of Pan-European channels', *European Journal of Communication* 17 (2): 183–203.

Chalaby, J., 2002b, *The de Gaulle Presidency and the Media: Statism and Public Communications*, London: Palgrave.

Chalaby, J., 1998, *The Invention of Journalism*, London: Macmillan.

Chalaby, J., 1997, 'No ordinary press owners: press barons as a Weberian ideal type', *Media Culture and Society* 19: 621–41.

Chalaby, J., 1996, 'Journalism as an Anglo-American invention: A comparison of the development of French and Anglo-American journalism, 1830s–1920s', *European Journal of Communication* 11: 303–26.

Chalaby, J. and Segell, G., 1999, 'The broadcasting media in the age of risk', *New Media and Society* 1: 351–68.

Chomsky, N., 1989, *Necessary Illusions: Thought Control in Democratic Societies*, London: Pluto.

Collins, R., 2002, *Media and Identity in Contemporary Europe: Consequences of Global Convergence*, Exeter: Intellect.

Collins, R., 1999a, 'The European Union audiovisual policies of the UK and France' in Scriven, M. and Lecomte, M. (eds), *Television Broadcasting in Contemporary France and Britain*, London: Berghahn Books.

Collins, R., 1999b, 'European Union media and communication policies' in Stokes, J. and Reading, A. (eds), *The Media in Britain*, London: Macmillan.

Collins, R., 1997, 'Unity in diversity: The European single market in broadcasting and the audiovisual 1982–1994' in Stavridis, S., Mossialos, E., Morgan, R. and Machin, H. (eds), *New Challenges to the European Union: Policies and Policy-Making*, Aldershot: Dartmouth.

Commission of the European Communities, 1983, *Interim report. Realities and Tendencies in European Television*, Brussels.

Corcoran, F. and Preston, P. (eds), 1995, *Democracy and Communication in the New Europe: Change and Continuity in East and West*, New Jersey: Hampton Press.

Coste-Cerdan, N. and Minon, M., 1993, 'The media markets in Europe: Evolution between

1980 and 1991' in Institute of Media Economics, *Media Industry in Europe*, Luton: John Libbe.

Cozens, C., 2002, 'Italian TV drops Berlusconi opponents', *Guardian*, 26 June.

Culik, J., 2004, 'The Czech Republic' in Kelly, M., Mazzoleni, G. and McQuail, D. (eds), *The Media in Europe*, London: Sage.

Curran, J., 1996, 'Reform of public service broadcasting', *Janvost – The Public*, 3 (3).

Curran, J. and Park, M.-J., 2000, *De-Westernising Media Studies*, London: Routledge.

Curran, J., Douglas, A. and Whannel, G., 1980, 'The political economy of the human-interest story' in Smith, A. (ed.), *Newspapers and Democracy*, Cambridge, MA: MIT Press.

Dahlgren, P., 2000, 'Media and power in transition in Sweden' in Curran, J. and Park, M.-J. (eds), *De-Westernizing Media Studies*, London: Routledge.

Dahlgren, P. and Sparks, C., 1991, *Communication and Citizenship: Journalism and the Public Sphere*, London: Routledge.

Danan, M., 2000, 'French cinema in the era of media capitalism', *Media, Culture and Society* 22: 355–64.

Daremas, G. and Terzis, G., 2000, 'Televisualization of politics in Greece', *Gazette* 62: 117–32.

Davis, H., Hammond, P. and Nizamova, L., 1998, 'Changing identities and practices in post-Soviet journalism: The case of Tatarstan', *European Journal of Communication* 13 (1): 77–97.

DCMS (Department for Culture, Media and Sport), 2004, *New EU Media Programme 2007–13*, letter to stakeholders, June, www.culture.gov.uk (accessed 15 June 2005).

de Bens, E., 1998, 'Television programming: More diversity, more convergence?' in Brants, K., Hermes, J. and Van Zoonen, L. (eds), *The Media in Question*, London: Sage.

de Bens, E., 1991, 'Flanders in the spell of commercial television', *European Journal of Communication* 6: 235–44.

de Bens, E. and Mazzoleni, G., 1998, 'The media in the age of digital communication' in McQuail, D. and Siune, K. (eds), *Media Policy: Convergence, Concentration and Commerce*, London: Sage.

de Bens, E. and Østbye, H., 1998, 'The European newspaper market' in McQuail, D. and Siune, K. (eds), *Media Policy: Convergence, Concentration and Commerce*, London: Sage.

de Bens, E. and de Smaele, H., 2001, 'The inflow of American television fiction on European broadcasting channels revisited', *European Journal of Communication* 16: 51–76.

de Bens, E., Kelly, M. and Bakke, M., 1992, 'Television content: Dallasification of culture?' in Siune, K. and Truetzschler, W. (eds), *Dynamics of Media Politics*, London: Sage.

de Grazia, V., 1998, 'European cinema and the idea of Europe' in Nowell-Smith, G. and Ricci, S. (eds), *Hollywood and Europe*, London: BFI.

de Mateo, R., 2004, 'Spain' in Kelly, M., Mazzoleni, G. and McQuail, D. (eds), *The Media in Europe*, London: Sage.

de Mateo, R., 1997, 'Spain' in Østergaard, B. (ed.), *The Media in Western Europe*, London: Sage.

de Mateo, R., 1989, 'The evolution of the newspaper industry in Spain 1939–87', *European Journal of Communication* 4: 211–26.

de Moragas Spa, M., Garitaonandia, C. and Lopez, B. (eds), 1999, *Television on your Doorstep*, Luton: University of Luton Press.

de Smaele, H., 1999, 'The applicability of western media models on the Russian media system', *European Journal of Communication* 14: 173–89.

de Tarle, A., 1981, 'The press and the state in France' in Smith, A. (ed.), *Newspapers and Democracy*, Cambridge, MA: MIT Press.

Deuze, M., 2004, 'What is multimedia journalism', *Journalism Studies* 5: 139–52.

de Vreese, C., 2003, Framing Europe: *Television News and European Integration*, Amsterdam: Askant.

de Vries, B. and Zwaga, W., 1997, 'Legislators or interpreters? On the relationship between journalists and their readers', *Media, Culture and Society* 19: 67–81.

Dhoest, A., 2004, 'Negotiating images of the nation: the production of Flemish TV drama, 1953–89', *Media, Culture and Society* 26: 393–408.

Dickinson, M. and Street, S., 1985, *Cinema and State: The Film Industry and the British Government 1927–84*, London: BFI.

Djerf-Pierre, M., 2000, 'Squaring the circle: public service and commercial news on Swedish television 1956–99', *Journalism Studies* 1: 239–60.

Donsbach, W. and Klett, B., 1993, 'Subjective objectivity: How journalists in four countries define a key term in the profession', *Gazette* 51: 53–83.

Donsbach, W. and Wenzel, A., 2002, Publizistik Heft 4: 373–87, quoted in Russ-Mohl, S., 2003, *Neue Zurcher Zeitung*, 14 February.

Downing, J., 1996, *Internationalizing Media Theory: Transition, Power, Culture*, London: Sage.

Downing, J., 1995, 'Media, dictatorship and the re-emergence of "civil society"' in Downing, J., Mohammadi, A. and Sreberny-Mohammadi, A. (eds), *Questioning the Media: A Critical Introduction*, London: Sage.

Druker, J., 2001, 'Naked bodies, runaway ratings' in Giles, R., Snyder, R. and DeLisle, L. (eds), *Reporting the Post-Communist Revolution*, New Jersey: Transaction Publishers.

Drummond, P., Paterson, R. and Willis, J. (eds), 1993, *National Identity and Europe: The Television Revolution*, London: BFI.

Dudrah, R., 2002, 'Zee TV-Europe and the construction of pan-European South Asian identity', *Contemporary South Asia* 11: 163–81.

Economist, 2002, 'Power in your hand: A survey of television', 18 April.

Eide, M., 1997, 'A new kind of newspaper? Understanding a popularization process', *Media, Culture and Society* 19: 173–82.

Ekecrantz, J., 1988, 'The rise and fall of national news in Sweden', *Media, Culture and Society* 10: 197–207.

Ellis, F., 1998, 'The media as social engineer' in Kelly, C. and Shepherd, D. (eds), *Russian Cultural Studies: An Introduction*, Oxford: Oxford University Press.

Esser, F., 1999, '"Tabloidization" of news: A comparative analysis of Anglo-American and German press journalism', *European Journal of Communication* 14: 291–324.

Esser, F., 1998, 'Editorial structures and work principles in British and German newspapers', *European Journal of Communication* 13: 375–405.

Esser, F., Reinemann, C. and Fan, D., 2000, 'Spin doctoring in British and German election campaigns: How the press is being confronted with a new quality of political PR', *European Journal of Communication* 15: 209–39.

Eurobarometer, 2002, 'Europeans' participation in cultural activities', European Commission, April.

Eurodata, 2004, 'Reality television: The end of a story or a new lease of life?', press release, 2 July.

European Audiovisual Observatory, 2003, *World Film Market Trends*, Strasbourg: Cannes Market.

European Federation of Journalists, 2003 (2002), *European Media Ownership: Threats on the Landscape*, Brussels, September.

European Music Office, 1996, *Music in Europe*, Brussels: EMO.

Everett, W., 1996, *European Identity in Cinema*, Exeter: Intellect.

Ezra, E. (ed.), 2004, *European Cinema*, Oxford: Oxford University Press.

Financial Times, 2002, 'Making the wrong headlines', 25 November.

Findahl, O., 1989, 'Language in the age of satellite communication', *European Journal of Communication* 4: 133–59.

Finney, A., 1996, *The State of European Cinema: A New Dose of Reality*, London: Cassell.

Fisk, R., 2002, 'Imagine if Blair tried to force Paxman off air. In Italy that sort of thing is about to happen', *Independent*, 5 June.

Forbes, J. and Street, S., 2000, *European Cinema: An Introduction*, Basingstoke: Palgrave.

Forgacs, D. and Lumley, R., 1996, *Italian Cultural Studies: An Introduction*, Oxford: Oxford University Press.

Fortunati, L., 2005, 'Mediatization of the net and internetization of the mass media', *Gazette* 67: 27–44.

Franco, J., 2001, 'Cultural identity in the community soap', *European Journal of Cultural Studies* 4: 449–72.

Franklin, B., 1997, *Newszak*, London: Arnold.

Gapper, J., 1999, 'Selling soap to Europe's viewers', *Financial Times*, 15 January.

Garitaonandia, C., 1993, 'Regional television in Europe', *European Journal of Communication* 8: 277–94.

Gavin, N., 2001, 'British journalists in the spotlight: Europe and media research', *Journalism* 2: 299–314.

Gavin, N., 2000, 'Imaging Europe: Political identity and British television coverage of the European economy', *British Journal of Politics and International Relations* 2: 352–73.

Gifreu, J., 1996, 'Linguistic order and spaces of communication in the post-Maastricht Europe', *Media, Culture and Society* 18: 127–39.

Giles, R., Snyder, R. and DeLisle, L., 2001, *Reporting the Post-Communist Revolution*, New Jersey: Transaction Publishers.

Gilson, Y., 2002, 'Europe and regional media: a two way street', European Journalism Centre, www.ejc.nl (accessed 15 June 2005).

Ginsborg, P., 2004, *Silvio Berlusconi: Television, Power and Patrimony*, London: Verso.

Glover, J., 1995, 'Factions and fiction', *Guardian*, 27 February.

Gott, R., 1990, 'A headache after the party', *Guardian*, 26 February.

Graffy, J., 1998, 'Cinema' in Kelly, C. and Shepherd, D. (eds), *Russian Cultural Studies: An Introduction*, Oxford: Oxford University Press.

Graham-Holm, N., 1999, *American Influence on Danish Journalism*, Center for Journalistik og Efteruddannelse, Danmarks Journalisthojskole.

Grantham, B., 2000, *Some Big Bourgeois Brothel: Contexts for France's Culture Wars with Hollywood*, Luton: University of Luton Press.

Grisold, A., 1996, 'Press concentration and media policy in small countries: Austria and Ireland compared', *European Journal of Communication* 11: 485–509.

Gross, P., 2003, 'New relationships: Eastern European media and the post-communist political world', *Journalism Studies* 4: 79–89.

Gross, P., 2002, 'Media and political society in Eastern Europe', *Media Development* 1: 28–32.

Grundle, S., 1997, 'Television in Italy' in Cornford, J. and Rollet, B. (eds), *Television in Europe*, Exeter: Intellect.

Grundmann, R., Smith, D. and Wright, S., 2000, 'National elites and transnational discourses in the Balkan War: A comparison between French, German and British establishment press', *European Journal of Communication* 15: 299–300.

Gulyas, A., 2003, 'Print media in post-communist East Central Europe', *European Journal of Communication* 18: 81–106.

Gulyas, A., 2002, 'Democratisation and the mass media in post-communist Hungary', *Media Development* 1: 33–8.

Gustafsson, K. and Weibull, L., 1997, 'European newspaper readership. Structure and development', *The European Journal of Communication Research* 22: 249–74.

Habermas, J., 1989, *The Structural Transformation of the Public Sphere*, Cambridge: Polity Press (first published in German in 1962).

Hadenius, S. and Weibull, L., 1999, 'The Swedish newspaper system in the late 1990s', *The Nordicom Review* 20: 129–52.

Hagen, L., 1997, 'The transformation of the media system of the former German Democratic Republic after reunification and its effects on the political content of newspapers', *European Journal of Communication* 12: 5–26.

Hainsworth, P., 1994, 'Politics, culture and cinema in the new Europe' in Hill, J., McLoone, M. and Hainsworth, P. (eds), *Border Crossings: Film in Ireland, Britain and Europe*, London: BFI.

Halliday, J., Curry Jansen, S. and Schneider, J., 1992, 'Framing the crisis in Eastern Europe' in Raboy, M. and Dagenais, B. (eds), *Media, Crisis and Democracy*, London: Sage.

Hallin, D. and Mancini, P., 2004, *Comparing Media Systems*, Cambridge: Cambridge University Press.

Hallin, D. and Papathanassopoulos, S., 2002, 'Political clientelism and the media: southern Europe and Latin America in comparative perspective', *Media, Culture and Society* 24: 175–95.

Halloran, J., 1993, 'The European image: Unity in diversity – myth or reality?', *Media Development* 4, 25–9.

Hankiss, E., 1994, 'The Hungarian media's war of independence', *Media, Culture and Society* 16: 293–312.

Hardt, H., 1988, 'The accommodation of power and the quest for enlightenment: West Germany's press after 1945', *Media, Culture and Society* 10: 135–62.

Harris, O., Kolovos, I. and Lock, A., 2001, 'Who sets the agenda?: An analysis of agenda setting and press coverage of the 1999 Greek European elections', *European Journal of Marketing* 35: 1117–35.

Harris, S., 2004, 'The Cinema du Look' in Ezra, E. (ed.), *European Cinema*, Oxford: Oxford University Press.

Harrison, J. and Woods, L., 2001, 'Defining European public service broadcasting', *European Journal of Communication* 16: 477–504.

Harrison, J. and Woods, L., 2000, 'European citizenship: Can audio-visual policy make a difference?', *Journal of Common Market Studies* 38: 471–95.

Harvie, C., 1994, *The Rise of Regional Europe*, London: Routledge.

Hayward, S., 1993, *French National Cinema*, London: Routledge.

Heinderyckx, F., 1993, 'Television news programmes in Western Europe: A comparative study', *European Journal of Communication* 8: 425–50.

Hellman, H. and Sauri, T., 1994, 'Public service television and the tendency towards convergence: Trends in prime-time programme structure in Finland 1970–82', *Media, Culture and Society* 16: 47–71.

Hemels, J., 1997, 'Social contextualisation of the press: The Dutch case', *The European Journal of Communication Research* 22 (3): 317–41.

Henning, V. and Alpar, A., 2005, 'Public aid mechanisms in feature film production: The EU MEDIA Plus Programme', *Media, Culture and Society* 27 (2): 229–50.

Henry, G., 1989, 'Public convenience: European broadcasters want to present a unified front against deregulation', *Listener*, 6 April.

Herman, E. and Chomsky, N., 1989, *The Political Economy of the Mass Media*, New York: Pantheon.

Hibberd, M., 2001, 'The reform of public service broadcasting in Italy', *Media, Culture and Society* 23 (2) 233–52.

Hickethier, K., 1996, 'The media in Germany' in Weymouth, A. and Lamizet, B. (eds), *Markets and Myths: Forces for Change in the European Media*, London: Longman.

Hill, A., 2002, '*Big Brother*: The real audience', *Television and New Media* 3: 323–40.

Hill, J., 1996, 'British film policy' in Moran, A. (ed.), *Film Policy: International, National and Regional Perspectives*, London: Routledge.

Hill, J. and McLoone, M., 1996, *Big Picture, Small Screen: The Relations between Film and Television*, Luton: John Libbey.

Hill, J., McLoone, M. and Hainsworth, P., 1994, *Border Crossing: Film in Ireland, Britain and Europe*, London: BFI.

Hirsch, M. and Petersen, V., 1998, 'European policy options' in McQuail, D. and Siune, K. (eds), *Media Policy: Convergence, Concentration and Commerce*, London: Sage.

Hirsch, M. and Petersen, V., 1991, 'Regulation of media at the European level' in Siune, K. and Truetzschler, W. (eds), *Dynamics of Media Politics*, London: Sage.

Hjarvard, S., 1999, *TV-nyheder i konkurrence*, Copenhagen: Samfundslitteratur.

Hjarvard, S., 1993, 'Pan-European television news: Towards a European political public sphere' in Drummond, P., Paterson, R. and Willis, J. (eds), *National Identity and Europe*, London: BFI.

Hoffmann-Riem, W., 1991, 'The road to media unification: Press and broadcasting law reform in the GDR', *European Journal of Communication* 6: 523–43.

Hollstein, M., 1983, 'Media economics in Western Europe' in Martin, L.J. and Chaudhary, A. (eds), *Comparative Mass Media Systems*, London: Longman.

Holm, H.H., 1998, 'Journalism education in Denmark: The challenges of the market and politics', Arhus: Danmarks Journalisthojskole.

Holtz-Bacha, C., 1991, 'From public monopoly to a dual broadcasting system in Germany', *European Journal of Communication* 6: 223–33.

Holtz-Bacha, C., 1990, 'Videomalaise revisited: Media exposure and political alienation in West Germany', *European Journal of Communication* 5: 73–85.

Hood, S., 1972, *The Mass Media*, London: Macmillan.

Horvath, J., 1997, 'The changing face of the mass media in Eastern Europe', http://www.heise.de/tp/r4/artikel/1/1214/1.html (accessed 15 June 2005).

Høst, S., 1999, 'Newspaper growth in the television era: The Norwegian experience', *The Nordicom Review* 20 (1): 107–28.

Hujanen, T., 2000, 'Programming and channel competition in European television' in Wieten, J., Murdock, G. and Dahlgren, P. (eds), *Television Across Europe*, London: Sage.

Hulten, O., 2004, 'Sweden' in Kelly, M., Mazzoleni, G. and McQuail, D. (eds), *The Media in Europe*, London: Sage.

Humphreys, P., 1996, *Mass Media and Media Policy in Western Europe*, Manchester: Manchester University Press.

Humphreys, P., 1994, *Media and Media Policy in Germany: The Press and Broadcasting Since 1945*, Oxford: Berg.

Husband, C., 1993, 'Europe, media and identities: The European Community and ethnic minorities', *Media Development* 4: 17–19.

Hutton, W., 1994, 'Moguls on the podium', *Guardian*, 30 March.

Index on Censorship, 1994, *Media Moguls and Megalomania* 23, September/October.

International Federation of Journalists, 2002, European Media Ownership: Threats on the Landscape, Brussels: International Federation of Journalists, www.ifj.org (accessed 15 June 2005).

Iordanova, D., 1999, 'East Europe's cinema industries: Financing structure and studios', *Janvost – The Public* 6: 45–60.

Iorwerth, D., 1995, *A Week in Europe*, Cardiff: University of Wales Press.

Jackel, A., 2004, 'Cinema in Europe' in Briggs, A. and Cobley, P. (eds), *The Media: An Introduction*, London: Longman, 2nd edn.

Jackel, A., 2002, 'Cinema in Europe' in Briggs, A. and Cobley, P. (eds), *The Media: An Introduction*, London: Longman.

Jackel, A., 1999, 'Broadcasters' involvement in cinematographic co-productions' in Scriven,

M. and Lecomte, M. (eds), *Television Broadcasting in Contemporary France and Britain*, Oxford: Berghahn Books.

Jackel, A., 1997, 'Cultural co-operation in Europe: The case of British and French cinematographic co-production with Central and Eastern Europe', *Media, Culture and Society* 19: 111–20.

Jackel, A., 1996, 'European co-production strategies: The case of France and Britain' in Moran, A. (ed.), *Film Policy: International, National and Regional Perspectives*, London: Routledge.

Jakubowicz, K., 2004, 'Poland' in Kelly, M., Mazzoleni, G. and McQuail, D. (eds), *The Media in Europe*, London: Sage.

Jakubowicz, K., 2001, 'The genie is out of the bottle' in Giles, R., Snyder, R. and DeLisle, L., *Reporting the Post-Communist Revolution*, New Jersey: Transaction Publishers.

Jakubowicz, K., 1990, 'Broadcasting in post-communist Poland: blazing new trails or treading a well-worn path?', *Media Development* (4): 5–6.

Jakubowicz, K. and Jedrzejewski, S., 1988, 'Polish broadcasting: The choices ahead', *European Journal of Communication* 3: 91–111.

Jarvie, I., 1998, 'Free trade as a cultural threat: American film and TV exports in the post-war period' in Nowell-Smith, G. and Ricci, S. (eds), *Hollywood and Europe*, London: BFI.

Jarvie, I., 1992, *Holllywood's Overseas Campaign: The North Atlantic Movie Trade 1920–1950*, Cambridge: Cambridge University Press.

Jarvie, I., 1990, 'The post-war economic foreign policy of the American film industry: Europe 1945–50', *Film History* 4: 277–88.

Jarvie, I., 1988, 'Dollars and ideology: Will Hays' economic foreign policy 1922–45', *Film History* 2: 207–21.

Jeancolas, J., 1998, 'From the Blum-Byres Agreement to the GATT affairs' in Nowell-Smith, G. and Ricci, S. (eds), *Hollywood and Europe*, London: BFI.

Jenkins, B. and Spyros, S., 1996, *Nation and Identity in Europe*, London: Routledge.

Johnson, O., 2001, 'Power from the people' in Giles, R., Snyder, R. and DeLisle, L. (eds), *Reporting the Post-Communist Revolution*, New Jersey: Transaction Publishers.

Johnson, O., 1998, 'East Central and Southeastern Europe, Russia and the Newly Independent States' in Merrill, J. (ed.), *Global Journalism*, London: Longman, 3rd edn.

Jones, T., 2003, *The Dark Heart of Italy*, London: Faber and Faber.

Jurkowicz, M., 2004, 'Ideas in our heads: Introduction of PSB as part of media system change in Central and Eastern Europe', *European Journal of Communication* 19: 53–74.

Jurkowicz, M., 1992, 'Coming to terms with press freedom in the former USSR', *Media Development* 2: 24–7.

Kaposi, I., 2004, 'European media landscape – Hungary', European Journalism Centre, www.ejc.nl (accessed 15 June 2005).

Kascuba, W., 1993, 'Everyday culture' in Shelley, M. and Winck, M. (eds), *Aspects of European Cultural Diversity*, London: Routledge.

Katus, J. and Volmer, W.F., 2000, *Government Communication in the Netherlands: Backgrounds, Principles and Functions*, The Hague: Sdu Publishers, 2nd edn.

Kelly, M., 1983, 'Influences on broadcasting policies for election coverage' in Blumler, J. (ed.), *Communicating to Voters*, London: Sage.

Kelly, M., Mazzoleni, G. and McQuail, D. (eds), 2004, *The Media in Europe*, London: Sage.

Kepplinger, H.M. and Kocher, R., 1990, 'Professionalism in the media world?', *European Journal of Communication* 5: 285–311.

Kevin, D., 2003, *Europe in the Media: A Comparison of Reporting, Representation and Rhetoric in National Media Systems in Europe*, London: Lawrence Erlbaum Associates.

Kilborn, R., 1993, 'Towards Utopia – or another Anschluss? East Germany's transition to a new media system', *European Journal of Communication* 8: 451–70.

Kiss, B., 2004, 'Hungary' in Kelly, M., Mazzoleni, G. and McQuail, D. (eds), *The Media in Europe*, London: Sage.

Klein, U., 1998, 'Tabloidised political coverage in *Bild Zeitung*', *Janvost – The Public* 5: 80–93.

Kleinstuber, H., 2004, 'Germany' in Kelly, M., Mazzoleni, G. and McQuail, D. (eds), *The Media in Europe*, London: Sage.

Kleinstuber, H., 1998, 'The digital future' in McQuail, D. and Siune, K. (eds), 1998, *Media Policy: Convergence, Concentration and Commerce*, London: Sage.

Kleinstuber, H. and Weischenberg, S., 2001, 'The contradiction of journalism in Germany' in Tunstall, J. (ed.), *Media Occupations and Professions*, Oxford: Oxford University Press.

Kleinstuber, H., Rossmann, T. and Wisener, V., 1993, 'The mass media' in Shelley, M. and Winck, M. (eds), *Aspects of European Cultural Diversity*, London: Routledge.

Knee, J., 1998, *Visions of the Future*, Paris: World Association of Newspapers.

Koch, T., 1991, *Journalism in the Twenty-First Century: Online Information, Electronic Databases and the News*, Twickenham: Adamantine Press.

Kocher, R., 1986, 'Bloodhounds or missionaries: Role definitions of German and British journalists', *European Journal of Communication* 1: 43–64.

Koukoutsaki, A., 2003, 'Greek television drama: Production policies and genre diversification', *Media, Culture and Society* 25: 715–35.

Kuenzli, R., 2004, 'Dada and surrealist film' in Ezra, E. (ed.), *European Cinema*, Oxford: Oxford University Press.

Kuhn, R., 1995, *The Media in France*, London: Routledge.

Laborde, A. and Perrot, M., 2000, 'Programme-making across borders: The Eurosud news magazine' in Wieten, J., Murdock, G. and Dahlgren, P. (eds), *Television Across Europe*, London: Sage.

Labour Research, 1992, 'Media moguls take on Europe', *Labour Research*, 7–10 February.

Lamizet, B., 1996, 'The media in France' in Weymouth, A. and Lamizet, B. (eds), *Markets and Myths: Forces for Change in the European Media*, London: Longman.

Latouche, S., 1996, *The Westernisation of the World*, Cambridge: Polity Press.

Lee, A., 1976, *The Origins of the Popular Press 1855–1914*, London: Croom Helm.

Leroy, P. and Siune, K., 1994, 'European elections and television', *European Journal of Communication* 9: 47–70.

Levinson, P., 1997, *The Soft Edge: A Natural History and Future of the Information Revolution*, London: Routledge.

Looseley, D., 1995, *The Politics of Fun: Cultural Policy and Debate in Contemporary France*, Oxford: Berg.

Lopez, B., Risquete, J. and Castello, E., 1999, 'Spain: Consolidation of the autonomic system in the multichannel era' in de Moragas Spa, M., Garitaonandia, C. and Lopez, B. (eds), *Television on your Doorstep*, Luton: University of Luton Press.

Lowe, G.F. and Alm, A., 1997, 'Public service broadcasting as cultural industry: Value transformation in the Finnish market-place', *European Journal of Communication* 12: 169–91.

Lumley, R., 1996, 'Peculiarities of the Italian newspaper' in Forgacs, D. and Lumley, R. (eds), *Italian Cultural Studies: An Introduction*, Oxford: Oxford University Press.

Maarek, P., 1997, 'New trends in French political communication: The 1995 presidential elections', *Media, Culture and Society* 19: 357–68.

Macdonald, S., 1993, *Inside European Identities*, Oxford: Berg.

Machet, E., 1999, 'Ten years of the Television without Frontiers Directive', *Intermedia* 27 (3): 40–3.

Machill, M., 1998, 'Euronews: The first European news channel as a case study for media industry development in Europe and for spectra of transnational journalism research', *Media, Culture and Society* 20: 427–50.

Mancini, P., 2000, 'Political complexity and alternative models of journalism' in Curran, J. and Park, M.-J. (eds), *De-Westernising Media Studies*, London: Routledge, 265–78.

Mancini, P., 1993, 'Between trust and suspicion: How political journalists solve the dilemma', *European Journal of Communication* 8: 33–51.

Marlière, P., 1998, 'The rules of the journalistic field: Pierre Bourdieu's contribution to the sociology of the media', *European Journal of Communication* 13: 219–34.

Mathijs, E., 2002, '*Big Brother* and critical discourse: The reception of *Big Brother* Belgium', *Television and New Media* 3: 311–22.

Mattelart, A., 2000, *Networking the World 1794–2000*, Minneapolis, MN: University of Minnesota Press.

Mattelart, A. and Palmer, M., 1991, 'Advertising in Europe: Promises, pressures and pitfalls', *Media, Culture and Society* 13: 535–56.

Maxwell, R., 1995, *The Spectacle of Democracy: Spanish Television, Nationalism and Political Transition*, London: University of Minnesota Press.

Mazdon, L., 1999, 'Cinema and television: From enmity to interdependence' in Scriven, M. and Lecomte, M. (eds), *Television Broadcasting in Contemporary France and Britain*, London: Berghahn Books.

Mazzoleni, G., 1997, 'Italy' in Østergaard, B. (ed.), *The Media in Western Europe*, London: Sage.

Mazzoleni, G., 1995, 'Towards a "videocracy"? Italian political communication at a turning point', *European Journal of Communication* 10: 291–319.

Mazzoleni, G., 1991, 'Media moguls in Italy' in Tunstall, J. and Palmer, M., *Media Moguls*, London: Routledge.

Mazzoleni, G. and Palmer, M., 1992, 'The building of media empires' in Siune, K. and Truetzschler, W. (eds), *Dynamics of Media Politics*, London: Sage.

McCain, T. and Lowe, G.F., 1990, 'Localism in Western European radio broadcasting: Untangling the wireless', *Journal of Communication* 40: 86–99.

McGregor, B., 1997, *Live, Direct and Biased*, London: Arnold.

McLachlan, S. and Golding, P., 2000, 'Tabloidization in the British press: A quantitative investigation into changes in British newspapers, 1952–1997' in Sparks, C. and Tulloch, J. (eds), *Tabloid Tales*, Boston, MA: Rowman and Littlefield.

McLoone, M., 1996, 'Boxed in: The aesthetics of film and television' in Hill, J. and McLoone, M. (eds), *Big Picture, Small Screen: The Relations between Film and Television*, Luton: University of Luton Press.

McNair, B., 2001, 'Media professionals in the former Soviet Union' in Tunstall, J. (ed.), *Media Occupations and Professions*, Oxford: Oxford University Press.

McNair, B., 2000, 'Power, profit, corruption and lies: the Russian media in the 1990s' in Curran, J. and Park, M.-J. (eds), *De-westernising Media Studies*, London: Routledge.

McNair, B., 1988, *Images of the Enemy*, London: Routledge.

McQuail, D., 2004, 'Introduction' in Kelly, M., Mazzoleni, G. and McQuail, D., *The Media in Europe*, London: Sage.

McQuail, D., 1998, 'Commercialization and beyond' in McQuail, D. and Siune, K. (eds), *Media Policy: Convergence, Concentration and Commerce*, London: Sage.

McQuail, D., 1995, 'Western European media: The mixed model under threat' in Downing, J., Mohammadi, A. and Sreberny-Mohammadi, A. (eds), *Questioning the Media: A Critical Introduction*, London: Sage.

McQuail, D., 1990, 'Caging the beast', *European Journal of Communication* 3: 313–31.

McQuail, D. and Siune, K. (eds), 1998, *Media Policy: Convergence, Concentration and Commerce*, London: Sage.

Meier, W. and Trappel, J., 1998, 'Media concentration and the public interest' in McQuail, D. and Siune, K. (eds), *Media Policy: Convergence, Concentration and Commerce*, London: Sage.

Meyer, C., 1999, 'Political legitimacy and the invisibility of politics: Exploring the European Union's communication deficit', *Journal of Common Market Studies* 37: 613–40.

Miege, B. and Salaun, J.-M., 1989, 'France: a mixed system. Renovation of an old concept', *Media, Culture and Society* 11: 55–66.

Miller, D. and Dinan, W., 2000, 'The rise of the PR industry in Britain, 1979–98', *European Journal of Communication* 15: 5–35.

Miller, T., 1996, 'The crime of Monsieur Lang' in Moran, A. (ed.), *Film Policy: International, National and Regional Perspectives*, London: Routledge.

Miller, T., Govil, N., McMurria, J. and Maxwell, R., 2001, *Global Hollywood*, London: BFI.

Mills, A., 1994, 'Rules, rights and quotas – new European angles on the new media business', *Intermedia* 22: 7–9.

Molnar, P., 2001, 'Transforming Hungarian broadcasting' in Giles, R., Snyder, R. and DeLisle, L. (eds), *Reporting the Post-Communist Revolution*, New Jersey: Transaction Publishers.

Moran, A., 1998, *Copycat TV: Globalisation, Program Formats and Cultural Identity*, Luton: University of Luton Press.

Moran, A., 1996, *Film Policy: International, National and Regional Perspectives*, London: Routledge.

Morgan, D., 1995, 'British media and European Union news', *European Journal of Communication* 10: 321–43.

Morley, D. and Robins, K., 1995, *Spaces of Identity: Global Media, Electronic Landscapes and Cultural Boundaries*, London: Routledge.

Mortensen, F., 2004, 'Denmark' in Kelly, M., Mazzoleni, G. and McQuail, D. (eds), *The Media in Europe*, London: Sage.

Moynahan, B., 1984, 'French "BBC" plan misfires as politics makes a comeback', *Sunday Times*, 7 October.

Mulvey, L., 1998, 'New wave interchanges: Celine and Julie and Desperately Seeking Susan' in Nowell-Smith, G. and Ricci, S. (eds), *Hollywood and Europe*, London: BFI.

Murdock, G., 2000, 'Digital futures: European television in the age of convergence' in Wienten, J., Murdock, G. and Dahlgren, P. (eds), *Television Across Europe*, London: Sage.

Murschetz, P., 1998, 'State support for the daily press in Europe: A critical appraisal', *European Journal of Communication* 13: 291–313.

Negrine, R., 1998, 'Models of media institutions: Media institutions in Europe' in Briggs, A. and Cobley, P., eds, *The Media: An Introduction*, London: Longman.

Negrine, R. and Papathanassopoulos, S., 1991, 'The internationalization of television', *European Journal of Communication* 6: 9–32.

Negus, K., 1993, 'Global harmonies and local discords: Transnational policies and practices in the European recording industry', *European Journal of Communication* 8: 295–361.

Nelson, M., 2001, 'Business reporting in Eastern Europe' in Giles, R., Snyder, R. and DeLisle, L. (eds), *Reporting the Post-Communist Revolution*, New Jersey: Transaction Publishers.

Neveu, E., 2001, *Sociologie du journalisme*, Paris: Edition La Découverte.

Neveu, E., 1999, 'Politics on French television: Towards a renewal of political journalism and debate frames?', *European Journal of Communication* 14: 379–409.

Newton, K. and Artingstall, N., 1994, 'Government and private censorship in nine western democracies in the 1970s and 1980s' in Budge, I. and McKay, D. (eds), *Developing Democracy*, London: Sage.

Norris, P., 2000a, *A Virtuous Circle: Political Communication in Post-industrial Societies*, Cambridge: Cambridge University Press.

Norris, P., 2000b, 'The internet in Europe: A new north-south divide', *Press/Politics* 5: 1–12.

Nowell-Smith, G. (ed), 1989, *The European Experience*, London: BFI.

Nowell-Smith, G., 1998, 'Introduction' in Nowell-Smith, G. and Ricci, S., 1998, *Hollywood and Europe*, London: BFI.

Nowell-Smith, G. and Ricci, S., 1998, *Hollywood and Europe*, London: BFI.

Ognianova, E. and Scott, B., 1997, 'Milton's paradox', *European Journal of Communication* 12: 369–90.

Ornebring, H., 2003, 'Televising the public sphere: Forty years of current affairs debate programmes on Swedish television', *European Journal of Communication* 18: 501–27.

Østbye, H., 1997, 'Norway' in Euromedia Research Group, *The Media in Western Europe*, London: Sage.

Østergaard, B., 1998, 'Convergence: Legislative dilemmas' in McQuail, D. and Siune, K. (eds), *Media Policy: Convergence, Concentration and Commerce*, London: Sage.

O'Sullivan, J., 2005, 'Delivering Ireland: Journalism's search for a role online', *Gazette* 67: 45–68.

Owen, K., 1986, 'Chirac tears state TV apart', *New Statesman*, 22 August.

Pandovani, C. and Tracey, M., 2003, 'Report on the conditions of public service broadcasting television', *New Media* 4: 131–53.

Palmer, M., 2001, 'Journalists and media professionals in France', in Tunstall, J (ed.), *Media Occupations and Professions*, Oxford: Oxford University Press.

Papathanassopoulos, S., 2002, *European Television in the Digital Age*, London: Polity Press.

Papathanassopoulos, S., 2001a, 'The decline of newspapers: The case of the Greek press', *Journalism Studies* 2: 109–23.

Papathanassopoulos, S., 2001b, 'Media commercialization and journalism in Greece', *European Journal of Communication* 16: 505–21.

Papathanassopoulos, S., 1997, 'The politics and the effects of the deregulation of Greek television', *European Journal of Communication* 12: 351–68.

Papatheodorou, F. and Machin, D., 2003, 'The umbilical cord that was never cut: The post-dictatorial intimacy between the political elite and the mass media in Greece and Spain', *European Journal of Communication* 18: 31–54.

Parenti, M., 1992, *Make Believe Media: the Politics of Entertainment*, New York: St Martin's Press.

Parenti, M., 1986, *Inventing Reality*, New York: St Martin's Press.

Pells, R., 1997, *Not Like Us: How Europeans Have Loved, Hated and Transformed American Culture Since World War II*, New York: Basic Books.

Petersen, V. and Siune, K., 1997, 'Denmark' in Euromedia Research Group, *The Media in Western Europe*, London: Sage.

Petley, J. and Romano, G., 1993, 'After the deluge: Public service television in Western Europe' in Downmunt, T. (ed.), *Channels of Resistance: Global Television and Local Empowerment*, London: BFI/Channel Four Books.

Pfetsch, B., 1996, 'Convergence through privatisation? Changing media environments and televised politics in Germany', *European Journal of Communication* 11: 427–51.

Picard, R., 1996, 'The rise and fall of communication empires', *The Journal of Media Economics* 9: 23–40.

Pieterse, J., 1991, 'Fictions of Europe', *Race and Class* 32: 3–10.

Porter, V. and Hasselbach, S., 1991, 'Beyond balanced pluralism: Broadcasting in Germany' in Dahlgren, P. and Sparks, C. (eds), *Communication and Citizenship: Journalism and the Public Sphere*, London: Routledge.

Porter, W., 1983, *The Italian Journalist*, Ann Arbor, MI: University of Michigan Press.

Pottker, H., 2003, 'News and its communicative quality: The inverted pyramid – when and why did it appear?', *Journalism Studies* 4: 501–11.

Powrie, P., 2003, 'Cinema' in Dauncey, H. (ed.), *French Popular Culture*, London: Arnold.

Pritchard, T., 1990, 'Continental currents', *Listener*, 8 November.

Reporters Sans Frontiers, 2003, 'A media conflict of interest: Anomaly in Italy', report 23, April, www.rsf.org/article (accessed 15 June 2005).

Reporters Sans Frontiers, 2002, 'Broadcast making fun of Berlusconi is censored', press release, 11 October, www.rsf.org/article (accessed 15 June 2005).

Rieffel, R., 1984, *L'Élite des journalistes*, Paris: PUF.

Roberts, M. and Bantimaroudis, P., 1997, 'Gatekeepers in international news: The Greek media', *Press/Politics* 2: 62–76.

Robins, K., 1993, 'The politics of silence: The meaning of community and the uses of media in the new Europe', *New Formations* 21: 80–101.

Roe, K. and de Meyer, G., 2000, 'Music television: MTV-Europe' in Weiten, J., Murdock, G. and Dahlgren, P. (eds), *Television Across Europe*, London: Sage.

Rollet, E., 2001, 'Connecting to the information age: A challenge for the European Union', *Gazette* 65: 371–86.

Roncarolo, F., 2002, 'A crisis in the mirror: Old and new elements in Italian political communication' in Kuhn, R. and Neveu, E. (eds), *Political Journalism: New Challenges, New Practices*, London: Routledge.

Rooney, D., 2000, 'Thirty years of competition in the British tabloid press: The *Mirror* and the *Sun* 1968–98' in Sparks, C. and Tulloch, J. (eds), *Tabloid Tales*, Boston, MA: Rowman and Littlefield.

Rui Cadima, F. and Braumann, P., 1999, 'Portugal: Analysis and perspective of regional television' in de Moragas Spa, M., Garitaonandia, C. and Lopez, B. (eds), *Television on your Doorstep*, Luton: University of Luton Press.

Russ-Mohl, S., 2001, 'Wall fall profits, wall fall losses' in Giles, R., Snyder, R. and DeLisle, L. (eds), *Reporting the Post-Communist Revolution*, New Jersey: Transaction Publishers.

Ruston, U., 1991, 'Romania: Lost planet in the Gutenberg galaxy', *Index on Censorship* 1: 5–6.

Salaverria, R., 2005, 'An immature medium: Strengths and weaknesses of online newspapers on September 11', *Gazette* 67: 69–86.

Salokangas, R., 1999, 'From political to national, regional and local: The newspaper structure in Finland', *The Nordicom Review* 20 (1): 77–106.

Sarikakis, K., 2005, 'Defending communicative spaces: The remits and limits of the European Parliament', *Gazette* 67: 155–72.

Sartori, C., 1996, 'The media in Italy' in Weymouth, A. and Lamizet, B. (eds), *Markets and Myths: Forces for Change in the European Media*, London: Longman.

Schepelern, P., 2004, 'Postwar Scandinavian cinema' in Ezra, E. (ed.), *European Cinema*, Oxford: Oxford University Press.

Schiller, H., 1969, *Mass Communications and the American Empire*, New York: Beacon Press.

Schoenbach, K., Lauf, E., McLoed, J. and Scheufele, D., 1999, 'Distinction and integration: Socio-demographic determinants of newspaper reading in the USA and Germany, 1974–96', *European Journal of Communication* 14: 225–39.

Schoenbach, K., Stuerzebecher, D. and Schneider, B., 1998, 'German journalists in the early 1990s: East and West' in Weaver, D. (ed.), *The Global Journalist: News People Around the World*, Cresskill, NJ: Hampton Press.

Schlesinger, P., 1997, 'From cultural defence to political culture: Media, politics and collective identity in the European Union', *Media, Culture and Society* 19: 369–91.

Schlesinger, P., 1993, 'Wishful thinking: Cultural politics, media and collective identities in Europe', *Journal of Communication* 43: 6–17.

Schlesinger, P., 1992, 'Europeanness – a new cultural battlefield?', *Innovation* 5: 11–23.

Schudson, M., 1978, *Discovering the News*, New York: Pentheon.

Schulz, W., 1998, 'Media change and the political effects of television: Americanization of the political culture', *Communications* 23: 527–42.

Schulz, W., 1997, 'Changes in the mass media and the public sphere', *Janvost – The Public* 57–69.

Scott, A., 2004, 'Hollywood and the world: The geography of motion picture distribution and marketing', *Review of International Political Economy* 11: 33–61.

Scriven, M. and Roberts, E., 2003, *Group Identities on French and British Television*, Oxford: Berghahn Books.

Scriven, M. and Roberts, E. (eds), 2001, 'Local specificity and regional unity under siege: Territorial identity and the television news of Aquitane', *Media, Culture and Society* 23: 587–605.

Seaton, J. and Pimlott, B., 1980, 'The role of the media in the Portuguese revolution' in Smith, A. (ed.), *Newspapers and Democracy*, Cambridge, MA: MIT Press.

Semetko, H., de Vreese, C. and Peter, J., 2000, 'Europeanised politics – Europeanised media? European integration and political communication', *West European Politics* 23: 121–41.

Sepstrup, P., 1989, 'Implications of current developments in West European broadcasting', *Media, Culture and Society* 11: 29–54.

Sequentia, 1995, 'Cinema in Europe: The first 100 years', March/April.

Servaes, J., 2001, 'The European information society: Much ado about nothing?', *Gazette* 64: 433–47.

Sinclair, J., 2004, 'Endemol: Formats and the future' in Sinclair, J. and Turner, G. (eds), *Contemporary Television*, London: BFI.

Siune, K., 1983, 'The campaign on television' in Blumler, J. (ed.), *Communicating to Voters*, London: Sage.

Siune, K. and Hulten, O., 1999, 'Does public service broadcasting have a future?' in McQuail, D. and Siune, K. (eds), *Media Policy: Convergence, Concentration and Commerce*, London: Sage.

Skogerbø, E., 1997, 'The press subsidy system in Norway: Controversial past – unpredictable future?', *European Journal of Communication* 12 (1): 99–118.

Smith, A., 1980, *The Geopolitics of Information: How Western Culture Dominates the World*, Oxford: Oxford University Press.

Smith, A., 1978, 'The long road to objectivity and back again: The kinds of truth we get in journalism' in Boyce, G., Curran, J. and Wingate, P. (eds), *Newspaper History*, London: Constable.

Snyder, L., Willenborg, B. and Watt, J., 1991, 'Advertising and cross-cultural convergence in Europe, 1953–89', *European Journal of Communication* 6: 441–68.

Sollinge, J., 1999, 'Danish newspapers: Structures and developments', *The Nordicom Review* 20 (1): 31–76.

Sondergaard, H., 1996, 'Fundamentals in the history of Danish television' in Bondebjerg, I. and Bono, F. (eds), *Television in Scandinavia: History, Politics and Aesthetics*, Luton: University of Luton Press.

Sorlin, P., 1999, '1957: A divided Europe. European cinema at the time of the Treaty of Rome', *Contemporary European History* 8: 411–24.

Sparks, C., 2000, 'The panic over tabloid news' in Sparks, C. and Tulloch, J. (eds), *Tabloid Tales: Global Debates over Media Standards*, Boston, MA: Rowman and Littlefield.

Sparks, C., 1991, 'From state to market: What Eastern Europe inherits from the West', *Media Development* 18 (3): 11–15.

Sparks, C. with Reading, A., 1998, *Communism, Capitalism and the Mass Media*, London: Sage.

Sparks, C. and Reading, A., 1994, 'Understanding media change in East Central Europe', *Media, Culture and Society* 16: 243–70.

Sparks, C. and Tulloch, J. (eds), 2000, *Tabloid Tales: Global Debates over Media Standards*, Boston, MA: Rowman and Littlefield.

Splichal, S., 1994, *Media Beyond Socialism: Theory and Practice in East-Central Europe*, Boulder, CO: Westview Press.

Splichal, S. and Sparks, C., 1994, *Journalists for the Twenty-first Century*, Norwood, NJ: Ablex.

Steemers, J., 2004, 'Europe as a television market' in Sinclair, J. and Turner, G. (eds), *Contemporary World Television*, London: BFI.

Street, S., 2004, 'From Ealing comedy to the British New Wave' in Ezra, E. (ed.), *European Cinema*, Oxford: Oxford University Press.

Street, S., 2000, 'Trainspotting' in Forbes, J. and Street, S. (eds), *European Cinema: An Introduction*, Basingstoke: Palgrave.

Sturmer, C., 1993, 'MTV's Europe: An imaginary continent?' in Downmunt, T. (ed.), *Channels of Resistance: Global Television and Local Empowerment*, London: BFI/Channel Four Books.

Svegfors, M., 1998, 'The newspaper in the ultra-modern age' in *Yearbook of the European Institute for the Media*, 97–106.

Syngellakis, A., 1997, 'Television in Greece' in Cornford, J. and Rollet, B. (eds), *Television in Europe*, Exeter: Intellect.

Syvertsen, T., 1992, 'Serving the public: Public television in Norway in a new media age', *Media, Culture and Society* 14: 229–44.

Syvertsen, T., 1991, 'Public television in crisis: Critiques compared in Norway and Britain', *Media, Culture and Society* 6: 95–114.

Szekfu, A., 1989, 'Intruders welcome? The beginnings of satellite television in Hungary', *European Journal of Communication* 4: 161–71.

Terzis, G. and Kontochristou, M., 2004, 'European media landscape – Greece', European Journalism Centre, www.ejc.nl (accessed 15 June 2005).

Texier, C., 1998, 'An overview of the current debate on press regulation in France' in Stephenson, H. and Bromley, M. (eds), *Sex, Lies and Democracy: The Press and the Public*, London: Longman.

Thompson, K. and Bordwell, D., 2003, *Film History*, New York: McGraw Hill.

Tincknell, E. and Raghuram, P., 2002, '*Big Brother*: Reconfiguring the "active audience" of cultural studies?', *European Journal of Cultural Studies* 5: 199–215.

Tracey, M., 1998, *The Decline and Fall of Public Service Broadcasting*, Oxford: Oxford University Press.

Trappel, J., 2004, 'Austria' in Kelly, M., Mazzoleni, G. and McQuail, D. (eds), *The Media in Europe*, London: Sage.

Trappel, J., 1991, 'Born losers or flexible adjustment? The media policy dilemma of small states', *European Journal of Communication* 6: 355–71.

Traquina, N., 1995, 'Portuguese television: The politics of savage deregulation', *Media Culture and Society* 17: 223–38.

Trenz, H., 2004, 'Media coverage on European governance: Exploring the European public sphere in national quality newspapers', *European Journal of Communication* 19: 291–319.

Triandafyllidou, A., 2003, 'Research note: The launch of the euro in the Italian media', *European Journal of Communication* 18: 255–63.

Truetzschler, W., 1998, 'The internet: A new mass medium?' in McQuail, D. and Siune, K. (eds), *Media Policy: Convergence, Concentration and Commerce*, London: Sage.

Tsaliki, L., 1995, 'The media and the construction of an "imagined community": The role of media events on Greek television', *European Journal of Communication* 10: 345–70.

Tufte, T., 1999, 'Denmark: New legislation, last minute rescue?' in de Moragas Spa, M., Garitaonandia, C. and Lopez, B. (eds), *Television on your Doorstep*, Luton: University of Luton Press.

Tumber, H., 1995, 'Marketing Maastricht: The EU and news management', *Media Culture and Society* 17: 511–19.

Tunstall, J., 2002, 'Trends in news and political journalism' in Kuhn, R. and Neveu, E. (eds), *Political Journalism: New Challenges, New Practices*, London: Routledge.

Tunstall, J., 2001, *Media Occupations and Professions: A Reader*, Oxford: Oxford University Press.

Tunstall, J., 1992, 'Europe as world news leader', *Journal of Communication* 42: 84–99.

Tunstall, J., 1977, *The Media Are American*, London: Constable.

Tunstall, J. and Machin, D., 1999, *The Anglo-American Media Connection*, Oxford: Oxford University Press.

Tunstall, J. and Palmer, M., 1991, *Media Moguls*, London: Routledge.

Tusa, A., 2001, 'A fatal error' in Giles, R., Snyder, R. and DeLisle, L. (eds), *Reporting the Post-Communist Revolution*, New Jersey: Transaction Publishers.

Tusa, J., 2001, 'Radio and the fall of communism' in Giles, R., Snyder, R. and DeLisle, L. (eds), *Reporting the Post-Communist Revolution*, New Jersey: Transaction Publishers.

UNESCO, 2003, *Institute for Statistics – Culture and Communication Sector*, Paris: UNESCO, March.

Van der Eijk, C., 2000, 'The Netherlands: Media and politics between segmented pluralism and market forces' in Gunther, R. and Mughan, A. (eds), *Democracy and the Media: A Comparative Perspective*, Cambridge: Cambridge University Press.

Van der Wurff, R., 2005, 'Impacts of the internet on newspapers in Europe', *Gazette* 67: 107–20.

Van Dusseldorp, M., 1998, *The Future of the Printed Press: Challenges in a Digital World*, European Journalism Centre, www.ejc.nl (accessed 15 June 2005).

Van Zoonen, L., 1991, 'A tyranny of intimacy: Women, femininity and television news' in Dahlgren, P. and Sparks, C. (eds), *Communication and Citizenship: Journalism and the Public Sphere*, London: Routledge.

Vartanova, E., 2004, 'Russia' in Kelly, M., Mazzoleni, G. and McQuail, D. (eds), *The Media in Europe*, London: Sage.

Vartanova, E., 2002, 'A global balancing act: New structures in the Russian media', *Media Development* 1: 13–16.

Venturelli, S., 2005, 'Europe's broadcast views', *Foreign Policy*, March/April.

Venturelli, S., 1998, *Liberalising the European Media: Politics, Regulation and the Public Sphere*, Oxford: Clarendon Press.

Vilches, L., 1996, 'The media in Spain' in Weymouth, A. and Lamizet, B. (eds), *Markets and Myths: Forces for Change in the European Media*, London: Longman.

Wagstaff, C., 1998, 'Italian genre films in the world market' in Nowell-Smith, G. and Ricci, S. (eds), *Hollywood and Europe*, London: BFI.

Wagstaff, C., 1996, 'Cinema' in Forgacs, D. and Lumley, D. (eds), *Italian Cultural Studies*, Oxford: Oxford University Press.

Wallraff, G., 1978, *Wallraff: The Undesirable Journalist*, London: Pluto Press.

Ward, D., 2003, 'State aid or band aid? An evaluation of the European Commission's approach to public service broadcasting', *Media, Culture and Society* 25: 233–50.

Wasko, J., 1994, *Hollywood in the Information Age*, London: Polity Press.

Weaver, D., 1998, 'Journalists around the world: Commonalities and differences' in Weaver, D. (ed.), *The Global Journalist: News People Around the World*, Cresskill, NJ: Hampton Press.

Weischenberg, S., Loffelholz, M. and Scholl, A., 1998, 'Journalism in Germany' in Weaver, D. (ed.), *The Global Journalist: News People Around the World*, Cresskill, NJ: Hampton Press.

Werner, O., 2002, 'Debating the euro', *Gazette* 64: 219–33.

Weymouth, A. and Lamizet, B., 1995, *Markets and Myths: Forces for Change in the European Media*, London: Longman.

Wheeler, M., 2004, 'Supranational regulation: Television and the European Union', *European Journal of Communication* 19: 349–69.

Wieten, J., 2000, 'Introduction – Television genres: borders and flows' in Wieten, J., Murdock, G. and Dahlgren, P. (eds), 2000, *Television Across Europe: A Comparative Introduction*, London: Sage.

Wieten, J., 1998, 'Reality television and social responsibility theory' in Brants, K., Hermes, J. and Van Zoonen, L. (eds), *The Media in Question*, London: Sage.

Wieten, J., 1988, 'The press the papers wanted? The case of post-war newsprint rationing in the Netherlands and Britain', *European Journal of Communication* 3: 431–55.

Wieten, J., Murdock, G. and Dahlgren, P. (eds), 2000, *Television Across Europe: A Comparative Introduction*, London: Sage.

Wigbold, H., 1979, 'Holland: The shaky pillars of Hilversum' in Smith, A. (ed.), *Television and Political Life: Studies in Six European Countries*, London: Macmillan.

Williams, K., 1997, *Get Me a Murder a Day!: A History of Mass Communication in Britain*, London: Arnold.

Williams, K., 2001, 'Demise or renewal? The dilemma of public service television in Western Europe' in Bromley, M. (ed.), *No News Is Bad News: Radio, Television and the Public*, Harlow: Pearson Educational Ltd.

Winston, B., 1998, *Media Technology and Society*, London: Routledge.

Wolf, M., 1989, 'Italy: From deregulation to a new equilibrium' in Nowell-Smith, G. (ed.), *The European Experience*, London: BFI.

Woolton, D., 1992, 'Journalists: The Tarpeian rock is close to the Capitol', *Journal of Communication* 42: 26–41.

Index